Contents

Part One:
The Business of Web Commerce   1

Part Two:
Laying the Groundwork for Your
Commerce Center   55

Part Three:
Building Your Web Commerce Server 139

Part Four:
Constructing and Managing Contact 271

Acknowledgments

Build A World Wide Web Commerce Center represents the combined efforts of many people from net.Genesis, as well as from people outside of net.Genesis. Inside net.Genesis the key participants in this book project include: David Angell, Senior Author/Editorial Director; Bahar Thompson, Director of Engineering; Eric Richard, Director of Product Development; Rajat Bhargava, President & CEO; Matthew Cutler, Director of Business Development; Neil Robertson, David Greenstein, Fernando Cruz, and Chad Engel, Software Engineers; Alex Fisher, Marketing Communications Manager; Marianne Cincotta (a.k.a. "The Goldfish Supplier"); and board members, Bradley Feld and Sean O'Sullivan.

Outside of net.Genesis, special thanks go to Bob Denny, Developer of WebSite; Kristina Lessing, Public Relations at Netscape Communications Corporation; and J. Allard, Internet Technologies Program Manager, Microsoft Corporation.

At John Wiley, a special thanks to Phil Sutherland, Senior Acquisitions Editor. Also thanks to Bob Ipsen, Director of Marketing; Jeff DeMarrais, Publicist; Kathryn Malm, Assistant Editor, and Frank Grazioli, Senior Managing Editor.

Introduction

The World Wide Web is the undisputed business medium of the 1990s and beyond. Until recently, though, tapping into this vast cybermarket was prohibitive for many businesses and other organizations because it required setting up a Unix server. The early adoption of TCP/IP into Unix's networking capabilities made Unix the choice for working on the Net, so it became the dominant multitasking operating system for Internet servers. Unix is a powerful operating system, but for the majority of PC-based businesses using Microsoft Windows it was a difficult—if not impossible—transition to the Unix realm. Without the resources to support an expensive and technically demanding Unix infrastructure, the only option was hosting a site on someone else's Unix computer connected to the Internet.

For the first time in the history of the Internet, millions of PC-based businesses and other organizations have the opportunity to easily and affordably build their own Web sites for conducting commerce on the Internet. The enabling technology behind this Web server revolution is Microsoft's new Windows NT operating system, which, together with tumbling Internet connection costs, powerful Pentium PCs, and easy-to-use Web server software allows firms of just about any size to establish a strategic foothold on the Web for publishing and conducting electronic commerce.

Windows NT is an industrial-strength version of Microsoft Windows that finally breaks the Unix barrier to building Web sites. Under its familiar Windows 95 interface is a powerful 32-bit multitasking, highly secure operating system made for the Internet. Using Windows NT as a Web server costs a fraction of what it costs to set up and operate Unix servers , so businesses are already picking up on Windows NT's robust capabilities. Windows NT/Intel platforms will surpass all Unix-based workstation sales in 1997.

With the advent of secure transaction protocols (secure socket layer and Secure-HTTP) the stage is now set for conducting commerce on the Web. A new crop of Windows NTbased Web server software that supports secure transactions has hit the shelves, and a new protocol from Visa and Master-Card called secure electronic transactions (SET) is bringing credit card transactions to full fruit on the World Wide Web.

Just as Windows NT and Web commerce is hitting its stride, competition among Internet service providers is dramatically driving down the cost of high-bandwidth connections. Not only are prices dropping for high-end digital connections, but new types of affordable service options such as ISDN are coming online. For as little as a few hundred dollars a month, your business Web site can be connected to the Internet around-the-clock and support 80,000 requests a day. Even the new 28.8Kbps modems with a dedicated analog telephone line that costs under $100 a month can support up to 20,000 requests a day.

The bottom line is that all these new trends in the interrelated technologies for building Web site afford you and your business exciting opportunities that can't be ignored. The World Wide Web levels the playing field for businesses to the point that any business can establish a full-blown Web site and operate it for the first year for the cost of a single-page advertisement in *PC Week* with a readership of 250,000. For the same money invested in a Web site, you get an entire business platform that can provide a great deal of content to a potential audience of over 30 million people worldwide.

Who Will Benefit from this Book?

The enabling technology behind establishing a Web site is only the tip of the iceberg. In-house Web site development comes from the same team effort that drives a business as a whole. A Web site is not a simple add-on to a business; it mirrors the business on the Internet. Every Web site requires a core of functional tasks orchestrated from a diverse collection of participants from technical, content, graphic design, information architecture, project management, and marketing domains. *Build A World Wide Web Commerce Center* will help any of the following:

- Businesses and other organizations that have no Web site presence on the World Wide Web

- Businesses and other organizations that are currently using a service to operate their Web site, but want to take control of the site

- Individuals interested in knowing how to build a sophisticated Web site

- Microsoft Windows users who are familiar with the fundamentals of the World Wide Web and want to establish a Web site without Unix or programming experience

- Business decision makers who know their companies need to establish a presence on the Web but have been held back by the expensive and technical Unix barrier

- Any departmental managers in larger organizations seeking a way to create their own Web presence

About this Book

Build A World Wide Web Commerce Center is designed to provide the entire webmaster team with an integrated blueprint that brings all the components of building a Web site into clear focus. It takes you through the entire process of establishing a Windows NT-based Web commerce server. Throughout this book, coverage of the business issues is blended in with the technical details of planning, setting up, and managing a Web commerce center. The goal of this handbook is to take what you already know about—your people, your products, your company—and integrate that into the realm of electronic commerce. It's not a theoretical book, but a practical one that cuts through the jungle of Web server, internetworking, security, and other topics to get any business up and running as a Web site.

How this Book Is Organized

Build a World Wide Web Commerce Center is organized into four parts, each of which takes you through a major subsystem of the entire process of establishing a Web site. You can jump in at any part to learn what you want, when you want. However, if you want the complete picture, take the full linear reading approach. The following sections provide an executive summary of each part of this book.

Part I: The Business of Web Commerce

Part I provides an orientation to "what's happening" on the Web to enable commerce and the radical technological changes that are breaking barriers to Web server entry. It covers new security protocols that allow credit card sales across the Internet. This part also outlines the new generation of affordable hardware, software, and telecommunications options available for PC-based businesses to build their own in-house Web sites. At the end is a valuable blueprint of business issues that surround the Web site building process.

Part II: Laying the Groundwork for Your Commerce Center

Part II creates the technical foundation for setting up a Windows NT-based Web server. It presents an overview of the core technical issues you need to understand to enter the Web server realm. From the overview, this part delves into the specifics of the PC hardware requirements for operating a Web site, how to set up Windows NT to operate as a Web site platform, and how to connect your Web server to the Internet via a dedicated connection. Once you complete this part, you're ready to choose, install, and operate your Web server software.

Part III: Building Your Web Commerce Server

Part III explains how to build your Web commerce server on top of your Windows NT platform. It presents an overview of the Web server software marketplace and the technical functions of Web server software. This part then goes on to cover the three leading Windows NT-based Web server software packages: Microsoft's Internet Information Server, Netscape's Commerce Server, and O'Reilly's WebSite Professional. It provides detailed, hands-on instructions for setting up and configuring each product to give you a feel for it. You'll learn how each product works through these test drives. After completing this part, you will know how to get your Web server up and running.

Part IV: Constructing and Managing Contact

Building on the foundation laid in Part III, Part IV covers the essential add-on tools that make your Web site a full-service commerce site. It covers working with the following three tools: Web site usage-tracking programs, which let you to stay on top of what's happening at your Web site; form-generating programs that let you create interactive forms for your customers to fill out online and collect the information into a database for processing without CGI programming; Web site conferencing software that creates interactive discussion groups, similar to network newsgroups except in the friendlier HTML environment. After covering the big three Web site enhancement tools, this part explains leading client/server multimedia applications, including Macromedia's Shockwave, Progressive Networks' RealAudio, and Adobe's Acrobat. This part ends with a discussion of future tools to watch, including Sun Microsystems' Java and other promising new technologies.

Part One

The Business of Web Commerce

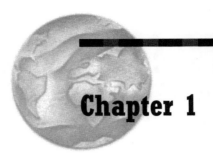

Chapter 1

Getting Down to Business on the World Wide Web

The rush is on for millions of small businesses to establish a presence on the World Wide Web. Everyone is scrambling for solutions to get a piece of the electronic commerce pie as the media, consultants, gurus, Internet service providers, software companies, and other players broadcast the loud sirens of opportunity. The first rule for coping with this crazy environment is keep your cool. The one constant of the Internet is change itself, so before jumping into the fray, read this chapter to get a sense of what is going on in the realm of the Internet and electronic commerce.

The Internet Changes Everything

Steven Levy's *How the Propeller Heads Stole the Electronic Future* (*The New York Times Magazine*, September 24, 1995) succinctly summed up the impact of the Internet on our future. What he observed was that the skyrocketing fortunes of the Netscape IPO (Initial Public Offering) "... had marked the moment when Wall Street finally realized what had been becoming increasingly apparent to computer users: a set of highly technical but reliably standardized communications protocols known as the Internet had established itself as the key to the electronic future." Levy went on to say, "The future would not be made by silver-haired telephone- and cable-company executives, ... but by companies like Netscape and their customers .... In short it was the end of the 500-channel dream, a myth constructed by the masters of media. They believed that the television set would extend its domain from the center of the entertainment universe to the worlds of commerce and information."

Levy's point was that the Internet, of which the World Wide Web is the biggest subset, has burst open the media monopolies. Every home or small business site is potentially a global broadcaster or marketer. As Levy states, "The road to information nirvana is via the ethos of the Internet, not the television or other traditional mass-media. The impact is more than just becoming a delivery medium for sound bites or 30-second spots; a Web site acts as a combination book, radio, magazine, mailbox, conversation parlor, bulletin board, and even television set in one. It brings unlimited channels of communications, community building, electronic commerce, and a full-blown version of interactivity to anyone connected to the global Internet." Millions of businesses and individuals can ditch the media gatekeeper and sell directly to the customer via the Web.

The power shift from the living room to the den or home office is already happening. According to *Broadcasting & Cable*, the World Wide Web is challenging the tower of power in media: the television. A Yahoo/Jupiter Web

User Survey reported that 61 percent of the respondents said they're watching less television and spending more time online.

The Internet Phenomenon in Numbers

The Internet has been growing from the start of its 26-year history, but the last two years have seen an astonishing expansion—with the Net more than tripling in size. The Internet is at the forefront of three to five years of tremendous growth and change as a new generation of key enablers unleashes mainstream uptake of the Internet. It's predicted that 97 percent of the future installed base hasn't come online yet. These vast numbers of people will make the Internet user demographics more closely resemble those of the general population than do current user demographics.

The Server Side of the Net

According to Mark Lottor's Domain Survey (http://www.nw.com/zone/host-count-history/), from July 1994 to July 1995, the number of hosts rose from 3.2 million to 6.6 million. North America had the largest number of host computers on the Net, with more than 4.5 million as of July 1995, up from 2.1 million in July of 1994. Western Europe showed the second largest amount of Internet growth, with 1.4 million hosts in July 1995. The growth rate for the Internet is greater outside the United States, which means the Net offers ever-expanding global marketing opportunities. The number of Web servers grew from 130 in June 1993 to 11,576 in December 1994, according to a net.Genesis survey. A more recent survey of all domain Web servers showed the number of Web servers rose from 18,957 on August 1, 1995, to 60,374 on December 1, 1995.

The User Side of the Net

The number of people using the Internet can only be estimated, but most analysts' estimates range from 20 million to 40 million people. International

Data Corporation (IDC) estimates the number to be 56 million at the end of 1995 and expects another 200 million users will join the Internet by 1999. Worldwide, the total number of individuals with Internet access is in the 35–40 million range. Expect to see that number grow to over 130 million by 1998.

As the Net becomes a bigger commercial market, more and more demographic studies are being conducted. The Emerging Technologies Research Group of FIND/SVP (http://etrg.findsvp.com) surveyed 2,000 U.S. households and found 3.4 percent of them are Internet users. The survey found that 31 percent of Internet users were self-employed professionals working from home. In the 1 million households that access the Internet directly, executives and teachers accounted for 50 percent of the total occupational profile. Of the estimated 30 million users on the Internet in 1994, more than 3 million were consumers, according to FIND/SVP. The bulk of the remaining Internet users came from academia, corporations, and government agencies. These online consumers are affluent and active users of all types of information, such as print, direct mail, and financial services.

The Third World Wide Web User Survey (13,000 respondents) conducted by Georgia Tech's Graphics, Visualization, and Usability Center (http://www.cc.gatech.edu/gvu/user_surveys/survey-04-1995/) from April 10 to May 10, 1995, found that U.S. Web users had a median age of 36, and the average European Web user was 31. About half (50.3 percent) of all respondents were married, 15.5 percent were female, and the overall average income of a Web user was between $50,000 and $60,000.

According to a demographic survey conducted by SRI International (http://future.sri.com) in Menlo Park, California, between February and May 1995, the Web consisted of two audiences. The first is the upstream audience, a group that comprises 50 percent of Web users but only 10 percent of the U.S. population. The upstream group's gender split was 77 percent male, 23 percent female. This group is upscale, highly educated (97 percent had some college education), and its members work in technical and academic fields, with professionals, scientists, and professors being the top three categories.

The second Web audience is a group comprising 50 percent of the Web and 90 percent of U.S. society. This group's gender split is 64 percent male, 36 percent female. Currently, most of those in the Web's second audience are students or recent graduates working in technical, managerial, or professional fields. Some 70 percent of them reported their age as under 30. This second group also included 11 percent 35- to 45-year-olds, whom the survey labeled Fulfilleds. The Achievers category (a stable, upscale, family-oriented segment; typically women in white-collar occupations such as management and sales) accounted for 6 percent of the Web population. The SRI study found the entire Web audience has a median yearly income of $40,000, but it also revealed a substantial number of low-income users (28 percent have yearly incomes of less than $20,000). With 89 percent of the other half having some college education, the study confirmed that education plays a big role in Internet participation.

Net Users by Company Size

Another interesting Internet user profile was done by O'Reilly & Associates. This survey looked at the use of the Internet by commercial users based on the number of employees in their companies (Table 1.1). The two largest groups of commercial users are those working in companies with fewer than 50 employees and those working in companies with over 10,000 employees.

TABLE 1.1 Internet Use by Commercial Users Based on Number of Employees

Number of Employees	Percent of Total Commercial Internet Users
<50	19%
51–100	7%
101–250	7%
251–500	9%
501–1,000	8%
1,001–5,000	16%
5,001–10,000	8%
>10,000	25%

What's a Web Site About?

Chances are you've already surfed the Web and viewed its meteoric rise from your Web browser window. And like many others, you may have authored your own HTML pages and placed them on someone else's Web server. Both of these forms of Web participation are passive. What defines a real Web presence is operating your own Web server that lets your business become a full-service storefront or a publishing service that can contain an entire hard disk of information, which can be delivered in an ever-expanding range of multimedia ways. This server operates on a computer connected to the Internet via a dedicated connection, making it available 24 hours a day, 7 days a week, 365 days a year.

To refresh your memory, the World Wide Web is built on top of the client/server model. The client and server are programs that communicate with one another. The client contacts the server and requests a piece of information. Web browsers such as Netscape Navigator, NCSA's Mosaic, and Microsoft Internet Explorer are clients that contact Web servers. The server's job is to wait around for connections from outside client machines, listen to their requests, and respond to or serve their requests.

Why Run a Web Site?

Running a Web server is like having a giant digital canvas on which you can paint your business presence in just about any way you want. It's not a static entity; it's a dynamic medium that represents a constant work in progress. A Web site offers a powerful outlet to conduct the full range of business activities on the Internet. Some of the key uses of Web sites on the Web include:

- **Publications and Information.** The Web promises to make publications and information from virtually all sources tremendously more useful and available. Publications and information filtered and packaged to match personal preferences and to offer convenience will motivate users to use and pay for Web-based content rather than traditional physical media. Similarly, the multimedia, real-time, and hyperlinked capabilities of the Web will materially distinguish Web-based content from traditional media.

- **Entertainment.** The Internet has already become rich with entertainment activities, including sports, movies, games, after-hours clubs, and more.

- **Shopping.** The interactivity and convenient browsing capabilities of the Web empower the buyer. The Web is increasingly being adopted as the first stop in evaluating, selecting, and buying goods and services.

Beyond the opportunities to engage in all types of business activities on the Web, a variety of benefits result from the efficiencies of operating online. Here are some of the key benefits of using a Web site for conducting business.

- **Communications.** Communications are being revolutionized by electronic capabilities, and new technologies riding on the back of the Web will continue this trend. New protocols continue to add new communication functionality.

- **Cost Efficiencies.** Business users are already finding significant advantages in improved communications and lowering the cost of many corporate activities by operating a Web site.

- **Publishing on Demand.** The traditional barriers to entry into publishing (size and scale) are no longer as important as engaging, compelling content. The Web offers exciting ways to deliver information on demand.

- **Electronic Distribution.** A Web site offers clear cost and time efficiencies to both businesses and customers for delivery of information, files, and software. Many companies are already using the Web as their main delivery option for software.

- **Online Commerce.** The ability to handle transactions over the Web is now a reality, with a number of options available for conducting commerce ranging from encryption to support for Visa or MasterCard transactions.

Small Is Beautiful

One of the most exciting benefits of the World Wide Web is that it levels the playing field for businesses. Although large companies were the early leaders in establishing Web sites, the Web's power as a sales vehicle is inversely proportional to the size of the seller; the small companies can do better than big ones because the Web's worldwide reach can instantly transform a small outfit into a global distributor. By contrast, large corporations that already have their distribution networks in place often find the Web to be a niche channel, with direct Web sales registering only a fraction of their total revenue. However, a small company can run a Web site for direct sales and see an exponential growth in revenue. Additionally, smaller businesses can be more nimble and more focused on the Web, which means they almost always can outmaneuver larger concerns, which typically take a much longer time to reach a conclusion and to act decisively.

The economics of running a Web site make it extremely attractive compared with the cost of traditional advertising and marketing costs. Any business can establish a full-blown Web site and operate it for the first year for the cost of a single-page advertisement in *PC Week* with a readership of 250,000. For the same money invested in a Web site, one gets an entire business platform that can provide a lot of content to a potential audience of over 30 million people worldwide.

The Electronic Commerce Climate

Gone are the days of the Internet as the exclusive bastion of academics and techies, although their numbers are still well represented. With the end of restrictions on commercial activities on the Net that were imposed by the federal government, the business of the Internet is business. The Internet's commercial domain (.com) was the fastest growing segment over the last two years and is now the largest domain. More than 76,000 commercial addresses were registered with the Internet as of July 1995. Every day approximately 150 new businesses connect to the Net.

Active Media (http://www.activemedia.com), a research firm in Peterborough, New Hampshire, conducted a survey to determine the number of commercial Web sites from September 1994 to August 1995. The study cited the Open Market Commercial Sites Index (http://www.directory.net) as the source of its data showing the number of commercial Web servers growing from 588 in September 1994 to more than 6,000 in May 1995. As of December 1995 the number was over 18,000!

The current state of commercial activities on the Web is a mixed bag, with some wild successes but also dismal failures. The key point to keep in mind is that Web commerce is in its infancy. The Web exploded on the scene so rapidly that the institutional activities associated with any new technology have yet to catch up. Any new technology always moves ahead of the way people have been doing things. For example, automatic teller machines where around for a number of years before they became accepted as a way to conduct banking. In the case of the Web, which is an entire medium for delivering a wide range of commerce functions, the same phenomenon is in place.

The real opportunity of the Web for your business is recognizing the gap between current and future environments. As people's attitudes and habits catch up with the technology, your business must be ready for action. In other words, commerce will come, but you need to prepare for it now by establishing your Web site, then add commerce functionality to be ready to grow with the trends.

Sales and Profits

Current sales and profit research supports the fact that electronic commerce hasn't yet caught on. Active Media estimated total sales on the Web at $118 million between September 1994 and August 1995. Of the companies surveyed, 21 percent had sales greater than $10,000 during the prior month. Of these, 2 percent grossed more than $100,000 and 1 percent more than $1 million from selling on the Web. Of the 195 active Internet marketers surveyed, 22 percent reported profits from online activities. An additional 40 percent said they expected to be profitable within 12 to 24 months. Fifteen percent said they never expect their Internet activities to be profitable, but they find them useful for public relations. Fourteen percent were totally disappointed or did not expect a financial return for three to five years.

The Bureau of Business Research at American International College located in Springfield, Massachusetts, surveyed executives at 48 Forbes 500 firms to gauge their plans for marketing and selling online. The companies surveyed had combined sales of more than $188 billion and more than 765,000 employees. The executives predicted, on average, that about 67 percent of the firms in their particular industry would enable customers to access marketing data and transact business online and that 39 percent of a firm's annual sales would come from the Internet and online services.

The Rochester Institute of Technology conducted a survey of Internet shoppers, questioning 378 users who had bought products over the Net between February and May 1995. The study found Net users to be young, predominately male, and well educated. Their average age was 32, 79 percent were male, and 67 percent had college degrees. The majority of purchases (64 percent) were for software, books, music, magazines, and hardware. Most of the respondents (88 percent) were very satisfied or somewhat satisfied with their purchases, and only 4 percent indicated any dissatisfaction.

Risks and Realities

Many players agree that the issue of security over the Internet is overblown. Because of the recent emergence of the Web and electronic commerce, it's being held to a higher standard than are other elements of people's day-to-day lives. According to Michael Goulde, a senior consultant with the Patricia Seybold Group, "It's easier to tap a telephone or get a credit card carbon than to put a sniffer on an Internet connection, grab a packet, and then put it together with other packets in the right sequence. The bigger issue is thwarting hackers from accessing large computer systems and getting whole files on and off the Internet." Security on the Internet is a complex arena of encryption, firewalls, and other tools. As with the evolution of other areas of the Internet and computing in general, the widespread deployment of security systems will be on off-the-shelf solutions. With the adoption of security protocols and systems for the Web, most browsers and Web server software can easily support enough security for retail transactions right now.

Note: *Chapter 3 explains security protocols used for commerce on the Web.*

The Zen of Growing Your Web Site

The best way to think of the Web itself is as a huge work in progress. It is driven by constantly changing standards and new technology. Entering the realm of Web site building requires a Zen-like understanding of the underlying forces that act as guides through this constantly shifting environment. A Web site requires learning, planning, implementing, evolving, and maintaining. It's a multifaceted medium in which being static means death. To run a compelling Web site takes a generalist management style to orchestrate the divergent components into a unified symphony that is a business presence on the Internet. The following sections provide the basic mantras to keep in mind as you go down the path of Web site building.

Stay in the Driver's Seat

When it comes to establishing a Web presence on the Internet, knowledge is power. As a business decision maker, you need to understand the issues, even if you plan to have other people oversee different functions. If you don't understand the tools and options available, you are giving your decision-making powers away to people who won't have the understanding of your business and customers. It's easy to let the popularized, mass-media version of the Web gold rush cloud your better business judgment. The Web is a communications and data-movement medium. How you use it determines its effectiveness to your business. Establishing a Web site demands that you use the time-honored principles that drive any business:

- Reduce the costs of doing business by improving efficiencies
- Increase sales and profits by reaching out to new customers
- Gain competitive advantage by harnessing new technologies
- Improve customer satisfaction by adding convenience

The Art of Being Incremental

Electronic commerce on the Web is a new business frontier because the technology, players, prices, and services involved in establishing a business presence are in a constant state of flux. Building a Web site is a multifaceted process with a long learning curve. Therefore, the best way to set up and maintain a Web site is in stages. The learning process never stops, as new technologies come online and old ones die. You need to keep ahead of a constant stream of new Web-serving products and services and incorporate those that will help you stay ahead of the crowd. Additionally, keeping your Web site well fed and current takes a coordinated effort that involves getting all your people learning new Web skills. You will continually add functionality and improvements to capture more and more of your business activities in the real world and mirror them on your Web site. Think incremental as you climb up your learning curve.

Your Web Site Product as Content and Interactivity

As a commerce medium, the Internet is different from traditional mass media. Content-based marketing, which is the packaging of your business information as a resource, is the rule of the Internet. Always find ways to add value to your message to deliver quality, filtered information. Content and interactivity are the ultimate products of the Web. The mere availability of raw content or activity will have limited attraction; rather, content and activity will be fused with applications that make them come alive.

Integrate Your Business into Your Web Site

The technology behind establishing a Web site is only the beginning. Its ability to project a business image in compelling ways to millions of Internet users is the most important task. In-house Web site development must come from the same team effort that drives your business as a whole. A Web site is not a simple add-on to your business; it's a mirror of your business on the Web. Every Web site requires a core set of functional tasks orchestrated from a diverse collection of participants. According to The Webmaster's Guild (http://www.webmaster.org/), a nonprofit organization for Webmasters, the seven essential functions required to run a Web site are technical, content, graphic design, information architecture, project management, marketing, and evangelism. Because these skills encompass so many areas, the Webmaster role is typically handled by a team of individuals. Selecting these people and organizational factors is the most difficult task that your business must address before its journey into Web commerce.

Be Technically Literate

The Internet grew from the realm of mainframe computers and large-scale networking, with their unfriendly operating systems and complex infrastructures. These systems are tended to by legions of technical people and programmers in a world of large corporate, enterprise computing. Enterprise networking is defined as managing the network infrastructure in a large enterprise. It involves the enormous effort of planning the integration of disparate networks and systems and managing them.

Enterprise networking is the realm of big budgets, Information Management systems, and high-priced technical people. Unfortunately, it is their collective mindset that still dominates the Web-serving industry. (Even Microsoft Windows NT comes from this realm.) These people can't understand why anyone would abandon expensive and technically demanding Unix-based systems to connect to the Internet, and they'll spend countless hours telling you why Unix-based systems are better than PC-based systems.

However, as a small business, you must go the PC-based way to Web serving or you won't get connected to the Internet. PC computing works on a completely downsized pricing structure compared with that for Unix-based workstations, from hardware and software costs to people costs.

For nonprogrammers to survive in this environment takes determination, but don't get discouraged. Technology and history are on your side. There is an explosion of new technology rapidly making the setting up and running of a Web site both cheaper and easier. These continuing trends in PC hardware, Microsoft Windows, off-the-shelf Web server software, and telecommunications work to the advantage of a small business looking to get connected to the World Wide Web. It has been the convergence of new technologies that is bringing the Web to the rest of us. Like the downward spiral that brought computing from mainframe computers to PCs, the next generation of PC-based Web-serving technology will downsize the whole process of establishing and operating a Web site.

Chapter 2

Why You Can Build Your Own Commerce Server Now

Computer industry guru Patricia Seybold recently stated, "If you're not an active Internet citizen by the mid-1990s, you're likely to be out of business by the year 2000." Unfortunately for many businesses, the complexity of establishing a Web server of their own has left them unconnected. For them, the only option was seeking outside hosting services, an approach that is initially less expensive than running an in-house server, but comes at a high cost in terms of control and organizational commitment. But technology marches on! Thanks to the downsizing in both cost and complexity, legions of businesses now have the opportunity to build their own in-house Web sites for conducting electronic commerce.

The Unix Barrier

The history of the Internet as a system is synonymous with that of Unix, a powerful operating system born in the early days of mainframes and mini-computers. These expensive, mature Unix systems, operated by large government, corporate, and educational institutions, were designed for the multitasking and other functions that form the foundation of the Internet. The transmission control protocol/Internet protocol (TCP/IP), the networking protocol that forms the basis of the Internet, was integrated into the Unix operating system early on. This marriage of TCP/IP and Unix has lasted 26 years, right up to the present. Unix-based computers have dramatically improved their price/performance with the introduction of powerful workstations from such companies as Sun Microsystems, Hewlett-Packard, and others. Although Unix is a powerful operating system designed for technical markets, for PC-based businesses raised on Windows, switching to Unix is a difficult—if not impossible—transition. Without the resources to support the more technically demanding Unix infrastructure, many businesses turned to hosting a site on someone else's Unix computer connected to the Internet.

Web Site Outsourcing

Because Unix-based systems have dominated the Internet, the only viable option for most PC-based businesses was to use a Web hosting service. Basically, a Web hosting service rents space on its computer system, which is already connected to the Internet via a high-speed dedicated connection. The Web pages are created by the client, the Web hosting service, or a third-party Web design service. Once the HTML documents are created, they're placed on a Web server, either as part of an electronic mall or as a standalone Web site. An example of charges for a basic Web site with a few HTML pages might be as follows:

- A one-time setup charge for up to 10 pages or around $500. This typically includes creating the Web documents using an HTML editor, with additional charges for scanned images.

- A monthly flat fee of $100 for keeping documents on the provider's server or a sliding-scale fee based on the volume of traffic the client site generates.

- A charge of $20 for each change made to the Web site, such as altering the text on a page.

Looking at these numbers, you might conclude that outsourcing is a viable option for your business. Certainly, the initial startup charge of the outsourcing option is considerably less than the do-it-yourself cost, and you can establish your Web presence a lot faster. However, in the long run, taking the do-it-yourself route to building a Web site is strategically a superior move for your business. Why? Read on.

The In-House Advantage

A Web site is the presentation of your business in a new medium, so the stakes are too high to leave it to an outside source. Your Web site should mirror the entire customer interaction with your business that goes on in real life—and even go beyond it. Think about all the systems in place to function in your business and think about mirroring them on your Web site.

The in-house approach offers two key strategic advantages over using a Web hosting service. The first is that your business gains critical self-education from operating an in-house Web server, which will carry your business into the future of electronic commerce. The second is that your business gains complete control over its presence on the Web. You must have the freedom to add new features and make constant changes to the site. The additional layer of the Web hosting service gets in the way of keeping your Web site fresh. In addition, charges made for changes can quickly add up. To recap, here are the key reasons your business should go the do-it-yourself Web-serving route:

- A Web site is highly dynamic: your company, your literature, and your products change, as do methods for delivering your content. The charges imposed by a hosting service for making any changes become sizable in this environment. Additionally, you must deal with lead times for getting a hosting service to implement changes on your Web site.

- Your business needs the flexibility to incorporate enhancements to your Web site. Among these are order forms, back-end databases, guest books, and maps, which are often desirable additions to your pages. For a number of reasons—among them, server security— Web hosting services often want to stick to providing simple text and graphics. Thus, if you had hoped to realize the real power of a server, you'll instead have to settle for text and a few graphics to define your Internet presence or pay significantly more.

- Your business can't afford to forfeit the critical self-education process involved with` operating a Web presence on the Internet. An effective site represents the true heart and soul of your business, taking the involvement and collective knowledge of an entire organization. A Web site provides valuable electronic commerce training for your business to project your image on the Web, generate revenue, increase efficiency, and improve customer service. The advantages of an in-house Web site transcend the higher startup cost and time commitment of your people to grasp the medium.

Web Server Technology for the Rest of Us

The enabling technology for the do-it-yourself Web server revolution is the convergence of the Windows NT operating system, more powerful PC platforms, tumbling Internet connection costs, and easy-to-use Web server software. Together these breakthroughs allow small businesses to establish a strategic foothold on the Web for publishing and conducting electronic commerce.

Windows NT: More Than a Pretty Face

Windows NT is a Unix-like, 32-bit multitasking, highly secure network operating system with the familiar Windows 95 GUI on top (Figure 2.1).

Microsoft designed Windows NT to handle enterprise client/server computing and to be an Internet server platform. Windows NT supports simultaneous connections, fault-tolerant disk support, advanced TCP/IP support,
scalability to run on multiple CPUs, and a lot more. Microsoft also designed
Windows NT to take advantage of the more powerful Intel Pentium-based
PCs as well as to work on powerful RISC-based CPUs, such as DEC's high-
performance Alpha microprocessor. NT comes in two flavors: NT Workstation for client machines and NT Server for server platforms. Both are well
suited to operate as Web-serving platforms. The Windows NT Server
provides an expanded collection of network services that make it a viable
option for enterprise networking as well as a Web server.

Note: *Chapter 7 covers working with Windows NT.*

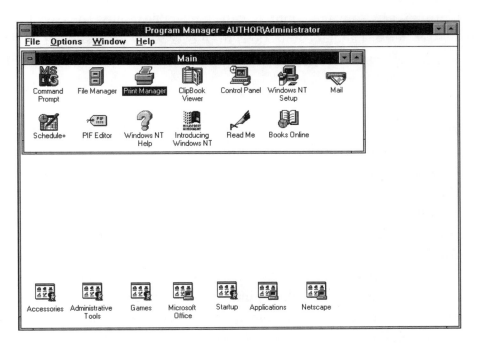

**FIGURE 2.1 The familiar face of Windows 95 on a powerful 32-bit
operating system.**

Can Windows NT Support a Busy Web Site?

Microsoft publishes information on several Internet servers, each running Windows NT Server. These are some of the busiest servers on the Internet, handling tens of thousands of connections a day. Used by more than 2 million customers on the Internet in its first year, Microsoft's FTP server runs on a quad processor Pentium-based computer with 128MB of RAM and is connected to the Internet by a T3 line. On average, 6,000 users connect to ftp.microsoft.com daily, making it one of the most accessed servers on the Internet. This server handles close to 300 simultaneous FTP sessions and over 300,000 file transactions per week. Microsoft's World Wide Web (www.microsoft.com) is running on similar computers with comparable results. The World Wide Web server handles connections from over 9,000 addresses per day, on average, and over 5,000 searches and 100,000 downloads daily, with processor time to spare.

Windows NT as a revolutionary alternative to Unix has not gone unnoticed in the computing world. International Data Corp. expects the worldwide workstation market in 1995 to reach 1,455,485 units, a 43% increase over 1994. Much of this growth can be attributed to the acceleration of Windows NT/Intel workstations. IDC goes on to state that Unix and Windows NT are not competing directly. Instead, it's in the nontechnical market that NT is growing, and NT is limiting penetration of Unix workstations into business applications. According to IDC, NT/Intel workstations will jump at a growth rate of 64%, and in 1997 their numbers will surpass those of all Unix/RISC workstation servers in unit shipments and revenue. Table 2.1 shows IDC-estimated volume of NT/Intel workstations compared with that of Unix/RISC workstations from 1994 to 1999.

TABLE 2.1 Estimated Volume of NT/Intel Workstations vs. Unix/RISC Workstations from 1994 to 1999

Worldwide Workstation Market by Operating System, 1993—1999

Units	1994	1995	1996	1997	1998	1999
Unix	759,138	920,485	1,034,200	1,147,400	1,264,800	1,390,300
NT	217,677	502,000	814,000	1,948,000	3,249,000	3,913,000

Why Use Windows NT for Web Serving

Windows NT is the first serious alternative to Unix-based Web servers. For Windows-based businesses, NT delivers Unix power but with a much easier interface. The result is an obvious reduction in the learning curve and infrastructure costs. The entire cost structure from the hardware to the Web server software is downsized from the more expensive Unix-based solutions. In a nutshell, here are the main features Windows NT offers:

- **Built-in Connectivity.** Windows NT includes a high-performance implementation of the Internet standard TCP/IP suite.

- **Ease of Use.** Windows NT is easy to set up and use, so it can put your business on the Internet almost immediately with a communications link provided by an Internet service provider.

- **Ease of Administration.** All Windows NT administrative tools use the familiar Windows user interface and are well integrated. Remote administration allows you to configure or monitor machines that are across the network. Event Viewer and Performance Monitor utilities show you the system status and performance of any computer on the network. The Windows NT implementation of TCP/IP is one of the first to use dynamic host configuration protocol (DHCP), which simplifies administration and configuration.

- **Security.** Windows NT provides the built-in resources you need to effectively secure your system on the Internet at the operating system and file levels. Directory and file access can be controlled by permissions.

- **Scalability.** Windows NT runs on Intel, DEC Alpha AXP, MIPS RISC, and PowerPC hardware, and it supports symmetrical multiprocessor machines. As a result, you can increase your system performance by upgrading your system hardware to include multiple CPUs without changing operating systems.

- **Performance.** Windows NT Server is designed to perform on the Internet, no matter how quickly the Internet grows or how your business requirements expand.

Why Not Use Windows 95

On the surface, Windows 95 and Windows NT look the same. However, the differences under the surface make Windows NT the superior choice for a Web server platform. One of the major differences between the two is that NT uses true preemptive multitasking, and Windows 95 uses shared multitasking. NT's preemptive multitasking allows true multitasking among several processes at the same time without affecting any one of them. In contrast, Windows 95 uses a system of multitasking that requires each process running on the system to share—one at a time—with other processes. This difference has a big impact on the performance of a Web server running on Windows. Web servers must be able to handle simultaneous processes to function optimally. Other advantages to Windows NT include unlimited resources, a true 32-bit operating system, and a protected environment.

The Pentium PC as a Server Platform

Windows NT is designed to take the full advantage of the Pentium processor. As is the case with most PC-based computing, more of everything in hardware is better. In using Windows NT as a platform for Web server, the important PC components are RAM and hard disk space. The basic Web server PC should include 32MB and a 1GB drive. The demands of using a PC for a Web site mean a more specific requirement for hardware. In many cases, for security and overall performance, you'll want to establish your NT-based server as a standalone unit that is dedicated for Web traffic.

———**Note:** *Chapter 6 covers more specifics on Web server hardware issues.*

A Web server running on a PC can almost saturate a T1 line, delivering over 100,000 transactions per hour based on a 5KB document size for a flat rate of over 2 million transactions per day. A 90MHz Pentium connected to the Internet via an ISDN line with 128Kbps can support more than 500,000 hits a day. If an average user takes 10 transactions, your Web site can support 50,000 people per day. Over the course of a business week, that translates to 250,000 people. Over a month, that translates to 1 million people! However, the overall capability of your Web server depends on the server's line speed, the clients' line speeds, and the average size of the document delivered.

Wiring a Web Server to the Net

A Web server needs to be accessible 24 hours a day, 365 days a year to the global Internet community. This means you need a dedicated connection for which you are charged a flat monthly rate instead of fees based on usage. Competition among Internet service providers (ISPs) is dramatically driving down the cost of higher-bandwidth connections. For example, at the high end of bandwidth spectrum, T1 (1.5Mbps) connections that used to cost $3,000 to $4,000 a month are now going for $1,500 or less. New types of less expensive dedicated connections are coming online, such as integrated services digital network (ISDN), Frame Relay, and Fractional T1 service.

———**Note:** *Chapter 8 explains dedicated Internet connection options.*

ISDN is one of the least expensive digital communications options. It's delivered to homes and businesses via standard telephone lines, so no new wiring is required. A single basic rate interface (BRI) line supports up to 128Kbps of digital bandwidth—without compression. Dedicated ISDN connections cost as little as a few hundred dollars a month, with prices sure to fall even more as ISDN becomes a mainstream service. You can even add multiple ISDN lines as needed to increase the bandwidth of your connection. According to Dataquest, over 2 million ISDN lines will be in service by 1999.

Even a Web site connected via a dedicate analog telephone line using a 28.8Kbps modem can support a moderately busy Web site. Based on an average document size of around 4KB and with various networking overhead taken into account, a 28.8Kbps connection can support 10,000 to 20,000 document requests per day.

Off-the-Shelf Web Server Software

Web server software coordinates the distribution of documents. A common term for a Web server is HTTP server, referring to the hypertext transport protocol that forms the basis of the Web. The server software performs these tasks:

- Provides control to determine who can access different levels of files and directories on the server
- Runs your CGI scripts and any external modules you write to add functionality to your Web pages
- Handles the input from image maps—special images that are capable of returning the user to the location that contained the original link to the server
- Logs the transactions that users make

Microsoft's Windows NT is ushering in a cornucopia of affordable Web server software packages. The competition is hot for Windows NT-based servers, and prices have fallen to between free and $1,499. Even the industry leader, Netscape Communications, has reduced its prices to stay competitive. Microsoft's Internet Information Server is bundled with Windows NT Server.

Although most of the early packages were for publishing only, the advent of secure transaction protocols on the Web has set the stage for secure Web server software. Web server software that supports only publishing is less expensive than Web commerce (secure) server software. However, the commerce version is the way to go. Even if you don't plan to implement a secure system immediately, you'll ultimately want your site to handle the full range of publishing, secure communications, and transaction processing.

Underneath the operation of commerce servers are the secure socket layer (SSL) and secure-HTTP (S-HTTP) security protocols. SSL is currently more popular because it's supported by the dominant browser Netscape Navigator. S-HTTP, developed by EIT (Enterprise Integration Technology) and supported by NCSA's Mosaic, is not in widespread use yet. A new protocol from Visa and MasterCard, called Secure Electronic Transactions (SET), promises to bring credit cards to full use on the Web.

Note: *Chapter 3 explains security protocols and payment options.*

The leading products in the Windows NT-based secure Web server market are Netscape Communications' Commerce Server (http://home.netscape.com/), O'Reilly & Associates' WebSite Professional (http://website.ora.com/), Microsoft's Internet Information Server (http://www.microsoft.com), The Internet Factory's Commerce Builder (http://www.aristosoft.com/), Process Software's Purveyor Encrypt WebServer (http://www.process.com/), and Spry's Safety Web Server (http://www.server.spry.com/).

Note: *Part Three explains working with Web server software.*

Tip: *Most of these Web server software publishers let you take a free 60-day test drive of their product by downloading the software from their Web sites.*

A Cornucopia of Web Server Enhancement Tools

Beyond Web server software, a variety of third-party tools let nontechnical Webmasters manage and enhance their Web sites. Setting up your site for conducting commerce requires a triad of core tools that form the foundation of your site. Web site usage-tracking software lets you track your Web site activity and generate valuable management information. As with any business

, you need to know what's happening with your investment. Leading ...cts for these tools include net.Genesis's net.Analysis (http://www.netgen /) and Interse's Market Focus (http://www.interse.com/).

n and database connectivity software lets your Web site interact with customers using on-screen forms. The information from these forms, which is then fed to a database file for processing, lets you solicit input from users for everything from surveys to orders. The leading form products are net.Genesis's net.Form (http://www.netgen.com) and Allaire's Cold Fusion (http://www.allaire.com/).

Establishing online discussion groups allows interaction with your company's customers or internal communications. This type of add-on software creates a network newsgroup system delivered via friendly Web documents. Leading software packages for creating discussion areas at Web sites include net.Genesis's net.Thread (http://www.netgen.com/) and O'Reilly's WebBoard (http://www.ora.com/).

Beyond the core tools is a growing number of enhancement tools to improve the delivery of information to Web users. Three new tools stand out as promising add-ons for delivering multimedia information via Web sites: Progressive Networks' RealAudio (http://www.realaudio.com/) for adding sound to your Web site, Macromedia's Shockwave (http://www.macromedia.com/) for generating multimedia documents, and Adobe's Acrobat (http://www.adobe.com/) for rich, platform-independent publishing. Other content development and management tools include Microsoft's FrontPage (http://www.microsoft.com/) and Adobe's PageMill.

Additionally, just over the horizon are new technologies, such as Sun's Java programming language and VRML (Virtual Reality Modeling Language), that promise to have a big impact on Web sites.

Note: *All these tools are covered later in this book.*

Chapter 3

Beyond Publishing and on to Commerce

Until recently, most Web sites focused exclusively on publishing information. It wasn't that businesses didn't want to handle transactions online; the barrier was in creating a secure infrastructure for handling sensitive information, such as credit card data. Like everything else on the Web, new developments in security allow even the smallest business to set up a Web site that includes the capabilities to securely handle orders and other sensitive information. This chapter presents the fundamentals of Web security protocols and encryption-based systems.

What Is a Secure Transaction?

The first step in discussing basic transaction security options is to define a secure transaction. A secure transaction of information messages possesses the characteristics discussed in the following sections. The first four—confidentiality, integrity, authenticity, and nonrepudiability—deal with protecting information delivered between a client and your Web server. The remaining three characteristics—host integrity, protection against spoofing, and virus protection—cover sensitive data once it's on your server or transactions between your organization and your bank or credit card processing vendor.

Confidentiality

Others cannot eavesdrop on an exchange even though your computer is broadcasting its message to the network, which is the equivalent of shouting something across a crowded room.

Integrity

The message received is identical to the message sent. Although a message crosses an open network that is connected to millions of other machines, you must have assurance that the message sent matches the one received.

Authenticity

You know with whom you are making the exchange. Over the Internet, you have none of the usual signals that provide authenticity, such as a signature, a recognized voice, or a familiar face. Your computer is exchanging information with someone else's computer.

Nonrepudiability

None of the parties involved in a transaction can deny that the exchange took place. Because you do not receive a return receipt, your correspondent can easily say, "I didn't receive your message." Conversely, if you change your mind about what you sent, you can say, "I didn't send it."

Host Integrity

Someone armed with a computer address, an account number, and a password cannot use that account for unauthorized activity. Host integrity is maintained when you isolate your computer from everyone else. This can be done physically, by ensuring that the wires to your network are not accessible to any people you don't trust. Another way is to place a second computer between your network and the Internet to broker transactions. This system is known as a firewall.

Protection against Spoofing

Hackers send messages from accounts they broke into, and the messages appear to come from legitimate servers. Alternatively, hackers can set up their computers to look like legitimate machines on the network and send spurious messages from them.

Virus Protection

Without the mechanism that guarantees a message is benign, downloading a virus to your local computer could be a mouse-click away. When you download software from the Web, you are accepting on blind trust that the computer you are communicating with is not harboring viruses.

Web Security Protocols

The hypertext transfer protocol, which forms the basis of the Web, offers no inherent security for transmission of data across the Internet. Two protocols can get around these problems: Secure-HTTP (S-HTTP) developed by Enterprise Integration Technology and secure socket layer (SSL) developed by Netscape. These protocols are part of the client and server software of the Web. Alternative methods of transmitting secure information are being developed by other companies. These strategies for commercial transactions will make conducting commerce on the Web far safer than sending your credit card number in the mail or giving it to an operator over the phone. The leading protocol emerging for credit card transactions is Visa/Mastercard's secure electronic transactions (SET), which is explained later in this chapter.

Both S-HTTP and SSL provide the foundation for using encryption to protect secure information. Encryption is, simply put, the process of encoding information so that only parties who understand the code can read that information. (Encryption is explained more fully later in this chapter.) Secure-HTTP and SSL differ in one basic way: S-HTTP is an application protocol, meaning it can be used for only HTTP transactions, whereas SSL is a protocol that can be implemented with any application protocol, including HTTP, FTP, Gopher, and telnet.

Secure-HTTP is a variation of HTTP, the standard protocol used on the World Wide Web. It's implemented in the same way that HTTP is implemented on current browsers and servers, but Secure-HTTP provides the ability for both servers and clients to send encrypted information. (Although Secure-HTTP is capable of communicating with both secure and insecure servers and clients, the security functions are disabled when it communicates with the latter). One of the more important features of S-HTTP is that it does not require the client to use a public key. Secure-HTTP supports three types of protection: encryption, which scrambles messages; authentication, which verifies that a message has not been changed since it was sent and that the name of the sender is accurate; and signature, which is the inclusion of a unique digital signature identifying the sender of the message.

Cryptography Primer

Most transaction security for sending sensitive information across the Internet depends on cryptography. Basically, cryptography is the scrambling of a message in a manner that makes it unreadable except for the person with the key to unscramble it. In a common form of cryptography, secret key cryptography, the sender uses a secret key or piece of data to encrypt or decrypt a given message. The sender must get both a secret key and the encrypted information to the receiver securely.

Public key cryptography (PKC) is a system based on a pair of keys, a public key and a private key, rather than a single key. The keys are related in such a way that information that is encrypted with the public key can be decrypted only with the private key. This means that, if you have a pair of keys, you can make the public key freely available to anyone who wants it without worrying about it. Anyone can send you a secret message using your public key to encrypt the message, but only you can decrypt the message using your private key.

When someone puts together a message to send to you and encrypts it with your public key, the computer also generates a message digest and attaches it to the message. The message digest is a small piece of data that results from performing a particular mathematical calculation on the message, acting as a digital fingerprint of the message. When you receive the message and decrypt it with your private key, your system also calculates the message digest. Then the digest that was created is compared with the one sent by the message. If they match, you know you received exactly what was sent. When you obtain a public key, it comes with a certificate, a piece of cryptographically secure information that guarantees that the key the sender obtained was yours. These certificates are generated by a trusted organization called a certifying authority (CA) that issues certificates on behalf of others.

RSA: The Keeper of the Algorithm

RSA was the first public key algorithm to support both encryption and authentication. Public key algorithms use a pair of keys—a public key and a private key—to encrypt and decrypt messages. You share your public key with the world, which means that anyone can use your public key to encrypt data meant for your eyes only. When you receive the encrypted data, you use your private key to decrypt it. Your private key always remains secret. When you want to send confidential data to other people, you use their public keys

Who Really Owns the RSA Security Software?

In a recent *InformationWeek* article titled "RSA, Feds in Digital Signature Fight: Security software maker asserts ownership of key technology patent," the question of Who Really Owns the RSA Security Software continues unresolved. The author stated that RSA Data Security Inc., which specializes in encryption software, is escalating its fight with the U.S. Government over patent rights covering digital signature technology. The government has a digital signature algorithm patent that it says covers the technology used in the digital signature standard (DSS) to authenticate codes that identify individuals or businesses. The government has made the algorithm available to the public for free. RSA contends that it owns the dominant patent covering digital signature technology and that technology must be licensed by companies and government agencies that want to use DSS. The National Institute of Standards and Technology in Washington is the agency handling the case.

to encrypt it, and they use their private keys for decryption. RSA, invented in 1977 by Ron Rivest, Adi Shamir, and Leonard Adleman, is the most popular public key algorithm and one of the strongest algorithms commonly used. The RSA algorithm is based on the idea that it is difficult to prime-factor a large number or break it down into its prime components. RSA's public and private keys are based on a pair of 100- to 200-digit prime numbers.

U.S. Government Restrictions on Encryption Technology

Believe it or not, in the age of the global Internet, software products that implement RSA and other cryptographic algorithms are defined as munitions by the U.S. State Department and covered under the International Traffic in Arms Regulation Act. This restriction prevents the full version of the RSA encryption algorithm from being exported outside the United States. Currently, the 128-bit key and beyond can be used to provide maximum security in the United States, while foreign users can use only the 40-bit key version of the RSA algorithm. The 40-bit key scheme is inadequate for security, and recent experience shows that it can be broken. The U.S. Government restriction on the encryption algorithms compels software companies like Netscape to publish two versions of its Web browser, one for the domestic market and the other for foreign markets. This division in the global marketplace is not compatible with the nature, structure, and history of the Internet and its users. Additionally, from the Web serving end of transactions, it means that foreign transactions come with higher risks.

Certificates and Certification Authorities

The process of implementing the public key cryptography system on a Web server—based on pairs of keys—requires getting a digital certificate before a server can support secure transactions. Only companies called certification authorities can issue certificates, and RSA is the leading certification authority. However, expect to see more CAs as commerce on the Web increases.

The digital certificate contains two groups of information. First is data on the certificate itself, including the name of the server, its public key, the certificate's validity dates, and the name of the CA. The second piece is the digital signature, which cannot be forged. The entire message is digitally signed by a Certification Authority that is known to many servers and can verify the relationship between a server and its public key. The CA generates a digital signature for the server and sends back a signed digital certificate. The certificate can then be published in a directory or attached to any message being sent across the network. Any other user can verify the authenticity of the certificate using the digital signature and the public key of the certification authority that signed the certificate. Once the certificate is known to be authentic, the information inside the certificate can be trusted.

Before the server can begin a secure connection with a client, the client needs to ensure that it is connected to a secure server, to verify the identity of the server, the client, and the server use authentication. After the server is authenticated, the client and server can encrypt data to each other and ensure the integrity of that data. The authentication process typically operates as follows:

1. The client sends a request to connect to the secure server.

2. Using the certificate it acquired from the CA, the server sends a signed digital certificate to the client. The server generates private and public keys before sending the request for a certificate.

3. The client authenticates the server by decrypting the digital signature and matching it with the certificate information. If the certificate was tampered with during the transaction, the digital signature won't match, in which case, the client terminates the connection to the server. If the certificate is valid, the server is authenticated.

4. The client generates a session key and encrypts it using the server's public key from the certificate (this way, only the server's private key can decrypt it). The session key is later used to encrypt data and ensure data integrity. The client sends the encrypted session key to the server.

5. The server receives the session key, which it uses to encrypt and decrypt the data it can then securely send and receive from the client.

Getting a Certificate

Certificates are required for using the security features of most popular Web server software. Before you can enable security on your server, you need to choose a certification authority, request a certificate, and install the certificate the CA sends you. The certificate is used to authenticate the server to client browsers before they begin a secure transaction. It can take anywhere from a day to two months or more to approve a certificate. After you contact a CA and gather the information you need, you can submit a request for a certificate. The typical cost is around $300 for setting up your account and $75 a year thereafter. To apply for a digital certificate, you typically provide the following to the CA:

- **Common name** is usually the fully qualified host name used in DNS lookups; for example, www.netgenesis.com.

- **E-mail address** is your business e-mail address. This is used for correspondence between you and the CA.

- **Organization** is the official legal name of your company. Most CAs require that you verify this information with legal documents (such as a copy of a business license).

- **Organizational unit** is optional information that describes an organization within your company. This can also be used to note a less formal company name (with the Inc., Corp., and so on).

- **Locality** is optional information that usually describes the city, principality, or country for the organization.

- **State or province** is usually required.

- **Country** is required as a two-character abbreviation of your country name (in the ISO format, the United States country code is US).

——**Note:** *Specific steps for getting a digital certificate are explained in Chapter 9.*

All Roads Lead to Taking Plastic

The ultimate form of all transactions is the use of credit cards because that's how we buy and sell goods. A business group led by MasterCard International and Visa International has announced plans for an industry-standard technology for protecting the security of electronic payments on the Internet. The new technical standard brings together previously warring camps, one led by Microsoft Corporation, the other by Netscape Communications Corporation. The standard, which should go into commercial use by the end of 1996, is intended to give merchants on the Internet a convenient, universally deployed means for protecting the privacy of online credit card transactions. For customers, the new technology promises a much higher level of security for electronic purchases than has been previously available on the Internet.

The software standard, called Secure Electronic Transactions (SET) will permit a user to send a credit card account number to a merchant in scrambled form. The scrambled number is unintelligible to electronic eavesdroppers and thieves, and even to the merchants receiving the payment. But a special code will enable a merchant to check electronically and automatically with the bank that issued the credit card number to determine that the user is the authorized owner of the card. The number-scrambling part of the system is based on a well-known and widely used national software standard known as the Data Encryption Standard. SET will be incorporated into Web server software as well as Web browsers.

Another important benefit of SET is that currently, many powerful types of encryption technology are barred from export because the government fears that foreign enemies may be able to conspire electronically. But the new credit card security standard will not be subject to such restrictions because it's designed to protect only financial information, not electronic messages or other types of computer documents.

Debit Account Transactions on the Web

Securing transactions via encryption between Web clients and Web servers supports credit card transactions. Another category of transaction technology available for commerce on the Web is the debit account method under which the end user and the Web server site establish accounts with a company that maintains accounts backed by real money. Transactions using this method involve moving digits between accounts. Although it's doubtful that these systems will replace the credit card as the premier transaction medium, they offer attractive options for Web commerce. They support the concept of an Internet-based information vending machine, which can sell information products at prices below standard for credit card transactions.

For example, you might sell an article for $1.00, which users pay when they download the information. These cybercoins get deposited automatically into a bank account, and you get real money. The automated transaction process allows a Web site to handle a large volume of low-priced products, just like a vending machine. The three leading players in this field are Cyber-Cash, DigiCash, and First Virtual.

CyberCash

CyberCash (http://www.cybercash.com) is a method that complements a secure Web server and browser using S-HTTP or SSL. CyberCash uses encryption to protect private messages and then sends those messages on top of the other protocols. A user establishes a "CyberCash persona," which sends information about the user to CyberCash after downloading the client information via anonymous FTP. The CyberCash client application is a stand-alone interface on a user's machine that is launched whenever the user needs to make a purchase using CyberCash. After requesting a purchase, the user is sent an online invoice form showing the total charge. The user then enters his or her credit card number and credit card information and submits it to the CyberCash server. All this information is encrypted using public and private key encryption technology. When the CyberCash server receives this request, the credit card is authorized by a bank or credit processing center, and the merchant's account is credited.

CyberCash maintains accounts for users who register their client software, so any two registered users can send money between CyberCash accounts. The electronic cash can be exchanged for real cash through a demand deposit in a bank, and the funds in CyberCash accounts are certified by participating banks. Currently, only Wells Fargo Bank is a participating bank.

DigiCash

DigiCash (http://www.digicash.com/) uses another model for electronic financial transactions called e-cash or electronic cash. The idea behind e-cash is that users have an account at an e-cash bank, from which they can withdraw e-cash, in the form of electronic coins. Each coin carries a bank signature to authenticate it. The e-cash is certified by a bank, and the bank can exchange real money for whatever amount of e-cash is spent. Like CyberCash, DigiCash uses its own client and server software, which works in conjunction with any Web browser or server.

The client software can be used to withdraw cash from the bank account; in other words, take e-cash from a server and store it on the local disk of the user. Then, the client software can send the e-cash from the local disk to the vendor to pay for a product or service. The user makes a connection to a vendor's shop using a regular Web client. When the user selects a link that requires payment, DigiCash shop software launches, making a request to the user's DigiCash client for payment.

The DigiCash shop software is simply the text-based version of DigiCash software, which can be used as either a server or a client—for a vendor or for a customer. Currently, Unix servers are the only servers that can use DigiCash shop software, but software is being developed for Windows NT. For servers that cannot run the software, DigiCash runs a remote shop server that will automatically handle transactions. The remote shop server uses a special directory set up on the Web server.

DigiCash's remote server accesses this directory over the Internet to get information such as the identity of the shop and owner, the goods for sale, and the prices of those goods. The bank account and local e-cash are both protected through public and private key encryption so that no one but the user can withdraw money from the designated bank account or local e-cash. Also, every payment in e-cash is unique, using authentication to identify the payment. If a user attempts to copy his or her local e-cash supply into a second file and spend that e-cash twice, the bank will not clear the payment.

All payments made with e-cash are anonymous, as with real cash. The e-cash is blinded, or made anonymous by the bank, when it is issued, meaning there is no way for the bank to connect a particular coin that has been issued to that same coin when it is spent. The value of the coin is verified by the bank without any reference to the user. In essence, the bank says, "Yes, this is real money," without asking, "Who are you and where did you get this money?"

A user includes an e-mail address when setting up a DigiCash account, allowing the bank to communicate with the user. The contact address is for administrative purposes only, not for purposes of identification. For example, if a bank needed to tell a user to look at a set of transactions or report that a key needed to be changed, it would use this e-mail address.

DigiCash is working on other ways of using e-cash, aside from transactions over the Internet. For example, a card with a computer chip on it, or a smart-card, can read the amount of e-cash from a user's disk, and then that card can be used like a credit card to make payments. Although the cards with computer chips were developed by DigiCash several years ago, DigiCash's cooperation with major credit card companies is leading to a wider acceptance of the e-cash system. This type of innovation could fully integrate electronic financial transactions and real world purchases, in effect making every PC an automatic teller machine combined with a shopping mall.

First Virtual

The First Virtual (http://www.fv.com/) solution to secure financial transactions on the Web uses no encryption. Users establish an account with First Virtual by sending e-mail with information about themselves, then call a toll-free number and enter a credit card number using a touch-tone phone. After these two steps, users are sent an account number and complete details about using the new account. Whenever a purchase is made using First Virtual, users transmit only the account number, and First Virtual automatically charges the credit card for that amount. The process is not much more complicated for vendors. First, the vendor submits the initial application, just like a regular user. Then, the vendor sends information about its checking account to First Virtual, and from that point on, any purchases made using First Virtual will be deposited directly to the e-mail account.

To prevent people from intercepting and using a First Virtual account number to make unauthorized purchases, every First Virtual purchase is confirmed by e-mail. A user makes a purchase, submitting only his or her account number. First Virtual uses that account number to retrieve the user's e-mail address and automatically send a letter requesting confirmation. Charges are made only after a reply is received from that user's e-mail address.

There is one major restriction on using First Virtual to authorize purchases, however: the only thing that can be paid for with a First Virtual account is information, in the broadest sense of the word. Nothing that First Virtual merchants sell is ever physically shipped to the consumer—it's sent over the Internet. This means that First Virtual can be used to buy anything from electronic artwork to software to literary works, as long as it can be transmitted to an electronic mail account. Also, First Virtual can be used to make donations and pay fees. This specialization reduces the possibility of fraud, because any information purchased will be sent to the account holder's electronic mail address, and not to a third-party impostor, even if the account number was used without authorization.

Chapter 4

The Business Side of a Web Site

The enabling technology behind establishing a Web site is a minor consideration; the heart and soul of your site comes from its full integration into your business organization. Paralleling the technological development process are the business and management aspects related to the constant feeding and caring of your Web site. This chapter presents a strategic overview of the key business elements required for a successful Web site.

Defining the Webmaster Team

In-house Web site development must come from the same team effort that drives your business as a whole because your Web site is not a simple add-on to your business, but a mirror of your business in cyberspace. Every Web site requires a core set of seven functional tasks orchestrated by a diverse collection of participants: expectation management, business strategy, domain expertise, content, information architecture, design, and technical knowledge. Within these functions, the Webmaster team must collectively possess knowledge of multiple fields as diverse as network configuration, graphic design, writing, marketing, software development, business strategy, and project management.

Who could make up your Web site team? The answer is as wide as possible a spectrum of people connected to your business: salespersons, information architects, PR and marketing people, techies or power users, visionaries, business strategists, information and layout designers, HTML authors, programmers, graphic designers, project managers, Web hackers, writers, content developers, network system administrators, and others.

The recurring themes running throughout all Webmaster functions are planning, implementing, and maintaining. Many of the functional tasks go on in parallel in different stages of the development cycle. The following outlines the basic components of each theme:

- **Planning.** involves sorting through the maze of options and developing a starting plan of action, complete with a list of action items and assignments. Expect ambiguity in this phase, but at least have a dynamic plan emphasizing points of reference in a steady path of demonstrable progress. At each stage of development modification can and will occur, so make your modification to the game plan and move on.

- **Implementing.** involves subcontracting action items and creating an infrastructure for constant communication and documented progress as well as coordinating and unifying the appropriate skill sets to match the function tasks. Project management plays a key role in this phase.

- **Maintaining.** means managing constant change. This phase requires evolutionary upgrading of skill sets to add new functionalities and enhancements to the Web site. It also involves establishing proper feedback mechanisms and evaluating results.

Expectation Management/Evangelism

Guy Kawasaki, former Apple Computer evangelist, defined his specialty as follows: "Evangelism is the process of convincing people to believe in your product or idea as much as you do. It means selling your dream by using fervor, zeal, guts, and cunning. In contrast with the old-fashioned concept of closing a deal, evangelism means showing others why they should dream your dream."

Selling a Web site presents a difficult challenge for evangelists because you have to walk a fine line between selling the vision and overselling it. Evangelizing for a Web site is the art of championing via strategic presentations, preparation, and anticipation. On the surface, all the hype about the Internet and the Web appears to make the job of selling a Web site easy, but it can also create expectations far beyond current realities. Expectation management is tricky, so the overriding rule of thumb is to undercommit and overdeliver. You'll need to manage the time to completion and overall quality issues to define your budget mix for establishing your Web site.

Business Strategy

The business strategy function crosses a wide range of issues, providing the conceptual framework for determining the business objectives of your Web site. What kind of business processes do you want to create online? Does your business want to begin with a few functions or all functions at once? Each function of your Web site, such as advertising, marketing, customer support, sales, market research, and product or service delivery, requires its own plan. Who is your audience? You need to understand what will motivate them, what they ultimately want, and what you can deliver.

The keys to developing a business strategy for your Web site are prioritizing, planning for success, doing competitive analysis, and budgeting. This planning stage will include prototyping systems and coordinating departments or groups within your organization. Another important part of this stage is investigating competitors and the latest technology options. Keeping up with new Web technologies helps maintain your site's freshness and excitement, so integrate realistic budgeting into your Web site strategy from the beginning. And finally, develop systems to gauge your Web site usage and feedback.

Domain Expertise

A key element to the success of your Web site is bringing specialized knowledge from diverse sources into focus for Web site content and operation. This is a team endeavor that can include customer service, PR, sales, advertising, administration, and others. Responsibility needs to be assigned, and new channels of communication and collaboration need to be opened. The ultimate success of the Web site will be determined by the success achieved by bringing your people's expertise to bear on your Web site. The role of knowledge sharing is important in keeping your site coordinated, so project management plays a pivotal role in keeping multiprocesses coordinated and working in harmony. Your business creates a valuable in-house resource by preserving and enhancing electronic skills.

Content

Much of what is on the Web today is nothing more than data, so for a Web site to stand out, its contents must be made to inform. Building meaningful content and delivering it within the electronic context takes a lot of hard work. A general rule of thumb for putting existing information on the Web is that everything you already have will probably have to be repackaged completely because the dynamics of content are rapid and subject to constant change. You also need to manage the appropriate amounts of content for each part of your Web site.

Information Architecture/Design

Information architecture is the design of understanding, making the complex clear. With the goal of your Web site to attract users, your information must be made available to each person in a way that is understandable and intuitive. The methods to create understanding for the user include context, metaphor, multiple points of entry, parallel tracks, and customization.

The online medium is the dynamic delivery system, allowing for information to be modified indefinitely and customized for user preferences. It's the information architect's or Web site designer's role to maintain continuity in the diversity of media through understanding the concept of identity. Identity is not just a logo, graphic language, color, typography, palette of elements or images; rather, it's present in every aspect of a company. It creates perceptions and beliefs, and it generates value and trust. So when people find those things to be clever, dumb, beautiful, bad, or unappealing, they file them away and create some new context into which they put that company.

For identity to migrate from the real world to the virtual world requires an understanding of not just visual design, but of the constraints and affordances of the medium as well. A company's identity on the Web must be consistent with the company's information, communication, and business objectives, which then strategically leverage the affordances of the medium.

Technical Infrastructure

The technical infrastructure includes all the components that come together to provide the platform for your company's content delivery via a Web site: the PC hardware, the Windows NT operating system, Web server software, the telecommunications connection to an Internet service provider, security, and technical Webmaster functions. These are core competencies that your business needs to master to begin the evolutionary process of growing your Web site. The technical infrastructure is subject to constant technological improvement. Your server platform will need to include as many enhancements and support features as possible to make the site attractive. The good news is the technical threshold for operating a Web site has been dramatically lowered so that nonprogrammers with a moderate amount of Windows and Internet experience can build a Web site.

Business Maxims for a Successful Web Site

Operating a Web site is technologically sexy, but a Web site's ultimate value to your business is how it impacts the bottom line. The following sections present the key business maxims to keep in mind as you develop your Web site plan.

Define the Success of Your Web Site

Evaluating the success of your Web site requires a means to measure that success. Without specifying clear goals that you want to achieve from your Web site, your business will never know if the end has been achieved, so you must determine why you want to invest resources in a Web presence. Selecting reasonable, achievable, and measurable goals at the start is the only way to be sure your efforts will pay off.

Give Something for Free

Web-based commerce must be packaged as "giving back to the Net" or, as Internet founder Vinton Cerf and others call it, the "gift economy" of the Internet. In planning a Web presence you must look beyond the immediate objectives of making a sale to incorporate a broader set of goals. The range of services, products, and information used to add value to a Web site is almost limitless. Many companies offer links to related sites, maintain directories of resources, offer free evaluation copies of their software, or provide other services. The best approach for each company depends entirely on its products, services, and areas of expertise. Gift-giving provides the foundation for bringing people to the site on a regular basis.

Always Be a Work in Progress

Change on the Web is the bread and butter of an effective Web site. All materials have life spans, so keeping your site fresh is a demanding task. Fortunately, the digital canvas of the Web provides an easy medium for making changes. And an ever-expanding cornucopia of tools for designing information helps to ensure that nothing stays the same very long on the Web. Think of your Web site as a farm stand that you must constantly restock with fresh produce to stay in business.

Get Something from Your Visitors

Learn as much as you can from your visitors on an ongoing basis by encouraging them to go beyond passive reading of documents into participating in discussion groups, filling out interactive forms, or sending e-mail. The Web is best put to use as a multidirectional communication medium. Because the cost of customer surveys or focus groups is expensive with traditional services, they are affordable to only large businesses. If you solicit input from your visitors, you can get valuable information for practically nothing. You have the power to conduct your own sophisticated surveys via your Web site.

Keep Them Coming Back

The first thing you need to do is to get people to your site, which you can do with online and offline campaigns. Once they get to your site, you need to make sure they keep coming back. The following sections suggest some actions you can take to bring people back.

Feed Curiosity

If you have a large site with too much to see in one online session, visitors will come back. The information and activities must not be confusing, but visitors should feel that there is a nugget just around the next corner, and that this is a valuable site.

Create Information Turnover

Provide at least some item that changes frequently or even every time someone visits. This may be a "What's New" feature or coverage of a current event broadly related to your industry.

Make Your Site an Indispensable Resource

Your page can offer links to existing databases, collections of Internet and Web guides, searching tools, or a repository of files. Related links become a springboard for surfing.

Create a Unique Event

The page can provide contests or giveaways. Other possibilities include first-person coverage of events or an ask-the-expert feature.

Entice Users with Constructive Engagement

Soliciting input from visitors is a must. Your site should include moderated discussion groups, surveys, interactive forms, and even software gadgets that make users want to come back.

Timing Is Everything

The convergence of new technologies makes establishing your Web site an option right now. You can start small and build up over time, but get started. The learning curve to master the Web serving realm is steep and steady. Even more important, although Internet access is not ubiquitous at the moment, it's only a matter of time until it will be. If you start creating a Web site today, you'll be ready to meet average computer users' expectations when they hit the Web. If not, you'll be playing catch-up. The knowledge you need to acquire continues to grow exponentially, so if you wait too long, you may never catch up.

Attract Attention

Your Web site can be the greatest site on the planet, but if people don't know it exists, all is lost. Making steady promotional efforts using both traditional forms of communication and new electronic methods such as links from other Web sites, Internet newsgroups, and e-mail is the way you get your customers to come to you. Once they arrive at your site, engage them with activity, filtered information, and other tools. The many new Web site enhancement tools allow your business to interact both ways with users, so make use of these tools.

Making Effective Use of Your Web Site

The Web offers a way for people to reach your business and find what they want. Over time, you can build your site to include the full functionality of marketing in the real world. The key business functions that a Web site can handle include public relations, customer service, prospect qualification, sales, customer feedback, and internal communications.

Public Relations

A well-positioned Web site can harvest good press in your industry trade journals. Use a What's New section to show off new products, your latest announcements, and other news. Journalists searching for information are regular users of these sections. Providing enough useful content about your company, products, and strategies in this section helps journalists write stories about your company. Consider the types of magazines that would access your site, and supply it with the appropriate text, images, sound bites, and video clips. The easier you make it for journalists to put together a story, the more often your business will appear in print.

Customer Service

The customer service function should be at the top of your list because a Web site is a convenient and effective way to deliver customer service. Connecting a database to your site lets customers find their own answers, which can save your business money. When you deliver your customer service via the Web, remember to treat your customers the way they expect to be treated in the Web medium, but always include a way to let them connect to a real person.

Prospect Qualification

The Web provides a powerful medium for the prospecting of potential sales. Most businesses can benefit from a Web site's inherent qualification capabilities, using them to dramatically shorten the sales cycle by providing a good deal of education for potential customers. The more potential customers get answers from your Web site, the more time your salespeople can spend closing sales.

Sales

A Web site can be integrated in the sales process at the point of customer contact with a sales person. For example, both the customer and sales person can share the same Web documents as the sales person leads the customer through an interactive demonstration.

Depending on the products your business sells, you can take orders online without the intervention of salespeople. Your Web site can support forms for users to select colors, styles, configurations, shipping methods, and payment terms. In fact, with new commerce enabling services now available for Web sites, there's no reason you can't support credit card sales online. You receive the credit card orders, then process them in the same way you do in the real world.

Customer Feedback

Online, interactive communication with your Web site customers and prospects allows your business to get valuable feedback through forms that visitors can fill out for surveys. Each phase of your product development, positioning, and promotion can include your customers' input. A web site can also contain areas where visitors can participate in moderated discussion groups to share information with other customers.

Internal Communications

Just as the Web offers better communication to prospects and customers, it can offer better communication internally. Use of a private Web site provides a valuable way to keep everyone in a company informed. It can be used to keep the sales force aware of product line changes and pricing updates or to deliver programs and files via a Web site.

Part Two

Laying the Groundwork for Your Commerce Center

Chapter 5

Web Server Technology Primer

Behind the operation of a Web site is a collection of technical issues that you need to understand, even if you're not involved in the actual mechanics of setting up and operating a Web site. A decision maker with an understanding of these concepts will be able to manage the project more effectively. This chapter explains the technical background information on the building blocks of establishing a Web site.

Web Protocols, Concepts, and Terminology

The World Wide Web encompasses a collection of standards and protocols. The HTTP (hypertext transfer protocol) is the protocol that provides the foundation of the Web. However, the Web supports the FTP (file transfer protocol), Gopher, WAIS, NNTP (network news transport protocol), Telnet, SMTP (for e-mail), and other protocols. All these protocols are hidden from the user as separate protocols. Web browser users see a standard interface, and they don't have to know whether the information is coming via one protocol or another. Another great feature of HTTP is that it doesn't restrict the types of objects that can be sent as long as there is a supporting viewer or helper application associated with a Web browser. The following sections provide an overview of the key elements and concepts that define the World Wide Web.

The Hypertext Transfer Protocol

HTTP is the glue that holds the World Wide Web together. Web servers and browsers use HTTP to communicate with each other. Every document request from a Web browser to a Web server is a new connection, or "hit," through which the document is transferred, then the connection is closed. Because HTTP is the primary protocol for distributing information on the World Wide Web, Web servers are often called HTTP servers. The basic transaction between a Web browser and a Web server via HTTP goes something like this:

1. The Web browser establishes a connection to the server via a unique URL address.

2. The browser makes a request to the server specifying a particular document to retrieve by clicking on a hyperlink.

3. The Web server sends the HTML document to the Web browser and disconnects the client.

4. The Web browser creates the document on the local machine.

HTTP is defined as a stateless protocol, which means it doesn't retain information about a connection from one request to the next. If a document contains inline images or multimedia objects, a separate connection must be established for each one. However, Netscape Navigator allows open multiple connections to retrieve multiple documents or objects in parallel.

The current version of the HTTP specification, 1.0, is supported by all leading Web servers and browsers. HTTP 1.0 supports the use of headers in documents, making it possible to pass along information for facilitating authentication, encryption, and user identification. The header is a block of information that precedes the main data, and when a Web browser requests data, the request transaction header can include the name of the Web client and other pertinent information. When a Web server responds to a request, the header it returns along with the requested data can include information about the status of the request, the number of bytes transmitted, and the content type.

Hypertext, Hypermedia, and Hyperlinks

Inherent in the concept of the World Wide Web are hypertext and hypermedia. Hypertext is textual material that includes links to other textual material, letting the user follow information in a nonlinear fashion. Hypermedia links different types of media, including the written word, graphics, video, and sound. Hyperlinks are links within Web documents that can take you to almost any resource on the Internet. Typically these are presented as colored or underlined text, icons, images, or image maps with hot spots.

Uniform Resource Locators

Uniform resource locators (URLs) are pointers to all kinds of objects located anywhere on the Internet. These objects can be files, newsgroups, Telnet sites, WAIS databases, and more. A URL is the unique address of a Web document or Internet object. All URLs have the following standard format:

```
protocol://machine_address/path/filename
```

"Protocol" in this format is the prefix that defines the protocol used as in ftp:// or telnet://. Network news is the only protocol that instead of being followed by the two forward slashes is followed by only a colon then the name of the newsgroup. Often URLs don't include filenames; for example, with the URL http://www.netgen.com, the browser can locate the server and the directory within the server, but not a specific document. Which document the server returns depends on the server setup. The URL path is not necessarily the same as the physical path of the file on the server; it is determined by how the Web site is mapped on the server.

Note: *Some URLs include a port specification if a nondefault port is used for the service. More on ports later.*

Hypertext Markup Language

The hypertext markup language (HTML) is the markup language that defines the structure of Web documents, but it does not define the exact formatting, which is left to the Web browser. In HTML, tags provide a functional description of a piece of a Web document without specifying how that text is to be rendered. For example, you can use a tag in HTML to identify a piece of text as a first-level header. However, each browser is then free to render that text in whatever format it uses for first-level headers. Beyond controlling the description of Web documents, HTML adds the ability to embed hypertext links into documents. These hypertext links, which can take the user to another Web document or any object on the Internet, are the information threads that form the structure of the World Wide Web.

The current version of HTML is 2.0, and the next version will be 3.0. Chapter 17 explains the key elements of HTML 3.0. Netscape has already added enhanced functionality to HTML 2.0 through the use of extensions that give users more control over the rendering of Web pages, and new tags allow users to center text and specify font size. These new tags were not in the official HTML specification, but many have become the de facto standard.

Multipurpose Internet Mail Extensions

Multipurpose Internet Mail Extensions (MIME) is an extensible system developed for sending multimedia data, such as graphics and videos, over

Internet mail. The Web adopted MIME as part of HTTP. By examining the type of a document, a browser can determine whether a it is HTML text that should be formatted and displayed or a sound file that should be passed to a helper application to be played through the computer's speaker system. Table 5.1 lists some common MIME types and filename extensions.

TCP/IP Primer

Transmission control protocol and Internet protocol (TCP/IP) is the collection of networking protocols that keeps the Internet as a whole connected. TCP/IP is not a single entity, but a set of software programs that provide network services such as remote logins, remote file transfers, and electronic mail. As a communications protocol it should handle errors in transmission, manage the routing and delivery of data, and control the actual transmission by use of predetermined status signals. IP resides at the network layer, and TCP operates in the transport layer of the networking model, which is explained later.

TABLE 5.1 Common MIME Types Supported by HTTP

Type	Description
Application/postscript	PostScript
Application/zip	PKZip file compression format
Audio/wav	Microsoft's .WAV format
Image/gif	CompuServe's GIF format
Image/jpeg	JPEG file format
Message/news	Usenet news message format
Message/rfc822	Internet e-mail message format
Text/html	HyperText Markup Language
Text/plain	Plain ASCII text
Video/mpeg	MPEG movie format
Video/quicktime	Quicktime movie format

To operate a Web server, your PC must be running TCP/IP as one of its networking protocols. Chapter 7 explains setting up and configuring TCP/IP in Windows NT, where it is built in.

TCP/IP is a packet-based network, which means data is transferred in packets. These packets include the data, error control, and routing information, and they can be routed independently across the Internet. Once they reach their intended destination, they are reassembled. Because TCP/IP is packet based, you can support multiple simultaneous connection on a Web sever, even over an analog line using a modem.

Internet Addresses

Network addresses are analogous to mailing addresses in that they tell a system where to deliver a diagram. TCP/IP uses a 32-bit address to identify a machine on a network and the network to which it is attached. IP addresses identify a machine's connection to the network, not the machine itself—an important distinction. Whenever a machine's location on the network is moved, the IP address must be changed, too. The IP address is the set of numbers such as 127.40.8.72, which uniquely identifies any device connected to the network.

IP (or Internet protocol) addresses are assigned only by the Network Information Center (InterNIC), although if a network is not connected to the Internet, that network can determine its own numbering. For all Internet accesses, though, the IP address must be registered with the NIC. The IP address must be in one of four formats, class A through class D, depending on the size of the network. The class is identified by the first few bit sequences, with up to four bits for class D. The class can be determined from the three (high-order) bits. In fact, in most cases, the first two bits are enough, because there are few class D networks.

Class A addresses are for large networks that have many machines. The 24 bits for the local address (also frequently called the host address) are needed in these cases. The network address is kept to 7 bits, which limits the number of networks that can be identified. Class B addresses are for intermediate-sized networks, with 16-bit local or host addresses and 14-bit network addresses. The typical domain name comes with a class C address. Class C networks have only 8 bits for the local or host address, limiting the number of devices to 256. There are 21 bits for the network address. Finally, Class D networks are used for multicasting purposes, when a general broadcast to more than one device is required. The lengths of the sections of the IP address have been carefully chosen to provide maximum flexibility in assigning both network and local addresses.

Domain Name Service

Instead of using the full 32-bit IP address, most systems on the Internet adopt more meaningful names for their devices and networks, usually reflecting the organization's name. Individual device names in a network can range from descriptive ones on small networks to more complex naming conventions on larger networks. Providing text-based names to act as pointers to IP addresses is referred to as the domain name service (DNS).

The domain name service uses a hierarchical architecture. The first level of naming divides networks into subnetworks, such as com for commercial. Below each of these is another division that identifies the individual subnetwork with a unique domain name, usually one for each organization. The organization's system manager can further divide the company's subnetworks as desired, with each network called a subdomain. The NIC also allows for a country designator to be appended. There are designators for all countries in the world, such as .ca for Canada and .uk for the United Kingdom. The Network Information Center (InterNIC) maintains the vast list of network names and the corresponding network gateway addresses.

Note: *See the Appendix "Webmaster Resources" for more information on Inter-NIC.*

The domain name service uses two systems to establish and track domain names: a name resolver and a name server. A name resolver on each network examines information in a domain name. If it can't find the full IP address, it queries a name server, which has the full NIC information available. The name resolver tries to complete the addressing information using its own database, which it updates. If a queried name server cannot resolve the address, it can query another name server, and so on, across the entire inter-network. There is a considerable amount of information stored in the name resolver and name server, as well as whole set of protocols for querying between the two. The details, luckily, are not important to an understanding of TCP/IP, although the overall concept of address resolution is important to understanding how the Internet translates between domain names and IP addresses.

Ports and Sockets

All applications or services that use TCP have a port number that identifies the application. On an Internet server, that number identifies where the application or service listens for data. Port number conventions have been adopted to allow better communications between TCP implementations, enabling port numbers to identify the type of service that one TCP system is requesting from another. Typically, port numbers above 255 are reserved for private use of the local machine, but numbers below 255 are for frequently used services. The default port for HTTP is 80, while the default port for SSL is 443. FTP's default port is 21, and Telnet's default port is 23.

Each communication circuit into and out of the TCP layer is uniquely identified by a combination of two numbers, which together are called a socket. The socket, whether on the sending or receiving machine, is composed of the IP address of that machine and the port number used by the TCP software. Because the IP address is unique across the internetwork and the port numbers will be unique to the individual machine, the socket numbers will also be unique across the entire internetwork. Thus, a process can talk to another process across the network, based entirely on the socket number.

The Architecture of TCP/IP

TCP/IP takes a layered protocol approach, which means each protocol layer is independent of the others. TCP/IP loosely follows the Open Systems Interconnection (OSI) model, which defines layers and protocols that computer networks must contain to control the interactions between computers. This reference model defines a framework for implementing protocols into seven layers: application, presentation, session, transport, network, data link, and physical.

The OSI Model

According to the OSI model, when information passes from computer to computer through a protocol, control of the data passes from one layer to the next, starting at the application layer. It then proceeds to the bottom layer of that same system, then to the next system, and then back up the hierarchy in that second system. The following defines the seven layers of the OSI reference model from the highest to the lowest level of the networking food chain.

ISO Seeks Global Standards through OSI

The OSI reference model was developed by the International Organization for Standardization (ISO), an association of member countries, each of which is represented by its leading standard-setting organization. For example, ANSI (American National Standards Institute) is that organization for the United States. ISO works to establish global standards for communications and information exchange.

The Application Layer

This is where applications reside. It's the interface point between the OSI model and the user. Common functions in this layer include opening, closing, reading, writing, and transferring files.

The Presentation Layer

This layer is responsible for the syntax of data between systems so the data is meaningful to both systems. It acts as a translator or formatter of data between different systems. This layer is also used for encryption.

The Session Layer

This layer manages the dialog between systems and is dependent on the transport layer for the connection. It ensures that data arrives at both ends of the link in a form meaningful to the applications operating at both ends.

The Transport Layer

This layer establishes transport connections between session entities. It detects if a packet has been routed and ensures that all of the data has been transferred.

The Network Layer

This layer handles the actual routing functions for moving data from one system to another and provides the addressing necessary to relay data. It enables the upper layers to be independent from the data transmission and switching technologies, and it performs the switching functions in routable protocols, such as IP.

The Data Link Layer

This layer defines the protocol that ensures that the data crossing the physical layer is reliable. Examples of the data link layer include the protocols used for local area networks (LANs) such as Ethernet and wide area networks (WANs) such as X.25. Synchronization, error control, and flow control are maintained here to maintain the validity and integrity of the transmission.

The Physical Layer

This layer represents the cabling of a network system that is the physical link between computers. It supports the point-to-point connections of two devices across the network, or multipoint connections. This layer supports the half- and full-duplex communication through either serial or parallel data paths.

The TCP/IP Model

TCP/IP consists of only five layers, performing the functions of OSI's seven. The differences between the OSI and TCP/IP models relate to the layers above the transport level, as well as those at the network level. TCP/IP combines the session and presentation layers into an application layer and combines the physical and data link layers into a network interface layer. The following describes the five layers of the TCP/IP model.

The Application Layer

This layer supports the protocols that form the basis of Internet applications, such as HTTP for the Web, file transfer protocol (FTP) for file transfers, and Telnet for remote login.

The Transport Layer

This layer adds transport data to the packet and passes it to the Internet layer.

The Internet Layer

This layer takes the data package from the transport layer and adds IP information before passing it on to the network. It also controls the action you initiate on your local host that is then performed or responded to on a remote host.

The Network Interface Layer

This is the network device as the host, or local computer, sees it. It's through this medium that the data is passed to the physical layer.

The Physical Layer

This bottom layer is the Ethernet, point-to-point protocol (PPP), or serial line interface protocol (SLIP) part of the network.

Key Elements of Building Your Web Site

Building a Web site from just the technical perspective involves working with a cluster of diverse technologies. This process, although quickly getting easier and less expensive, first requires grasping the key elements that come together to operate as your Web site. The following sections present a bird's-eye view of the key issues in building a Web site from the technology stand-point.

Note: *All these topics are covered in greater detail later in this book; for now we'll look at the big picture.*

Network Connections

A Web site must be accessible to the Internet 24 hours a day, 7 days a week, and 365 days a year. To make it this accessible requires getting a dedicated connection to the Internet, which means a telecommunication line for which service is billed at a flat monthly rate rather than measured. Network connections are measured in terms of bandwidth, or the speed at which the network transmits data to the Internet. The higher the bandwidth, the more expensive the service and the more volume of users your site can handle.

The cost of bandwidth is coming down, but it's still not cheap. However, there are several affordable options for operating a moderately busy Web site with 10,000 to 80,000 hits per day. You can use a dedicated 28.8Kbps modem that will support 10,000 to 20,000 hits per day or connect to the Internet via an ISDN line, which can support about four times the capacity of the 28.8Kbps modem. The 28.8Kbps modem option with a dedicated connection can run as little as $100 a month. ISDN runs around $200 to $500 a month for a dedicated connection. From these two low-end bandwidth connections, the scale moves up to Frame Relay, Fractional T1, and T1, which cost from $500 to $2000 per month.

Internet service providers are your link to connecting to the Internet via dedicated lines. They typically work with the local telephone company to get your line set up. Depending on the telephone company that services your area, your service experience, as well as the cost, will vary. The cost of getting a dedicated connection typically includes two components: the telephone company charges and the charges levied by the service provider. Wading through the tangle of telecommunications is probably the most difficult part of your journey toward establishing your own Web site. Your first line of defense is carefully choosing an Internet service provider. If you don't already have a domain name, you'll also usually establish it via the ISP before you can begin operating your Web site.

The other piece of the Internet connection is the networking device that connects your PC to the TCP/IP-based Internet. The TCP/IP functionality for your Web site comes from Windows NT. To connect to the Internet via dedicated voice line, you need a 28.8Kbps modem, and to connect to the Internet via ISDN, you need a device called a terminal adapter. The cost of this device varies depending on its capabilities.

PC Web Server Hardware

A new generation of PC-based hardware using the Intel Pentium and P6 processors combined with Windows NT, a robust 32-bit multitasking version of Windows, opens up affordable Web server platform options. In selecting these options, two determining factors of a Web server are the number of processes the machine is trying to do at one time and the number of users making requests to the server at one time. Key factors to consider in getting your PC-based server hardware are memory capacity, CPU speed, and disk speed. A Web server is not processor intensive, so CPU speed has little to do with bottlenecks. However, what you do need is a lot of memory. A Web server should run with at least 16MB RAM with 32MB to 64MB even better because having the server software in memory makes the server work a lot faster than if you had to swap out to read from disk.

Most server software works such that each time a connection is made to the server (that is, each time it receives a request), the server makes a copy of itself to handle the request. The more requests there are, the more copies of the server will be vying for memory space. If there isn't enough memory to go around, the system starts using temporary space on the hard drive. It swaps out the process of copying data from memory into a space on the hard disk. The bottom line in the comparison of memory access with hard disk access is that memory access is on the order of a hundred thousand times faster than disk access.

Following are some PC hardware configurations based on how many users connect to your Web site per day:

- For 25 to 50 users a day, a suitable server should have at least 16MB of memory, roughly 25MB of free hard disk space, and a 33MHz 486 processor.

- For 50 to 200 users a day, a server should have 20MB to 32MB of memory, roughly 50MB to 100MB of available hard disk space, and a 66MHz 486DX2 or 60MHz Pentium.

- For 200 or more users a day, a server should have 32MB to 64MB of memory, 200MB or more of unused hard disk space, and a 66MHz to 90MHz Pentium or dual-Pentium processor configuration.

Secure Web Server Software

Once you have chosen your hardware platform and installed Windows NT, you need to add your Web server software. Web server software that allows you to handle secure activities by using encryption and decryption is what you need to conduct commerce on the Web. A variety of commercial secure server programs is available, including Netscape's Commerce Server,

O'Reilly's Web Site Professional, and Microsoft's Internet Server. Prices for these software packages run anywhere from free to $1,499, but they are falling rapidly. Many of these Web server software publishers let you take a free 60-day test drive of their product by downloading the software from their Web sites.

With the advent of secure transaction protocols on the Web, there is no real reason not to get the secure Web server software instead of the unsecured versions for publishing only. Although Web server software used for publishing only is less expensive, the secure Web server software is the way to go. Even if you don't plan to implement a secure system immediately, you'll ultimately want your site to handle the full range of publishing, secure communications, and transaction processing.

As you recall, SSL (secure socket layer) and S-HTTP (Secure-HTTP) are the leading security protocols supported by Web browsers. SSL is currently more popular because it's supported by the dominant browser, Netscape Navigator. S-HTTP, developed by NCSA and supported by Mosaic, is not in widespread use yet. A new security protocol, SST (secure transaction technology), is an open specification jointly developed by Microsoft and Visa International. This secure transaction method promises to become a major player because it extends the current bankcard system to the Internet.

Web Server Security in Perspective

A hot topic on the Internet is security. For operating a Web commerce server, security issues break down into two components. The first involves establishing a secure system for handling sensitive data ranging from private communications to credit card or purchase order transactions online. This functionality is part of the Web server software, which supports the security protocols, such as SSL or S-HTTP. The second major area of security—and the one discussed here—is protecting your Web site from unauthorized attacks. Typically, this function lies at the hardware and operating system level.

Security starts with planning to integrate a Web server into your organization's existing network. Connecting to the Internet exposes your business in both good and risky ways. In general, a Web server is not a major security risk for small businesses that want to keep it separate from their internal network. It's connecting a network to the Internet that opens the system to potential attacks and requires advanced security systems, such as firewalls and proxies.

Firewalls and Proxies

A firewall system imposes a specially configured gateway machine between the outside world and the site's internal network. To minimize your risk, a computer called a firewall is used as a buffer zone between your private network and the Internet. A firewall protects you by keeping unauthorized individuals from directly accessing the machines on your private network and preventing them from seeing anything that's running behind your firewall. You can either use a firewall or refrain from connecting a system or machine that has sensitive data. Firewalls create a moat of protection for the internal network.

Firewall systems come in a variety of configurations, but they all fall into roughly two categories. The first category relies on a dual-homed gateway, a conventional computer with two separate network interface cards. One interface is connected to the inner network and the other to the outside world. There is no direct traffic between the two networks, so to provide access to the Internet from the internal network, programs known as proxies run on the gateway machine. A proxy's job is to accept requests from a machine on the internal network, screen it for acceptability according to the rules set up by the site's security stance, then forward it to a remote host in the outside world. Firewalls based on the dual-homed gateways are usually the most restrictive. Outgoing calls are restricted to the number of services for which the proxy software is available, and all network-aware programs on the inner network have to be modified to work with the proxies. In particular, for Web browsers to call out, there have to be proxies in place that can forward each of the protocols that Web browsers support, including Telnet, FTP, Gopher, and WAIS as well as HTTP itself. Incoming calls are generally not allowed across a dual-homed gateway; if they are, they involve a two-step process in which outside users are first required to log into the gateway and then Telnet to an internal host.

The second category of firewall configurations is called a screened-host gateway or packet-filtered gateway. This setup uses a network router or software to filter the network packets that pass between the outside world and the inner network. Packets can be filtered by several criteria, including their source and destination addresses, their source and destination ports, and whether or not they're initiating a connection. A screened-host gateway is usually configured so that the router allows through only those packets bound for the bastion host. All other packets are rejected. As far as the outside world is concerned, the only accessible machine on the inner network is the bastion host. In this respect the two schemes have the same appearance when viewed from outside.

In contrast to the previous scheme, the router can be set up to allow hosts in the inner network to initiate connections with outside services to receive packets in response to those connections. From the vantage point of users on the inner network, the firewall is a one-way mirror: they can see out, but the rest of the world can't see in. Because outgoing connections are not entirely risk free, many sites opt to cloud the one-way mirror. Outgoing connections to essential services, such as Telnet, FTP and e-mail, are allowed, while others are forbidden. A Web-friendly firewall would also allow outgoing packets bound for the HTTP, WAIS, and Gopher ports. An additional advantage of the screened-host gateway is its flexibility. By allowing selected inbound packets to travel to other than the bastion, it can open holes in the firewall to grant access to selected hosts and services.

Keeping the Web Away from Your Internet Network

For security at the simplest level, yet with the most protection for your internal network, build a standalone Web server (Figure 5.1). This method means

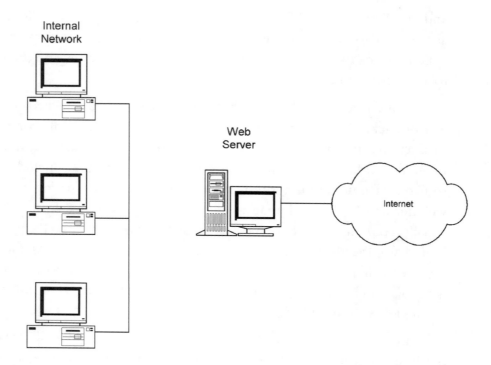

FIGURE 5.1 The physical isolation of your Web server from your internal network.

using a dedicated PC that isn't connected to your internal network. The dedicated connection to the Internet from the Internet service provider connects directly and exclusively to that PC. This is a reasonable option for a small business because it protects internal data from being exposed to the Internet and it allocates the full resources of the PC and the Internet connection to serving Web users. On the down side, of course, is that the lack of any network connection requires working on that specific machine to manage and maintain the Web server. In a small one- or two-office business, this may not be a problem, but for larger organizations it would be.

The Two-Ethernet-Card Solution

A step above the standalone approach is using the two-Ethernet-card solution, as shown in Figure 5.2. One Ethernet card directs TCP/IP packets to a

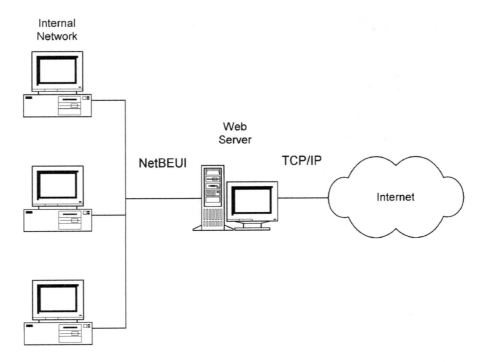

FIGURE 5.2 The two-Ethernet-card solution separates the TCP/IP protocol from your internal network packets.

router that communicates with the Internet, and the other Ethernet card
directs packets to the internal network, such as NetBIOS for Windows
networks. By setting up the card using Windows NT, you can ensure that
packets from one network cannot mix with packets from the other network.
In this way the two networks operate separately on the PC. Using the multihoming features of a Web server software package, you can allow the same
Web site to be accessed from the internal network as well as from the Internet. This option allows networked users in your organization to provide
input to the Web server from their nodes. It also allows multiple people
throughout your organization to contribute to the Web site from their locations instead of physically working on a single PC. This is typically the least
expensive option for a small business operating its own internal network.

The Software Firewall Option

A growing number of vendors are offering firewall software that runs on Windows NT. Some software firewall vendors include Raptor Systems' Eagle NT (http://www.raptor.com/), Network 1 Software and Technology's Fire-Wall/Plus (http://www.network-1.com/), LANOptics's Guardian (http://www .netguard.com/) and Microsoft's firewall product code-named Catapult (http: //www.microsoft.com/).

Chapter 6

Under the Hood of Your Web Server PC

Your hardware platform is the operating foundation of your Web site, and its performance plays a big role in the delivery of your documents on the Web. This chapter explains the hardware requirements for running an optimal Web server as well as other options to enhance the operation of your Web site.

What You Need to Run a Web Server

The demands on a PC's processor are not that tough for operating a basic Web server that delivers documents to users. PCs that are 486-based and up can handle the demands of a moderately active Web server. However, using a Pentium system is strongly recommended for meeting the demands made by Windows NT and for running external programs in conjunction with your Web server.

Beyond the CPU, there are several important pieces of your Web server, such as memory capacity and disk speed, that play an important role in its performance. For memory, consider 16MB a minimum, with 32MB to 64MB more realistic. The more memory it has, the faster your Web server performs because it can work with information in memory instead of swapping it out from a hard disk.

Swapping slows performance, so during peak loads a Web server can slow down dramatically. Your Web server should never have to swap out memory, except during really busy peak loads. Otherwise, users will be left waiting beyond the normal time they expect to receive the results of their requests.

Going the Intel CPU Route

One of the features of Windows NT touted by Microsoft is its portability. Currently, this means Windows NT can run on an Intel-compatible CPU or an ARC system-compliant RISC computer (MIPS R4000 or better). However, given the economic realities of the computer marketplace, the Intel-based PC rules in terms of offering affordable hardware for most PC-based businesses. The economics of buying and maintaining your Web server equipment are heavily slanted to the Intel-based PC. The scale and competition in PCs ensure better consumer benefits market than in the RISC workstation market. In addition, the adoption of Windows NT to RISC has been slow and is not projected to reach any kind of critical mass. The best strategy for most PC businesses is to stay with the Intel architecture when it comes to running a Windows NT-based Web server.

The current Pentium class of CPUs offers the computing power for running a powerful Web site. Beyond the Pentium processors, a growing number of vendors are offering Pentium Pro workstation-class systems designed for 32-bit operating systems, such as Windows NT. The Pentium Pro systems support the symmetrical multiprocessing (SMP) architecture inherent in Windows NT that lets you operate a system spread out over multiple CPUs.

The Pentium Pro will radically alter the server landscape. It promises to deliver workstation-class computing capabilities within reach of millions of smaller enterprises that lack the resources and technical expertise required to set up and maintain a Unix-based system. Compared with $10,000-plus for workstations based on chips such as Digital Equipment Corp.'s Alpha, the PowerPC 604, and Sun's UltraSparc, the Pentium Pro systems are running under $8,000.

SRAM Requirements

Although you can use an Intel 386 system to run your Web site, doing so is simply foolish. The processing bottlenecks inherent in the 386 architecture will quickly alienate your Web site users. Windows NT is a multithreaded preemptive multitasking system that requires much larger cache memory than a conventional single-thread operating system. All Intel 486SX or better CPUs employ a CPU cache, which is a small amount of static RAM (called SRAM) closely coupled to the CPU. It exchanges data with the CPU at speeds much higher than those of the normal dynamic random access memory (DRAM) used in most PCs. In order to operate at CPU speeds, SRAM caches have to have very high memory access speeds of 20 nanoseconds compared with the 70 nanoseconds of conventional DRAM. The 20-nanosecond static RAM's extremely high price tag resulted in a two-tier architecture for 386 CPUs. The first tier uses a small amount of the very fast SRAM, which in turn is refreshed from DRAM.

Because 386 processors do not include any internal cache memory, the 386 system isn't an option for running Windows NT. The Intel 486 series processor has an 8KB on-chip cache, and the Pentium processor has a 16KB on-chip cache. More cache RAM dramatically improves your Web server's performance.

Thanks for the RAM Memory

Windows NT is a memory hog that, according to Microsoft, requires 12MB RAM. However, based on reality, you should have a minimum of 16MB RAM (over and above the CPU cache). The additional cost of the RAM more than pays off in improved performance. Beyond the basic 16MB recommendation, various Windows NT options may require additional memory. In fact, to be effective, a Web server on top of your Windows NT platform should have at least 32MB of RAM. You can determine the amount of additional memory required to run your Web server by subtracting 16MB (NT RAM requirement) from the application publisher's recommended configuration.

Hard Disk Issues

The bottom line on hard disk capacity is get a 1GB drive. It is not that expensive today, so there's no need to skimp here. The official Microsoft requirement for Windows NT Server is 90MB of hard disk space, and 75 for NT Workstation.

Besides the basic storage space requirements to be considered in selecting a hard disk for a Windows NT system, there is the disk controller. Windows NT's preemptive multitasking uses asynchronous I/O (asynchronous input/output). This feature means the CPU can request to read information from a disk file while continuing to work on other tasks. It waits for the hard disk controller to inform it that the request is complete.

The performance of Windows NT is significantly enhanced if you select a better type of disk controller, such as SCSI (small computer system interface). Windows NT's preference for SCSI-based CD-ROMs and tape drives also makes the SCSI approach the best. The best performance will be achieved with intelligent disk controllers, which can carry out operations independently of the system's CPU. Check out the Windows NT hardware compatibility list to find out what hard disk controllers are supported by Windows NT.

CD-ROM

CD-ROM should be considered essential for all Windows NT-based Web servers. Microsoft distributes Windows NT on CD-ROM, as well as most

Web server software, and utilities on CD-ROMs. Currently, Windows NT supports a limited range of CD-ROM controllers—mostly ones based on SCSI. So, again, you're going to need a controller and CD-ROM from the Windows NT hardware compatibility list.

Given that SCSI is the best supported controller type for both CD-ROM and tape backup, SCSI makes sense as the primary transport mechanism for your hard disks as well, allowing you to have just one disk controller for the entire system. Because SCSI also supports use of the various disk array options supported by Windows NT Server, use SCSI as the standard disk controller type for your Windows NT Web server. Consult the latest Windows NT hardware compatibility list for the names of supported CD-ROMs and controllers.

Choosing the Right Bus

Your PC's system bus architecture becomes extremely significant with Windows NT, especially in a high-performance configuration. Currently available buses include ISA, EISA, MCA, VESA, and PCI Local Bus. The bottom line on bus architecture is there are only two real contenders for a Windows NT platform: VESA and PCI.

VESA

The local bus is basically the extension of the high-speed parallel bus used by RAM on the computer's motherboard to peripheral devices. Early local bus implementations were proprietary, varying from manufacturer to manufacturer. However, the need to standardize on a nonproprietary local bus architecture for video cards drove the Video Electronic Standards Association (VESA) to define the VL-Bus (VESA local) standard. VL-Bus provides a relatively high-speed 32-bit connection.

PCI

Intel developed a competing standard, Peripheral Connect Interchange (PCI), which eliminates the limits of the local bus technology. PCI has emerged as the new industry standard for high-speed peripherals. When considering PCI for NT, consult the current NT hardware compatibility list to make sure the system you are considering is supported and the peripherals you require are available for that system's bus.

Network Adapter Cards

Windows NT requires a network adapter card to operate. As with other hardware, check the Windows NT hardware compatibility list to make sure your adapter card is supported. You can have several adapters installed on your system. For example, you may want to create a dual home gateway system for you Web server. One network adapter card handles your local NetBEUI network, while the second adapter card handles TCP/IP system backup.

Your Windows NT-based server platform should include a backup device to preserve the valuable content you plan to use with your Web site. Using a backup system makes a full copy of your system in case you experience any problems. The time and effort it takes to reconstruct Windows NT and your Web site make the investment in a backup system well worth the price. A simple backup program built into Windows NT supports only tape-drive devices with SCSI interfaces and a limited range of other tape drives. In order to use NT's built-in backup, you'll need a compatible tape device from the Windows NT hardware compatibility list. A wide range of NT-compatible tape drives is available—consult the latest Windows NT hardware compatibility list.

Upgrading an Existing System

If you're making the jump to Windows NT on an existing PC, you need to make sure the hardware is supported by Windows NT via the availability of drivers for your current hardware. Because Windows NT is relatively new, many hardware vendors are just creating drivers for their hardware. Check the Windows NT Hardware Compatibility List to see if your hardware is supported. If it's not listed, check with the hardware vendor. Often they'll have the new drivers available at their Web or FTP site for you to download.

Chapter 7

Setting Up NT as Your Web Serving Platform

Windows NT is an industrial-strength version of Windows designed for enterprise client/server computing and well suited to operate as a Web server platform. Under its familiar Windows graphical user interface (GUI) is a Unix-like, 32-bit multitasking, highly secure network operating system. NT takes Windows into the world of client/server computing as well as matching the operating system to 32-bit Pentium processors. This chapter examines Windows NT's workings and provides hands-on instructions for setting NT for running your Web server.

Windows NT Server and Windows NT Workstation

Windows NT, being a client/server-based operating system, is sold in two flavors: Windows NT Server and Windows NT Workstation. As their respective names imply, the server version is for running a dedicated server, and the workstation version is for client computers. You can use Windows NT Workstation as a peer-to-peer networking solution without NT Server. Each Windows NT Workstation computer can support up to 10 connections from other Windows NT Workstations. Think of Windows NT Workstation, which lists for $319, as a more powerful version of Windows 95. The limit of 10 simultaneous connections for Windows NT Workstation applies not to connections to the Web server, but to connections in which users login on your local network to access the machine running Windows NT Workstation. If you're already using a Windows for Workgroups or Windows 95 network, you can connect the Windows NT Workstation machine to that network.

If you're building an internal network around Windows NT, you'll need NT Server to handle server-related tasks, such as file sharing and printing management. Windows NT Server supports more than 10 simultaneous login connections, such as for file- and print-share connections. It includes a sophisticated collection of network administration tools, directory replication, fault-tolerant disk support, Macintosh File System support, multiuser Remote Access Service, and advanced TCP/IP support (DHCP, WINS, etc.). Windows NT Server lists for $699. Microsoft also sells a NT Server "value package" that includes 10 client licenses as well as the Microsoft Internet Information Server for $999. You don't need to use Windows NT Server as the operating system running your Web site. Most Web server software will work on both NT Workstation or NT Server. However, the Microsoft Internet Information Server requires NT Server to run. Third-party Web server software packages, such as Netscape's Commerce Server or O'Reilly's Website Professional, work with both versions of NT.

Windows NT's Architecture

Windows NT is secure, scalable, and portable. It takes full advantage of 32-bit processing power, and it can exploit more than one CPU. NT employs an architecture in which no application program is permitted direct access to the hardware or to protected portions of the operating system. All such access is mediated by the NT Executive, which performs the requested access on the application's behalf. All operating systems have a kernel containing the minimum set of functions that must be kept in memory. For example, in DOS, the kernel is BIOS (basic input/output system). The other parts of DOS that aren't necessary all the time are stored on disk and loaded into memory only when needed. In Windows NT the equivalent of the BIOS is not a part of the kernel, but instead is part of the NT Executive. At the core of the Executive lies the microkernel, which comprises only those services that are absolutely required to remain in memory at all times.

The NT microkernel is so small that on multiprocessor system, one copy is executed on each CPU. Windows NT also support symmetric multiprocessing, which means Out of the box, Windows NT Workstation supports one or two CPUs, and Windows NT Server supports up to four. Supporting more processors requires a customized software, which is provided by the hardware manufacturer.

In Windows NT, applications cannot access low-level drivers or hardware services without the intervention of the operating system. Hardware is

From VMS to WNT

Windows NT was developed by Dave Culter, who developed VMS from Digital Equipment Corporation (DEC). Windows NT (which stands for new technology) is an interesting twist on the VMS name. When you take the letter in the alphabet before W (V) for Windows, before N (M) for New, and before T (S) for technology, you get VMS.

isolated from the drivers and the Hardware Abstraction Level (HAL). Security is provided whenever the application and operating system interact.

Windows NT Security

Windows NT includes a sophisticated security system built on the concepts of file ownership and specific access permissions. These permissions can be granted on a per-file or per-directory basis, making it possible to isolate each user's files from other users on the system.

Windows NT was designed to be certifiable at the federal government's C2 security standard. To provide a truly secure operating system, every file and every device in the system must have an owner.

Windows NT File Systems

Windows NT supports the familiar file allocation table (FAT) system that's standard for DOS, Windows 3.1 and Windows for Workgroups 3.11, and NTFS (New Technology File System), which is designed to exploit Windows NT's security and fault-tolerance features. In most cases, you'll want to use the NTFS file system for your Web and FTP serving functions. However, you can partition your hard disk for both FAT and NTFS. NTFS provides features that enables Windows NT to restore the state of the file system in the event of a power failure or other disk errors. Windows NT provides automatic conversion of file names to standard DOS-style 8.3 names for DOS and Windows 16-bit applications.

Windows NT version 3.51 supports directory and file compression.The compression delivers around a 50 percent reduction in space for most text files, and 40 percent on program files.

Preemptive Multitasking and Multithreading

Windows NT's preemptive multitasking matches powerful Unix preemptive multitasking features. The process of having multiple processes accomplished simultaneously by a CPU is called asynchronous I/O. The Windows

NT Task Scheduler switches these processes in and out of the CPU or multiple CPUs based on various criteria.

Windows NT adds a substantial extension to preemptive multitasking with multithreading. A thread is a low-overhead process that can be switched by the task scheduler. A single process may have many threads. Use of multithreading can significantly improve productivity in such applications as databases.

NT Memory Management

Windows NT runs a sophisticated memory management subsystem that uses a demand-paged virtual memory. Memory in the form of pages are freely moved between memory and a hard disk at the command of the memory manager. Whenever a program attempts to access memory that's not physically present in the machine, a page fault is generated. The NT Executive then takes over and loads in the requested memory. This process is automatic and transparent—and it means that programs can behave as though they have nearly unlimited memory space.

Windows NT 3.51 and Windows NT 4.0

Windows NT 4.0, the latest version of NT, supersedes Windows NT 3.51 and includes significant improvements. The following are just some of the new enhancements for Windows NT 4.0:

- **Windows 95 User Interface** (Workstation and Server). NT 4.0 sports the Windows 95 interface instead of the old Windows 3.11 interface used by Windows NT 3.51. This friendlier interface lets you use the same techniques used for Windows 95 to work with NT. Additionally, many of NT's tools and utilities have been redesigned to be easier to use.

- **Windows Explorer** (Workstation and Server). The Windows Explorer operates like the File Manager. This is a handy tool for browsing and managing files, drives, and network connections. Opening Windows Explorer presents a view of your PC's contents in a hierarchy or tree format, allowing you to easily view the contents of drives and folders.

- **Internet Explorer 2.0** (Workstation Only). This is the latest version of Microsoft's Web browser for Windows NT.

- **Hardware Profiles** (Workstation and Server). The Hardware Profiles feature allows you to create a list of hardware configurations used for specific tasks.

- **DNS Name Server** (Server Only). This enhancement includes a Domain Name Server built-in.

- **Microsoft Internet Information Server** (Server Only). Microsoft's Web, FTP, and Gopher server software are included in this improvement. The Web server software is a secure version that supports SSL.

- **Improved Remote Access Service Support**. Improved RAS makes using Windows NT with a modem or ISDN connection to the Internet.

Working with NTFS

NTFS, the file system of choice for establishing your Web server. Before you install your Web server software, you'll need to install NTFS or partition your hard disk for NTFS. The following sections explain how NTFS file security system works.

Using the Disk Administrator (NT 3.51)

Windows NT makes hard disk management easy with the Disk Administrator program. The Windows NT's Disk Administrator provides tools for managing disks, allowing you to create partitions on hard disks. It provides a graphical view of disk partitions as well as a centralized tool for disk management and maintenance. When you double-click on the Disk Administrator icon in the Administrative Tools group in the Program manager, the Disk Administrator dialog box appears, as shown in Figure 7.1.

In many computer systems, adding a new hard drive disrupts the order of existing drive letter assignments. In Windows NT, Disk Administrator allows you to statically assign drive letters so that this does not happen. Once assigned, drive letters are maintained when another drive is added to the system.

To assign a drive letter, follow these steps:

1. Select the partition or logical drive you want to assign to a letter.
2. Select Tools/Drive Letter.
3. When the Assign Drive Letter dialog box appears, select the assignment option you want.
4. Click on OK.

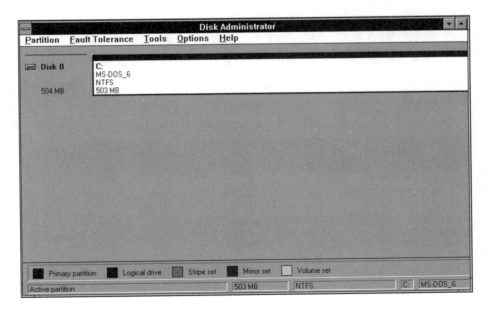

FIGURE 7.1 The Disk Administrator dialog box.

Drive letters for CD-ROM drives can be set with the Tools|CD-ROM Drive Letters command.

A primary partition is a subdivision of a physical disk; up to four primary partitions can be created per disk. A primary partition cannot be subdivided. In Intel-based systems, the primary partition of your C drive is the partition from which you boot the system. Only one of the four primary partitions can be designated an extended partition. In contrast, an extended partition is created from free space on your hard disk and can be subpartitioned into logical drives.

To create a primary partition on a hard disk do the following:

1. Select the free space area on a disk.

2. Select Partition/Create.

3. When the Create Primary Partition dialog box displays the minimum and maximum size for the partition, it also displays a text box labeled Create Partition of Size, in which you now enter the new partition size.

4. Click on OK.

On Intel-based computers, the system partition that contains the hardware-specific files needed for booting must be marked as active. To mark a partition as active for Intel-based computers, select the partition that contains the necessary startup files. Select Partition|Mark Active, then click on OK. An extended partition can be set up and used to create multiple logical drives or to be part of a volume set.

To create an extended partition, follow these steps:

1. Select the free space area on a disk.

2. Select Partition/Create Extended.

3. When the Create Extended Partition dialog box displays the minimum and maximum size for the partition and a text box named Create Partition of Size, enter the appropriate size.

4. Click on OK.

To create logical drives within an extended partition, select the space in the extended partition, select Partition/Create, enter the size of the logical drive in the Create Logical Drive dialog box, and click on OK. To delete a partition, volume, or logical drive, select the partition, volume, or logical drive you want to remove. Select Partition/Delete, then select Yes to confirm your delete request. Once a partition has been created, it must be formatted for use with the Tools|Format command.

Setting Directory and File Permissions (NT 3.51)

You can control who has access to your files and directories, as well as the extent of that access, using Windows NT's permissions. You can limit access on any shared directory, but you can restrict access to files only on NTFS partitions. Windows NT's set of standard permissions can be set for files and directories as shown in Tables 7.1 and 7.2.

TABLE 7.1 Windows NT Directory Permissions

Standard Permission	Access allowed
No Access	None.
List	Displays a directory's files and attributes. you can move to any subdirectory within the directory.
Read	Includes all rights from the List permission, plus you can display the owner and permissions of a directory. This permission also allows the same Read access as for file permissions for all files in the directory (see the following).
Add and Read	Includes all the rights from Read permissions, plus you can create subdirectories, add files to the directory, and change the attributes of a directory.
Change	Includes all the rights from Add and Read, plus user can delete the directory or any subdirectories

TABLE 7.1 Continued

Standard Permission	Access allowed
	below it. This permission also allows the same Change access as for file permissions for all files in the directory.
Full Access	Includes all the rights from Add and Read and Change permissions. Users can also change permissions for a directory or delete subdirectories and the files in them (no matter what their permissions). Users can also take ownership of the directory. Full Access allows the same Full Access permissions as for file permissions.

TABLE 7.2 Windows NT File Permissions

Standard Permission	Access Allowed
No Access	None.
Read	Displays the file's data and let's you view the file's attributes.
Change	Beyond Read activities, you can can launch program files, change the file's attributes, and display the file's owner and the permissions assigned to the file.
Full Access	Beyond the Read and Change activities, you can change or append data to the file.

To set permissions on a directory:

1. Select the directory from the directory panel. Choose Security|Permissions or select the Permissions button from the toolbar (the button with the key). The Permissions dialog box shown in Figure 7.2 appears. Note that whether the changes you make affect subdirectories and files depends on the setting of the Replace Permissions on Subdirectories and Replace Permissions on Existing Files check boxes.

2. Change permissions, add new user permissions, or delete existing permissions.

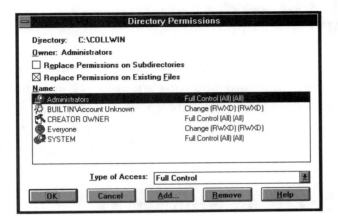

FIGURE 7.2 The Directory Permissions dialog box.

- To change a permission, select the name of the user group or the individual user you want to change. Select the permission type from the Type of Access pull-down list. Then click on OK.

- To add a user permission, click on Add. Select the name(s) of the users or user groups you want to add and click on Add. The name(s) are added to the Add Names box. When all users have been added, click on OK.

- To delete a user permission, select the user, then click on Remove.

3. Click on OK to return to the File Manager window.

Setting file permissions is done in a similar manner to setting directory permissions. By default, the File Permissions dialog box shows the permissions that are inherited from the directory in which it is contained. To manage file permissions, first select one or more files from the file panel of the File Manager. Next, choose Security|Permissions or select the Permissions button from the toolbar (the button with the key). Select the user(s) you want to remove or change, or click on Add to grant user(s) permission to selected file(s).

Working with TCP/IP in Windows NT (3.51)

TCP/IP is the glue of the Internet. Windows NT supports TCP/IP natively, but you have to install and configure it on your Windows NT PC. After that, you're ready to run Web server and FTP software on your PC and make the connection to the Internet. Before you can install and configure TCP/IP on Windows NT, you must be logged in as Administrator or as a member of the Administrator's group.

Installing TCP/IP on Windows NT

You can install the TCP/IP components of Windows NT when you first set up your system or any time later. This section assumes you've already installed Windows NT and are adding TCP/IP functionality. To install the TCP/IP protocol and utilities on your Windows NT server, do the following:

1. Open the Control Panel and double-click on the Network icon. The Network Settings dialog box appears (see Figure 7.3).

2. In the Network Settings dialog box, click on the Add Software button to open the Add Network Software dialog box (see Figure 7.4).

3. Select the TCP/IP Protocol And Related Components in the Network Software list box, and then click on the Continue button.

4. The Windows NT TCP/IP Installation Options dialog box appears (see Figure 7.5 and Table 7.3). The TCP/IP Internetworking, Connectivity Utilities, and Simple TCP/IP Services option is already checked to install TCP/IP, so click on the OK button. (You'll learn about the other options later.)

5. Windows NT Setup displays a message asking for the full path to the Windows NT distribution files. Provide the appropriate location and click on the Continue button; Windows NT starts copying the necessary files. You can specify a drive letter for floppy disks, a CD-ROM drive, or a shared network directory.

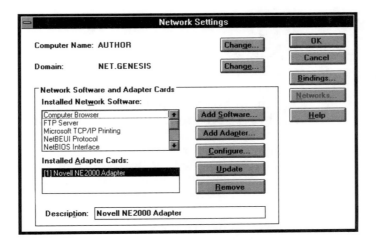

FIGURE 7.3 The Network Settings dialog box.

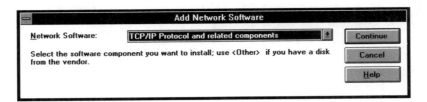

FIGURE 7.4 The Add Network Software dialog box.

TABLE 7.3 Available Components in the Windows NT TCP/IP Installation
Options Dialog Box

Option	Description
TCP/IP Internetworking	Includes TCP/IP, NetBIOS over TCP/IP and Windows Sockets interfaces, DHCP and WINS client software, and the TCP/IP diagnostic utilities. This is installed automatically.
Connectivity Utilities	Installs the TCP/IP utilities. Select this option to install connectivity utilities finger, ftp, lpr, rcp, rexec, rsh, telnet, and tftp, and the diagnostic utilities arp, hostname, ipconfig, lpq, nbtstat, netstat, ping, route, and tracert.

TABLE 7.3 Continued

Option	Description
SNMP Service	Installs the SNMP service, which allows this computer to be administered remotely using remote management tools. This option also allows you to monitor statistics for TCP/IP services using Performance Monitor. Performance Monitor is a tool included with Windows NT that gathers statistics and sets alarms for certain system components. It can be helpful in telling you whether or not your server is overworked.
TCP/IP Network Printing Support	Allows this computer to print directly over the network using TCP/IP. Select this option if you want to print to Unix print queues or TCP/IP printers that are connected directly to the network. This also must be installed if you want to use the Lpdsvr service so that Unix computers can print to Windows NT printers.
FTP Server Service	Allows files on this computer to be shared over the network with remote computers that support the file transfer protocol (FTP) and TCP/IP. Select this option if you want to use TCP/IP to share files with other computers.
Simple TCP/IPServices	Provides the client software for the Character Generator, Daytime, Discard, Echo, and Quote of the Day services. If you have other computers on your network that support these protocols, installing the Simple TCP/IP Services enables your Windows NT machine to respond.
Enable Automatic DHCP Configuration	Turns on automatic configuration of TCP/IP parameters for this computer. Select this option if there is a DHCP server on your internetwork to support dynamic host configuration.

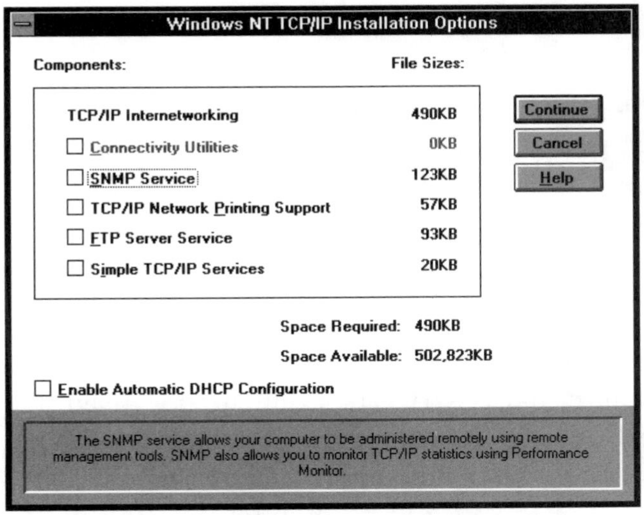

```
┌──────────────────────────────────────────────────────────┐
│ ─        Windows NT TCP/IP Installation Options           │
├──────────────────────────────────────────────────────────┤
│  Components:                              File Sizes:      │
│  ┌──────────────────────────────────────┐  ┌───────────┐  │
│  │  TCP/IP Internetworking        490KB │  │ Continue  │  │
│  │  ☐ Connectivity Utilities       0KB  │  ├───────────┤  │
│  │  ☐ SNMP Service               123KB  │  │  Cancel   │  │
│  │  ☐ TCP/IP Network Printing     57KB  │  ├───────────┤  │
│  │       Support                        │  │   Help    │  │
│  │  ☐ FTP Server Service          93KB  │  └───────────┘  │
│  │  ☐ Simple TCP/IP Services      20KB  │                 │
│  └──────────────────────────────────────┘                 │
│                                                            │
│              Space Required:   490KB                       │
│              Space Available:  502,823KB                   │
│  ☐ Enable Automatic DHCP Configuration                     │
│  ┌──────────────────────────────────────────────────────┐ │
│  │ The SNMP service allows your computer to be          │ │
│  │ administered remotely using remote management tools. │ │
│  │ SNMP also allows you to monitor TCP/IP statistics    │ │
│  │ using Performance Monitor.                           │ │
│  └──────────────────────────────────────────────────────┘ │
└──────────────────────────────────────────────────────────┘
```

FIGURE 7.5 TCP/IP Installation Options dialog box.

Configuring TCP/IP

For TCP/IP to work on your computer, it must be configured with the IP addresses, subnet masks, and default gateway for each network adapter on the computer. Microsoft TCP/IP can be configured using two different methods. If there is a dynamic host configuration protocol (DHCP) server on your internetwork, it can automatically configure TCP/IP for your computer. This option requires running a Windows Server on your network, in which case your TCP/IP installation will usually be handled by a system administrator.

DHCP automatically assigns IP addresses and provides management of those addresses. When you select this option, you are installing the server portion of the software. The client software must be installed on each workstation on your network. Since Internet hosts have static IP addresses, you do not need to install this portion when making your Windows NT Internet server. If this server is to be accessed through TCP/IP from other clients on the local network, you might need to install it.

The second method is to configure TCP/IP manually. After the TCP/IP software has been copied to your Windows NT computer, you need to provide some configuration information: the IP address of your machine and the IP address of the default gateway machine you use to connect to the Internet. These IP addresses are given to you by your Internet service provider. Remember, you must be logged on as a member of the Administrators group in Windows NT for the local computer to configure TCP/IP, following these steps:

1. Choose the OK button in the Windows NT TCP/IP Installation Options dialog box, and the TCP/IP Configuration dialog box appears automatically. Or if you are reconfiguring TCP/IP, start the Network option in the Control Panel. In the Installed Network Software list box, select TCP/IP Protocol in the Network Settings dialog box and choose the Configure button. Either way, the TCP/IP Configuration dialog box appears.

2. In the Adapter list of the TCP/IP Configuration dialog box, select the network adapter for which you want to set IP addresses. The Adapter list contains all the network adapters to which IP is bound on this computer as well as all adapters installed on this computer. You must set specific IP addressing information for each bound adapter with correct values. The bindings for a network adapter determine how network protocols and other layers of network software work together.

3. Enter the IP address of your computer in the IP Address field.

4. Enter the subnet mask, which for most connections will be a Class C subnet mask of 255.255.255.0.

5. In the Default Gateway field, enter the IP address of the Internet Service Provider's gateway machine. This IP address is provided by your service provider. If you're using a router, this entry will be the IP address of the router.

6. Click on the OK button.

Configuring TCP/IP to Use DNS

Although TCP/IP uses IP addresses to identify and reach computers on the Internet, users typically use the domain name system (DNS), which is a static naming service that provides standard naming conventions for IP computers. Typically, your Internet service provider maintains a DNS server, which you need to reference as part of your connection. You need to tell Windows NT Workstation running TCP/IP the IP address of that DNS server, which is supplied by your Internet service provider. Here's how to configure TCP/IP to use DNS on Windows NT Workstation:

1. In the Control Panel, choose the Network option. In the Installed Network Software list box of the Network Settings dialog box, select TCP/IP Protocol and choose the Configure button.

2. In the TCP/IP Configuration dialog box, choose the DNS button. The DNS Configuration dialog box appears, as shown in Figure 7.6.

3. In the DNS Configuration dialog box, you may type a name, usually your computername, in the Host Name box. Optionally, you may type in a domain name, which is the name you get when you register at InterNIC.

4. In the DNS Search Order box, type the IP address of the DNS server that will provide name resolution. Then choose the Add button to move the IP address to the list on the right. Your Internet service provider provides this IP address to you. You can add up to three IP addresses for DNS servers. The servers running DNS will be queried in the order listed.

5. Choose the OK button. When the TCP/IP Configuration dialog box reappears, choose the OK button. When the Network Settings dialog box reappears, choose the OK button. The settings take effect after you restart your computer.

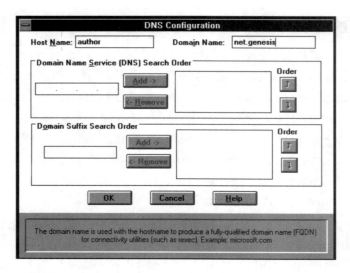

FIGURE 7.6 The DNS Configuration dialog box.

Working Windows NT 4.0

Windows NT 4.0 uses the friendlier Windows 95 interface and includes redesigned tools for working with directories, files, and TCP/IP. The following sections explain setting directory and file permissions, using the disk administrator, and installing and configuring TCP/IP.

Setting Directory and File Permissions (NT 4.0)

Setting directory—called folders in Windows NT 4.0—and file permission is performed much the same way as in Windows NT 3.51. However, in NT 4.0 you use the Windows NT Explorer, which has the look and feel of the File Manager in NT 3.51. To set permissions on a directory or file in NT 4.0, do the following:

1. Choose Start|Programs|Windows NT Explorer. The Windows NT Explorer window appears (Figure 7.7).

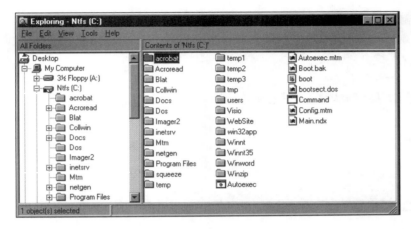

FIGURE 7.7 The Windows NT Explorer window.

2. Select the file or directory from the Folders panel, then choose File|Sharing. The Properties dialog box appears.

3. Click on the Security tab to display permissions settings (Figure 7.8).

4. Click on the Permissions button. The Permissions dialog box appears (Figure 7.9).

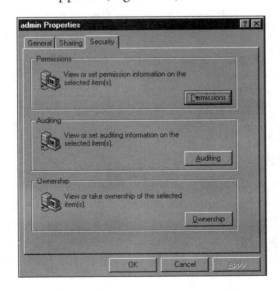

FIGURE 7.8 The Security tab in the Properties dialog box.

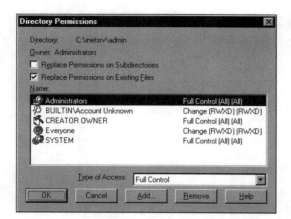

FIGURE 7.9 The Permissions dialog box.

5. Choose the type of access you want from the Type of Access setting. If you want to specify users, click on the Add button.

6. After setting your permissions, click on OK.

Using the Disk Administrator (NT 4.0)

The Disk Administrator in Windows 4.0 is similar to that of NT 3.51. To access the Disk Administrator in NT 4.0, choose Start|Programs|Administrative Tools|Disk Administrator. The Disk Administrator window appears, as show in Figure 7.10. This window is like the one in NT 3.51, except it includes a view menu option to switch between a volume's display and the default Disk Configuration display.

Installing and Configuring TCP/IP in Windows NT 4.0

For TCP/IP to work on your computer, it must be configured with the IP addresses, subnet masks, and default gateway for each network adapter on the computer. After the TCP/IP software has been copied to your Windows NT computer, you need to provide some configuration information: the IP address of your machine and the IP address of the default gateway machine you use to connect to the Internet. These IP addresses are provided by your

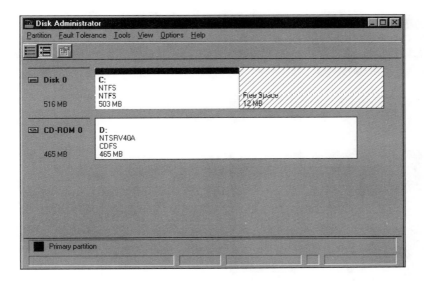

Figure 7.10 The Disk Administrator window in NT 4.0.

Internet service provider. Remember, you must be logged on as a member of the Administrators group in Windows NT for the local computer to configure TCP/IP.

1. Installing and configuring TCP/IP for Windows NT 4.0 is considerably more streamlined in NT 4.0 than in NT 3.51. The following steps explain how to install TCP/IP in Windows NT 4.0, if you did not already install it during setup: Open the Control Panel and double-click on the Network icon. The Network dialog box appears (Figure 7.11).

2. In the Network dialog box, click on the Protocols tab, then click on the Add button. The Select Network Protocol dialog box appears (Figure 7.12).

3. Select the TCP/IP Protocol from the Network Protocol list, then click OK. A Windows NT Setup dialog box appears, prompting you for the path of your Windows NT files. Enter the path and click on Continue. Windows NT copies the necessary files to your hard drive.

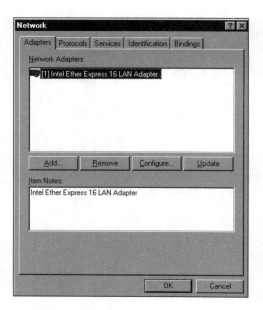

FIGURE 7.11 The Network window.

4. Click on the Close button in the Network dialog box. The Microsoft TCP/IP Properties dialog box appears (Figure 7.13).

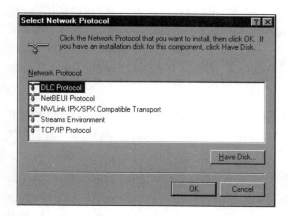

FIGURE 7.12 The Select Network Protocol dialog box.

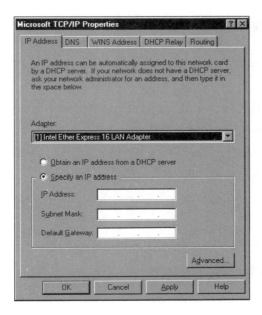

FIGURE 7.13 The Microsoft TCP/IP Properties dialog box.

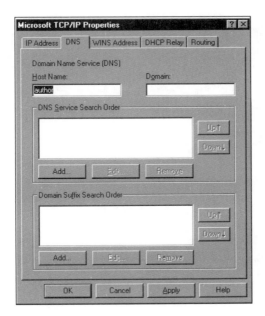

FIGURE 7.14 The DNS tab.

5. In the IP Address tab, enter the IP address of your machine in the IP Address field, the subnet mask in the Subnet Mask field, and the default gateway of your Internet Service provider in the Default Gateway field.

6. Select the DNS tab (Figure 7.14) to display settings for specifying your Internet service provider's DNS server(s).

7. Click on the Add button under the DNS Service Search Order group. The TCP/IP DNS Server dialog box appears.

8. Enter the IP address of your DNS server, then click on the Add button.

9. Repeat steps 7 and 8 for each DNS server IP address.

10. Click OK. Windows NT prompts you to restart NT. Click on the Yes button.

Chapter 8

Getting Wired to the Net

Getting your Web server connected to the Internet is the most difficult and typically the most expensive part of establishing your Web server. To connect a Web server requires a leased line that remains a dedicated connection to the Internet 24 hours a day, 365 days a year. Entering the world of dedicated Internet connections requires a basic grounding in telecommunications, networking, and Internet service provider issues. This chapter provides a foundation for you to make intelligent Internet connection choices.

The Two Paths You Can Take

There are two ways you can connect your own Web site to the Internet. The first is via a Web hosting service, which places your own Web server platform at the Internet service provider's (ISP's) premises. This approach reduces the high cost of getting high-bandwidth access to the Internet because the ISP leverages its existing high-speed digital connections and spreads out over multiple Web servers. You manage the Web server remotely via the Internet. Web hosting services is a better approach than establishing a Web presence by placing your HTML documents on someone else's machine, which would severely restrict your activities on that server. In the Web hosting service model, you can run whatever you want on your own machine, make as many changes as you want, and add programs and all kinds of other functionality as needed. Typically the cost of operating a Web site at a Web hosting service includes a one-time setup charge, a flat monthly rate, and a sliding scale monthly charge based on the amount of traffic your Web site is generating. This type of arrangement can get expensive if your site becomes popular.

In the long run getting a dedicated connection from an Internet service provider directly to your premises is strategically the best option. The initial learning and startup costs of this option are higher, but the expertise you gain from climbing this learning curve will place your business at a competitive edge in the move to electronic commerce. The two cost components of your dedicated connection are the leased, dedicated connection established through an ISP in conjunction with your local telephone company and the ISP's charge for your connection to the Internet. With dedicated connections, you lease the line and pay a flat fee that is independent of the usage level. In most cases, using standard dial-up service for running a dedicated Web server costs considerably more than a dedicated connection.

Dedicated Internet Access Primer

Before delving into Internet connections, it's important to understand how the underlying telecommunications functions work. Traditional data and voice networks connecting any two locations within the U.S. use a local and a long-distance provider. The local access provider connects your premises to its nearest central office (a telephone company switching facility), where the call is then handed off to the long distance access provider. The process is mirrored at the receiver's end, where the long distance company hands off the call to the local access provider. The geographic location of the hand-off points on the long-distance network is referred to as Point of Presence (POP). Local access in the U.S. is generally provided by the seven regional Bell operating companies (RBOCs), Ameritech, Bell Atlantic, Bell South, NYNEX, Pacific Bell, Southwestern Bell, and US West. In addition, many smaller local access providers such as AT&T, MCI, and Sprint provide long distance access for telecommunication services.

In order to get your own Web server connected to the Internet on a dedicated line, you need an Internet service provider that offers leased line connections. Finding the least expensive leased-line connection as well as an ISP that offers good service requires shopping around; check both local and national ISPs. Typically, ISPs charge a one-time setup fee for setting up the line, and in many cases the equipment. In addition, there's a monthly fee for Internet access. These fees usually don't include telephone company charges. If the leased line goes outside your local telephone company's long distance service area (LATA), a long-distance company must provide the line. In most cases, you'll want to tackle the process of establishing a dedicated connection using an ISP because it is already working with the telephone companies and can get you connected more smoothly.

Note: *See the Appendix for a comprehensive listing of Internet service providers.*

Although the cost of a dedicated connection has dramatically fallen, it is still not cheap. Generally, prices are directly proportional to the amount of data a line can handle, so selecting the right type and amount of bandwidth and the right type of access service is critical. Dedicated connections that support operating a Web server range in speed from 28.8Kbps to 45 Mbps. For many small businesses, the range is from 28.8Kbps to 256Kbps. Three types of dedicated connection services are available:

- Analog services, which represent the low end of the connection food chain in both bandwidth and cost. The maximum bandwidth for this option is 28.8Kbps.

- Switched digital services, including Switched 56 and ISDN. These forms of connections represent a midrange in digital connections, with bandwidth ranging from 56Kbps to 128Kbps.

- High-speed, dedicated services, including Frame Relay, Fractional T1, and T1 lines represent the high-end of Internet connections in both bandwidth and cost.

High-End Dedicated Connections

A T1 connection, the most common of the high-end connections, provides enough bandwidth for dozens of Web servers. Each 1/6 of a T1 line is 256Kbps. With a T1 connection, document transfers of several hundred kilobytes will appear instantaneous on a connected Web browser. A T1 connection to the Internet costs between $1000 and $3000 per month for the Internet service itself, plus the leased line charges, which frequently exceeds the cost of Internet access. Many ISPs offer fractional T1 access, usually in multiples of 128Kbps. A fractional T1 line at 128Kbps will run around $800 a month. A T3 connection, which is fast enough to serve hundreds of networks, is used by only major Internet service providers and the Internet backbone itself. T2 connections are typically used only inside the telephone system.

Just because a service provider gives you a T1 connection doesn't mean you will always get T1 speed. If, for instance, your service provider has 20 T1 customers feeding into a single T1 connection to the Internet, you will be competing with 19 other customers for the same T1 bandwidth. The same principle applies to your service provider's provider and so on; it's difficult to tell how fast your connection will really be. However, this is not necessarily a problem because Internet traffic is sent in short bursts (packets) rather than steady streams. On high-speed lines, it's common for customers to use only a tiny fraction (less than 5 percent) of the total bandwidth available to them. As long as only one customer sends packets, each customer has access to the full line speed. When packets are sent at the same time, customers see a temporary reduction in data throughput.

To accommodate many customers feeding off the same line while ensuring adequate speed for each, service providers monitor their Internet feed to make sure that only a fraction of the total bandwidth is being used. For example, if a service provider's Internet feed has only 25 percent utilization on average, 75 percent of the full line speed is available to any individual customer who needs it. Feeding several customers off a single line is thus a very useful practice—each customer can transfer data very quickly in bursts when necessary but can benefit from the lower cost of sharing an Internet feed with several other customers.

Midrange Dedicated Connections

Switched 56Kbps service is the oldest of the midrange communications technologies. In many cases, it's more expensive than the newer, more powerful ISDN services, with a 56K connection to the Internet usually costing $500 to $1,000 per month.

Two new bandwidth technologies are offering connection options that are generally cheaper than T1 connections: ISDN and Frame Relay. ISDN (integrated services digital network) recently became widely available. It is available as a dial-up service, but a growing number of telephone companies and

Internet service providers are offering dedicated ISDN service. A single ISDN line delivers 128Kbps of digital communications. You can add lines to increase the bandwidth in increments of 128Kbps. Depending on where your business is located, ISDN may qualify as a low-cost dedicated connection, typically priced at $250 to $500 a month.

Frame Relay is a relatively new technology that is used to link multiple locations more economically than running leased lines to each site. In Frame Relay, all sites connect to a central frame relay switch at the telephone company, forming a start network. If an Internet service provider already has a connection into a frame relay switch, customers need only obtain a local loop from the switch to their location. Frame Relay is a packet switching protocol with speed ranges from 56Kbps to 45 Mbps. Pricing, as for all other services, involves installation charges and monthly usage charges. The monthly usage charge for 56Kbps Frame Relay is around $200 to $300. Installation charges can sometimes be as high as $1,000. You'll also need a DSU/CSU and a router that supports routing IP over Frame Relay protocol.

Low-End Dedicated Connections

A low-end option in both bandwidth and cost for Internet connections is using a dedicated voice-grade line with a 28.8Kbps modem. A 28.8Kbps connection can support 10,000 to 20,000 Web server requests per day, at a monthly cost of under $100. Additionally, the analog option uses inexpensive and familiar technology. No networking experience is needed.

Calculating Bandwidth Needs

To come up with an accurate estimate of your bandwidth needs, remember that some documents will be more popular than others. Most of the transfers a typical Web site sees are at the home page, which as a rule of thumb should be downloadable in 10 to 20 seconds. Times longer than these turn away users. The average size of a Web site is 4 to 6Kb. The formula for calculating capabilities for data transmission for your Web site is the capacity of the connection divided by 8-bits, which converts into bits-per-second. For example, taking a 28.8Kbps line and dividing it by 8 (number of bits) equals approximately 3.6Kbps. If you reduce this amount for TCP/IP overhead, you might get 3Kbps or 3,600Kbps per hour. That figure divided by an average document size of 5Kb shows that your site can support 720 hits per hour for a daily maximum of 17,280 hits. Remember that hits are individual document requests. Users will typically make several hits, say an average of 10, as they explore your site. The result is your site can support a maximum of 1,728 users per 24-hour period. In the real world, a Web site typically has peak and non-peak times, so this maximum number is theoretical, but it does give an idea of the capacity of site using even a 28.8Kbps modem. To help keep your document size small and increase throughput, keep your home page small by reducing inline images. Also remember that the average network speed depends on both the client's network connection and yours. If the client network is slow, your network server slows down because it waits for remote clients to receive data.

Internet Connections: More Than Just Bandwidth

Bandwidth is the capacity of any data communications line. The amount of data that gets through in a specific amount of time is called throughput, which takes into account factors besides the size of the connection to determine the true bandwidth of a connection. Not all bandwidth is delivered as promised, so it's important to take a look at an Internet service provider's performance. If its network is being slowed down by large amounts of packet loss or long delivery times, called latency, you are not getting the delivery rate you're paying for. The service providers own network can create a bottleneck that can hamper your connection, no matter what the bandwidth between the ISP and your premises. The following sections cover key criteria for determining the performance of an ISP.

Packet Loss, Latency, and Throughput

As explained earlier, bandwidth by itself is not the only determining factor in choosing a connection. Latency and packet loss also can have a dramatic impact on your Internet connection if they slow down your Web server's delivery of information to users. Network packet loss happens when a packet doesn't make it to its destination within a reasonable amount of time and must be resent. Latency, which is the time it takes to get data from one point to another, impacts Web users in terms of the amount of time it takes for a user to get the request from the browser to the server, followed by the time it takes to get the data from the server back to the browser. Throughput, the total amount of data that gets from one point to another in a certain period of time is connected to both packet loss and latency. An Internet service provider's latency determines how long it takes data to travel across its network to the Internet.

Ping Your ISP

A simple way to evaluate an ISP is to ping its host machines and evaluate the statistics that are returned. A ping returns four important statistics that will help you evaluate the ISP's performance: the minimum, average, and maximum latencies and the percentage of packets that were lost. An acceptable packet loss range is one to four percent. Good latency times for a local Internet service provider should be less than 50ms (milliseconds). Use ping over a period of time to develop a chart of statistics that will give you a reasonable profile of what kind of service you can expect from the ISP.

Upgrade Path

In most cases, you'll want to upgrade your connection as your Web site grows. It's usually an incremental cost for upgrading within the same type of connection such as from a Fractional T1 to a larger bandwidth within a T1 connection. Upgrading gets expensive when you change from one technology to another. For example, going from the older 56Kbps connection to a

Fractional T1 will be expensive because of new installation costs and equipment. At the lower-bandwidth connections, such as a 28.8Kbps, the cost of converting to say ISDN is less costly than dealing with higher-bandwidth solutions. You should figure out your upgrade plan before you commit to your dedicated connection and keep in mind that making changes in your Internet connection can take time—from a few days to months.

Going the Modem Route

The 28.8Kbps modem connected to a dedicated analog line to an Internet service provider provides a reasonable connection for small Web sites. It's also the least expensive and easiest to set up and operate. Based on an average document size of around 4–6KB and with various networking overhead taken into account, a 28.8Kbps connection can support 10,000 to 20,000 requests per day. Assuming an average of 10 requests per user, that translates into 1,000 to 2,000 people per day. The cost of getting a dedicated 28.8Kbps connection to the Internet averages under $100 a month, and the cost of a 28.8Kbps modem is around $200. You don't need any communications software to run your Web site using this method. Windows NT includes the Remote Access Service (RAS) that lets you easily make the TCP/IP connection to your Internet Service provider. Working with Windows NT RAS is explained later in this chapter.

Going the ISDN Route

ISDN is one of the most exciting digital technologies for Web serving. For millions of individuals and small businesses relegated to slow modem connections to the Internet, ISDN offers an exciting new era in digital communications. What's even more revolutionary about ISDN is the price, with basic service costing as little as $25 a month. In addition, ISDN is delivered right to your home or office by the telephone company using the same wiring as for your regular telephone service.

ISDN is delivered via two B channels and one D channel that together make up the Basic Rate Interface (BRI). The two B (bearer) channels are the bread and butter of an ISDN connection. Each B channel supports 64Kbps of data communications or voice, and the two can be combined to act as a single pipeline using standard ISDN equipment. The D channel is a conduit for network instructions and typically includes extra capacity for X.25 data. ISDN delivers greater connection stability because it's digital. According to AT&T a voice line connection has a reliability rate of about 75 percent; a digital connection of about 100 percent.

ISDN is a great solution for operating an in-house Web server. Unfortunately, the telephone companies have been treating ISDN as a dial-up service based on usage charges, which usually make ISDN an unfeasible option for operating a Web server. Telephone companies, long used to operating in a shadowy world of monopolies and regulated tariffs, have been slow to respond to the potential of ISDN. However, a growing number of Internet service providers are offering dedicated ISDN service via Centrex service. Centrex service allows the Internet service provider to use telephone company switches as a PBX system with lines fanning out from the telephone company switch to end-user premises. This service typically runs around $300 to $500 a month by the time the telephone company charges are factored in.

ISDN's benefits are obvious, but establishing ISDN service is not as easy as it should be, starting with the lack of uniform ISDN availability, pricing, and service. The U.S. has seven regional telephone companies as well as a number of smaller independent telephone companies, each of which handles ISDN service independently, resulting in a lack of uniformity across the country. Adding to this confusion is the complex process of ISDN service pricing, which comes through the application of complex cost allocation and recovery rules established by both federal and state regulators.

The best way to explore the ISDN service option is through Internet service providers. If ISDN is available in your area, these providers have already been working with the local telephone company. Getting answers from your telephone company can be difficult. And because the total cost of your ISDN service is a combination of the telephone company charges plus the cost of the Internet service provider's connection, why not go to the source? See Appendix A for a list of ISDN-related resources.

Although most large metropolitan areas in the U.S. have ISDN service available, there are pockets of ISDN inaccessibility. The biggest barrier to ISDN availability is an 18,000-foot limit on the delivery of ISDN service from a telephone company facility, called a central office, to customer sites. This technological limit is imposed by the delivery of ISDN over standard telephone wiring. With repeaters—devices that amplify or regenerate the data signal to extend the distance—this limit can be extended. ISDN also may not be available if the central office in your area isn't equipped to handle ISDN service.

Note: *For a comprehensive listing of Internet access providers offering ISDN service, check out Dan Kegel's ISDN page (http://alumni.caltech.edu/~dank /isdn/).*

Through the ISDN Ordering Maze

The first configuration option for ISDN service is that each B channel needs to configured by the telephone company to handle voice, data, or a combination of the two. Within the standard 2B+D configuration for ISDN service, the circuit switched data (CSD) option supports the data transmission speeds of up to 64Kbps uncompressed for each B channel. Circuit switched refers to the type of connection established via ISDN, which is a fixed pathway through the telephone system for the duration of the call. The CSD option is the one you use for connecting to the Internet (or any other network).

To use a telephone, fax, or modem with your ISDN line, you must have at least one B channel support circuit switched voice (CSV). The alternate circuit switched voice/circuit switched data (CSV/CSD) option lets you use a

B channel for either option. The CSV/CSD option is the best choice for at least one B channel if you want to add analog equipment to an ISDN line. If you want to use more than one device at a time on your ISDN line, you also need to specify a multipoint configuration option, which allows the operation of multiple devices on the ISDN line that can connect to different hosts. If you're going to use only one device and connect to a single host such as an Internet access provider, specify a point-to-point configuration.

You also need to know the type of switch used by the telephone company for your ISDN service. A switch refers to electronic facilities that route telephone traffic from one destination to another. You see references to these switches in all ISDN documentation because compatibility between your ISDN equipment and the telephone company's switches is necessary for communication via ISDN. The leading digital circuit switches used by the telephone companies are AT&T's 5ESS (Electronic Switching System) and Northern Telecom's DMS-100. The AT&T 5ESS uses Custom or National ISDN 1 (NI-1) software, and the DMS-100 uses NI-1.

As part of ordering your ISDN service, you need to tell the telephone company the equipment you plan to use on the ISDN line. The telephone company will assign a SPID (service profile identifier) number for each B channel or each device connected to the ISDN line at the time it activates your service. SPIDs let the telephone company switch know which ISDN services a given device can access. They typically look like a telephone number with additional digits at the end. You use these SPIDs to configure your ISDN devices so that they can communicate with the ISDN switch at the telephone company.

The End of the Line

For ISDN as a network to recognize your connection, you must have a network termination (called NT1). The NT1 function can be incorporated into a standalone device to plug in ISDN and analog devices or integrated into an ISDN device. The important thing to remember is that you can have

NT1 function for only the termination of your ISDN service, regardless of the number of devices connected.

Standalone NT1 devices that include ports for connecting two ISDN devices sell for under $200. Leading standalone NT1 device vendors include Alpha Telecom (http://iquest.com/~ati_usa/), Tone Commander (http://www.halcyon.com/tcs/), Motorola (http://www.mot.com/), and AT&T (http://www.att.com/). Other NT1 devices include ports for connecting both ISDN and analog devices (via an RJ-11 telephone jack) and sell for around $400. The two leading NT1 Plus products include Alpha Telecom's Super NT1 (http://iquest.com/~ati_usa/) and IBM's 7845 ISDN Network Terminator Extended (http://www.ibmlink.ibm.com/oi/spec/abs/G2214199.html).

The NT1 function is also embodied in a number of PC ISDN adapters. For example, you can get an ISA bus card for connecting your PC to ISDN that has the NT1 built-in. Keep in mind that any ISDN device used to connect your PC to the Internet that includes built-in NT1 but does not include another port for connecting another ISDN or analog device restricts the use of your ISDN line to connecting only your PC.

Connecting Your PC to the Internet via ISDN

A cornucopia of ISDN hardware for connecting PCs to the Internet via ISDN is hitting the shelves. Most products are available in either U-interface or S/T-interface. From the NT1 outward through your ISDN line jack to the telephone company switch is defined as the U-interface. Any ISDN device labeled as supporting the U-interface includes the NT1 function built in. The S/T-interface defines any ISDN device that requires an NT1 device to plug into an ISDN line.

Most ISDN devices for connecting your PC to the Internet also support Point-to-Point Protocol/Multilink Protocol (PPP/MP), which allows Internet connections using both B channels. However, make sure the Internet access providers support PPP/MP on their side of the connection. Many Internet access devices also include support for file transfer compression, which can mean a fourfold increase over the 128Kbps rate. However, a compression scheme is good only if it's supported on both ends of the connection. The good news about compression is that the Stac Hardware and Lempel Ziv Algorithm are already de facto compression standards.

For connecting single PCs to the Internet, the main ISDN hardware option is a standalone device that connects to your PC's serial port or adapter cards that communicate via a COM port or Ethernet. Many Internet access providers sell these devices as part of a connection package, or you can purchase them at computer resellers. If you don't purchase equipment from an Internet access provider, check to find out what ISDN equipment the provider supports before you buy. The best place to keep up with Internet connection devices for your PC is on Dan Kegel's ISDN Page (http://alumni.caltech.edu/~dank/isdn/).

The Ethernet-Based ISDN Adapter Card

The leading low-cost, Ethernet-based ISDN adapter card is the Combinet EVERYWARE 1000 Series. Plugging directly into the PC's ISA Bus, the Combinet EVERYWARE 1000 Series adapter card looks like an Ethernet adapter card to your PC's software. Ethernet provides a faster way than the serial route for your PC to communicate to ISDN, and the EVERYWARE 1000 is compatible with popular network operating systems. You can get it with or without data compression and built-in NT1. All models include an S/T-port for adding another ISDN ready device. The cards come with a Windows-based utility to set up and configure the card on your system.

To use the EVERYWARE 1000, you need a network operating system running on your PC. If you don't have a TCP/IP stack running as part of your network operating system, you'll need to use network version of an Internet application such as Chameleon NFS. Because the EVERYWARE 1000 is a network-based ISDN adapter, you can also use it to connect to non-TCP/IP networks and communicate in their native environment. For more information on

Combinet products, check out the Cisco Systems Web site at http://
www.cisco.com. Cisco bought Combinet in 1995.

The Serial Connection

Another popular product to connect a PC via ISDN to the Internet is the
Motorola BitSURFR Pro (http:// www.mot.com/), which connects to your
PC via a serial port. Many Internet service providers support this product,
and it supports two B channels. It's easier to install than an adapter card or
an Ethernet solution. However, because it uses serial communications, the
speed it delivers data is less than the full 64Kbps because of the overhead of
asynchronous communications.

Registering Your Web Site

Typically as part of getting wired to the Internet, you need to establish your
domain name. As explained in Chapter 5, the Internet uses an addressing
scheme called the domain name system (DNS). For the most part, domain
names indicate the name and type of service or organization that owns or
supports the service. When you establish a connection, you choose a domain
name that is your unique Internet address. In most cases, your domain name
is the same as your business name. A domain name lets you capitalize on any
name recognition associated with your business name. Your business e-mail
addresses and other server addresses are typically tied to your domain name.
Because domain names are registered, you need to make sure the name you
want is available. When you establish a connection to the Internet via a
service provider, it typically registers your domain name with an organization called InterNIC.

Defining Your Domain Name

Domain names are organized in a hierarchical fashion with the most specific
(computer name or user name) at the left and the most general top-level
domain name to the right. For example, dangell@netgen.com translates to

the user dangell at the netgen host computer, and .com is the top-level domain specification. A domain name consists of two or more alphanumeric fields, separated by a dot (a period). No spaces are allowed in a domain name, but you can use the underscore (_) to indicate a space. Each field consists of some combination of letters A through Z (in either uppercase or lowercase), the digits 0 through 9, and the hyphen (-). Don't use the period (.), at sign (@), percent sign (%), or exclamation point (!). These characters are used by domain name servers and other network systems to construct e-mail addresses. Domain names are not case sensitive, so it doesn't matter whether letters are uppercase or lowercase.

In most cases, businesses register using the .com top-level domain, which stands for commercial. However, U.S. businesses can also register under the .us top-level domain, which is the geographical domain for the United States. In most cases, you don't want to limit yourself to a geographical domain name. However, if you can't use your business name as a .com domain name because it has already been used, you may want to use the .us top-level domain. If you are running a nonprofit organization, you may be able to use the .org top-level domain.

As explained in Chapter 5, the two main types of addresses, domain names and IP addresses, work together on the Internet. Each computer that uses TCP/IP protocols is distinguished from other computers on the Internet by a unique IP address. If you plan to connect a LAN to the Internet, you need a class C IP address, which lets you subdivide your domain name. You can use a class C IP address to supply a name for each of your computers, or you can create subdomains for other servers or services.

Checking the Availability of a Domain Name

Registration of domain names is handled by InterNIC, a collaborative project of three organizations (AT&T, General Atomics, and Network Solutions Inc.) supported by the National Science Foundation. AT&T manages InterNIC directory and database services, and Network Solutions Inc. manages the network registration services. General Atomics was dropped as a provider of Information Services because of poor performance.

The easiest way to check if a domain name is available is to use the Whois page at the interNIC web site (http://rs.internic.net/rs.internic.html). Using an HTML form, you can enter a name and in the text box. If the name is taken, information appears about the organization that is using the name. If it's available, a response comes back indicating its availability.

Policies have been put in place to ensure that the registration of domain names is for Internet use and not the capture of domain names. In the early days of domain name registration, just about anyone could get a domain name without regard for a business's ownership of the real name. An example is the famous MTV case. The InterNIC now has broader powers to denied applications.

When you apply for a domain name, you must have an operational name service from at least two operational Internet servers for that name. Typically, establishing an account with an Internet service provider will take care of this even if you don't have your own Web server up and running.

Registration of Your Domain Name

Until recently, the National Science Foundation funded Internet registration services, but on September 13, 1995, fees were levied for domain name registration and maintenance. The funds received from these fees will replace the funding provided by the NSF and provide funding for other Internet activities. The registration fee for a new domain name is now $100 (U.S.). New domain names are valid for two years from the date that the registrar activates them. The registration fee is nonrefundable. For each registered domain name, there is a maintenance fee of $50 per year, due on the anniversary date of the domain name activation. This annual fee will keep the domain name valid for one year. Payment must be made in advance each year.

To register for a domain name you must have at least an active primary and secondary name server up and running on the Internet. Your service provider will have these servers running for you to use as part of the application. The key people associated with your domain name must have electronic mailboxes. Once Registration Services receives your complete application, it will send you an acknowledgment via electronic mail or postal mail.

Web Server Security from the Internet Connection Side

Security is always a concern in providing services on the Internet. How you connect your Windows NT server to the Internet is probably the most important part of your overall security. You can choose from five different models when deciding to make your Internet connection. The following sections describe different models from which you can choose, in order from the most to the least secure.

Bridge and Router Primer

All networks are based on protocols, which specify how network communication occurs. TCP/IP is the networking protocol that forms the basis of the Internet, NetBEUI (NetBIOS Extended User Interface) is the network protocol for Windows-based networking, and IEEE 803.2 is the protocol that defines an Ethernet network at the physical layer of network signaling and cabling. Windows NT supports multiple networking protocols.

Communicating across different network protocols (networks) is referred to as internetworking. There are two classes of internetworking functions: bridges and routers. A bridge is a simple device that passes data from one network to another. A router, the more sophisticated device, allows data to be routed to different networks based on the packet address information associated with the data. A bridge is typically connected to a single PC via an Ethernet adapter or a small LAN to connect to only one protocol at a time. All the traffic is from a single protocol, such as NetBEUI, to another single protocol, such as TCP/IP. A wide area network (WAN) is created by the connection of two or more networks that are physically isolated from one another. In other words, when you connect your Web server to the Internet, you're creating a WAN.

Isolating Your Web Server from Your Internal Network

The most secure way to provide Internet services is to isolate your Web server from your internal network. This is not only the most secure way to connect to the Internet, but the easiest to plan and configure. Two-way IP communication exists between your server and the Internet, but no traffic passes to your production LAN. If your system is damaged, you rebuild it with backups. The biggest drawback to this model is that you cannot share files between the corporate network and your Web server.

You can connect a standalone Web server via a 28.8Kbps modem using PPP through Windows NT Remote Access Service (RAS). If you're using a digital connection to your Internet service provider, such as ISDN, you can use an ISDN adapter card that inserts in your PC. This type of card emulates Ethernet for maximum throughput between your PC and the connection. You can also use a standalone router connected to your Web server via an Ethernet adapter card. However, this option is overkill unless you plan to connect a LAN to your Internet connection.

Isolating the TCP/IP Protocol from Your Network Protocol

The protocol isolation option offers slightly less security but has a few more usability advantages. It involves installing two network adapters in your Windows NT Internet server, one of which is bound to the IP protocol and connected to the Internet. The other adapter is bound to the internal network protocol and uses this protocol to communicate with other network clients. It's very useful if you want to be able to place files on your server for Internet clients to access so that resources—are accessible from either direction.

However, the LAN clients cannot directly access the Internet. Keep in mind that, theoretically, a hacker could penetrate this security model, but it would be very difficult because the server does not perform protocol conversion or routing. The network adapter card used for connecting to the Internet goes out to a bridge or router device that connects to the Internet service provider. The other network adapter card connects the Web server as a PC on the local network. This allows files to be delivered to the Web server via the local network. However, the files must be manually moved on the system.

Using Windows NT's Remote Access Service

Windows NT's Remote Access System (RAS) is a built-in application for establishing a wide-area network (WAN). When you establish a Web server that connects via an Internet service provider, you're establishing a WAN, which is basically a LAN-style connection over telecommunications lines. Windows NT RAS supports PPP and SLIP protocols for TCP/IP networks, you can use RAS to connect to the Internet via a modem or ISDN. RAS works well with modems as long as the modems on both sides of the connection are compatible and supported by RAS.

Both NT Workstation and Server can function as RAS clients: a local user logged in to the system console can connect over the WAN to another RAS server. The single-user RAS Server provided with Windows NT Workstation allows one user at a time to access the Windows NT system remotely over the WAN, while the Windows NT Server version supports multiple users logged in at one time. Before you install RAS, all hardware should be installed and working. Depending on your network and requirements, you may need the following hardware setup before installing RAS:

- Network adapter card with a certified Network Driver Interface Specification (NDIS) driver

- Compatible modems (see the *Hardware Compatibility List* or the Remote Access Setup program)

- An ISDN card, if you are using an ISDN line

Installing RAS (NT 3.51)

If you do not have Microsoft's Remote Access Service already installed on your Windows NT Platform, you'll need to install it before you can make a dial-out call to an Internet service provider.

Caution: *Windows NT 3.51 makes changing difficult. You must completely uninstall Remote Access Service, then reinstall it and reenter all your information. Windows NT 4.0 dramatically improved working with RAS, as explained later in this chapter.*

To install the Remote Access service, do the following:

1. Start the Windows NT Control Panel and select the Network Settings icon. The Network Settings Dialog box appears (Figure 8.1). If you haven't created a Computer name and Workgroup name for your system, click on the Change button to add them.

2. Click the Add Software button. The Add Network Software dialog appears (Figure 8.2) with a list of items you can install. Select Remote Access Service from the list, and click the Continue button. You will be asked to type a path for the installation disks or CD. Once you've entered the path, Remote Access Service Setup copies the necessary files to your hard disk.

3. When the Add Port dialog appears, select a communications port to use from this list. RAS setup then displays a message box asking to confirm the detection of a modem on your system. Make sure your modem is connected and turned on. Click on OK. Your modem device name appears in the Configure Port dialog box (Figure 8.3).

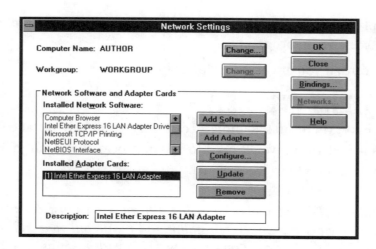

FIGURE 8.1 The Network Settings dialog box.

4. Select one of the three possible Port Usage settings-Dial out only, Receive calls only, or Dial out and receive calls. Unless you intent to call your computer running your Web site from another computer, choose Dial Out only and click OK. The Remote Access Setup dialog box appears (Figure 8.4).

5. Choose Continue. In the Network Configuration dialog box that appears define the dial-out protocol you'll be using. NetBEUI and TCP/IP are selected by default.

6. Choose OK to return to the Network Settings dialog box.

7. Click OK to complete the setup. After Network Setup is complete, restart the computer when you are prompted to do so. Setup creates a Remote Access Service group in Program Manager.

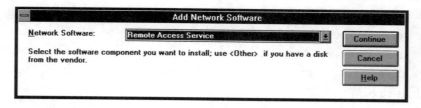

FIGURE 8.2 The Add Software dialog box.

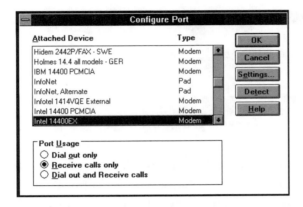

FIGURE 8.3 The Configure Port dialog box.

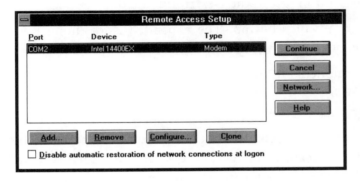

FIGURE 8.4 The Remote Access dialog box.

Setting Up RAS for Making the Connection (NT 3.51)

Once your computer reboots from the installation of RAS, the Remote Access Service group window appears (Figure 8.5) in the Program Manager window. To configure RAS for making the call to your Internet Service Provider, you need to create a Phone Book entry as explained in the following steps:

1. Double-click on the Remote Access icon in the Access Service group window. A message box appears informing you that the Remote Access Service phone book is empty. Click OK.

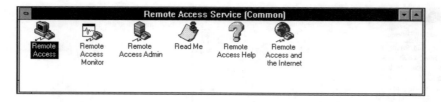

FIGURE 8.5 The Remote Access Service group window.

2. Click on the Add button. The Add Phone Book Entry dialog box appears (Figure 8.6). Enter an entry name that will appear in the Remote Access window in the Entry Name field. Enter the dial-in telephone number for your Internet service provider and optionally, add description text in the Description field.

3. Click on the Advance button. The expanded Add Phone Book Entry dialog box appears (Figure 8.7).

4. Click on the modem button to display the Modem Settings Dialog box (Figure 8.8).

5. Click on the down arrow of the Initial speed (bps) setting and select the maximum speed of your modem. Choose each of the three Hardware Features, then click OK. You're returned to the expanded Add Phone Book entry dialog box.

6. Click on the Network button, and the Network Protocol Settings dialog box appears (Figure 8.9).

7. Select the PPP radio button, then click on the TCP/IP and the Request LCP extensions (RFC 1570) check boxes.

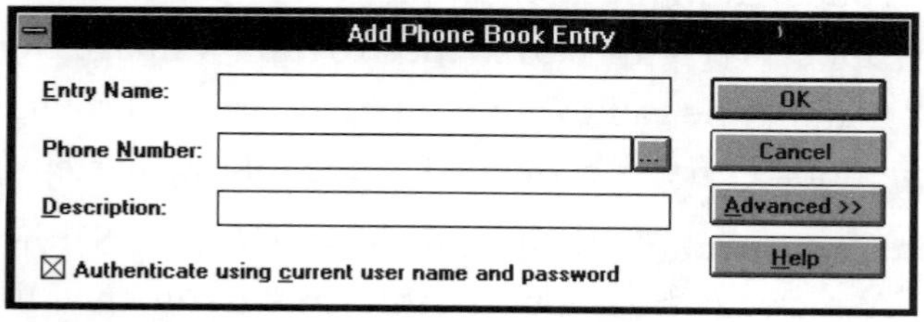

FIGURE 8.6 The Add Phone Book Entry window.

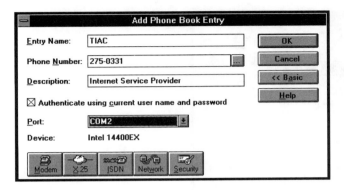

FIGURE 8.7 The expanded Add Phone Book Entry dialog box.

8. Click on the TCP/IP Setting button. The PPP TCP/IP Settings dialog box appears. (Figure 8.10).

9. Click on the required specific IP address radio button and enter your assigned IP address, which is supplied by your ISP. Click on the Use specific name server addresses radio button, then enter the ISP provider-supplied IP address for DNS servers. Activate the Use VJ header compression and Use default gateway on remote network settings.

10. Click OK to exit the PPP TCP/IP Settings dialog box, then click OK to exit the Add Phone Entry dialog box. The Remote Access window appears (Figure 8.11). You now need to configure the RAS

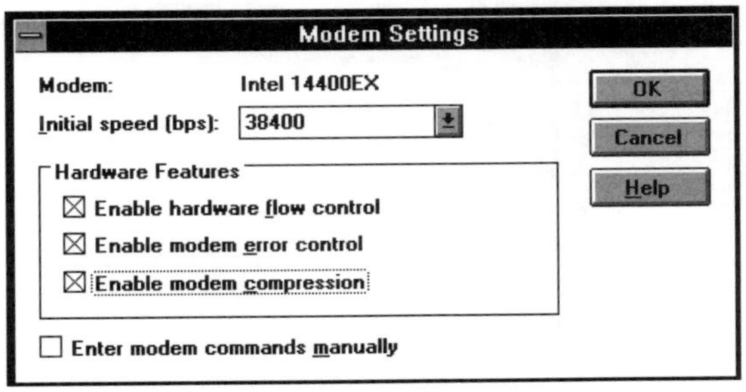

FIGURE 8.8 The Modem Settings dialog box.

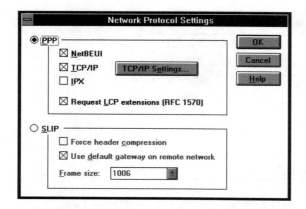

FIGURE 8.9 The Network Protocol Settings dialog box.

programs switch.inf file using the Windows NT NotePad program. This file provides a template for creating a logon script to enter your user login and password for connecting to your ISP's system.

11. Open NotePad from the Accessories group and choose the File|Open command in NotePad. Change to the c:\winnt35

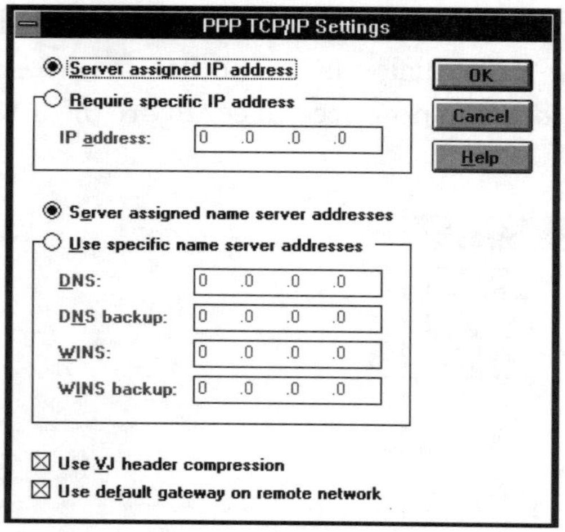

FIGURE 8.10 The PPP TCP/IP Settings dialog box.

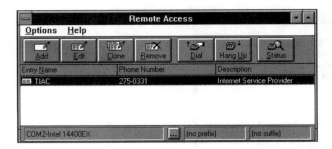

FIGURE 8.11 The Remote Access window.

\system\ras directory, change the *txt entry in the File name field to *.inf, and double-click on the switch.inf file.

12. Navigate down to the end of the switch.inf text file and enter the following lines:

[*add entry from Add Phone Book Entry dialog box's Entry Name field*]

```
COMMAND=
OK=<match> "login"
COMMAND=YourUSERId<cr>
OK=<ignore>
OK=<match> "password"
COMMAND=YourPassWord<cr>
OK=<ignore>
```

13. Change the YourUserID and YourPassWord entries to your actual user ID and password for logging on to your ISP machine, choose File|Save, then File|Exit.

14. Open the Remote Access window, and click on the Security button. The Security Settings dialog box appears (Figure 8.12).

15. Click on the Accept any authentication including clear text radio button, and click on the down arrow beside the After dialing field. Select the name you entered in the brackets [ ] of your NotePad entry. Click OK twice to return to the Remote Access dialog box.

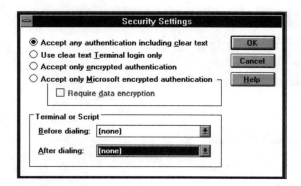

FIGURE 8.12 The Security Settings dialog box.

Making Your Connection (NT 3.51)

Making the connection to your ISP once you configured RAS is easy. In the Remote Access window simply double-click on the entry name. RAS dials your Internet service provider and logs on. Once you're connected, your machine running TCP/IP is connected to the Internet. Running the Web server software on your PC automatically makes your computer an active Web server.

Installing RAS in Windows NT 4.0

Windows NT 4.0 dramatically improves Remote Access Service by making it easier to install, set up, and reconfigure. For example, RAS in NT 3.51 did not allow you reinstall a different modem without removing the entire program, then reinstall it all over again. The following steps explain how to install RAS in NT 4.0.

1. Start the NT Control Panel and select the Network icon. The Network dialog box appears.

2. Select the Services tab, then click on the Add button. The Select Network Service dialog box appears (Figure 8.13).

3. Select Remote Access Service, then click on OK. The Windows NT Setup dialog box appears, prompting you for the path for your NT files.

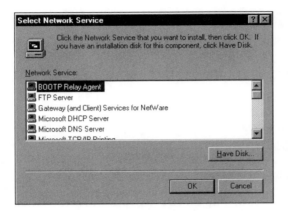

FIGURE 8.13 The Select Network Service dialog box.

4. Enter the path and click on Continue. Windows NT copies the Remote Access Files to your system.

The Remote Access Setup dialog box appears (Figure 8.14).

5. Click on the Add button. The Add Port dialog box appears (Figure 8.15).

6. Select the port and click OK. The Setup program displays a dialog box telling you to turn on your modem so that it can detect it. Turn on your modem, then click OK. After detecting your modem, NT displays the Configure Port dialog box with your modem entry selected (Figure 8.16).

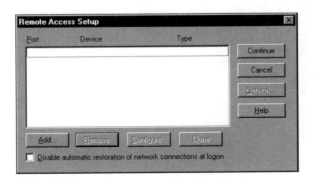

FIGURE 8.14 Remote Access Setup dialog box.

FIGURE 8.15 Add Port dialog box.

7. Click OK. NT returns to the Remote Access Setup dialog box.

8. Click on the Network button. The Network Configuration dialog box appears with the NetBEUI and TCP/IP option selected. Click on the NetBEUI option to turn it off, then Click OK twice to return to the Remote Access Setup dialog box.

9. Click on the Continue button to return to the Network dialog box, then click on the Close button. The Microsoft TCP/IP Properties dialog box appears (Figure 8.17). The entries in this dialog box were set up when you configured TCP/IP, as explained in Chapter 7.

10. Click OK. NT prompts you to restart your computer. Click on the Yes button to restart it.

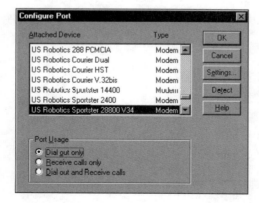

FIGURE 8.16 The Configure Port dialog box.

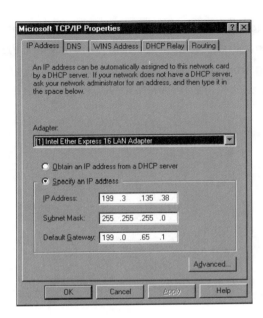

FIGURE 8.17 The Microsoft TCP/IP Properties dialog box.

Setting Up RAS for Making the Connection (NT 4.0)

Once your computer reboots from the installation of RAS, the Remote Access Service option is available in the Start|Programs menu. To configure RAS for making the call to your Internet Service Provider, you need to create a Phone Book entry. The procedure is almost identical to the way you do it in Windows 3.51, except you choose Start|Programs|Remote Access Service |Remote Access to display the Remote Access window. See "Setting Up RAS for Making the Connection (NT 3.51)" for instructions on setting up RAS.

Making Your Connection (NT 4.0)

Making the connection to your ISP once you configure RAS is easy. In the Remote Access window simply double-click on the entry name or select the entry then click on the dial button. RAS dials your Internet service provider and logs on. Once you're connected, your machine running TCP/IP is connected to the Internet. Running the Web server software on your PC automatically makes your computer an active Web server.

Part Three

Building Your Web

Commerce Server

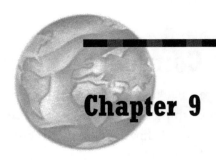

Chapter 9

Web Server
Software Primer

After getting through the maze of Windows NT, Internet connections, and other technical issues, you're ready to enter the Web server software realm. Web server software is the essential delivery mechanism for your Web site. It runs on top of your Windows NT platform as a service, ready and waiting for Web browsers to come calling. Like everything else associated with the Internet and the World Wide Web, the Web server market is in a state of rapid change. The good news is most of the changes are moving in the right direction in terms of costs and ease of use. This chapter offers you a focused game plan for choosing Web server software and presents an overview of the process involved in getting your digital certificate so that you can communicate via encryption for commerce.

Recapping Commerce vs. Publishing

Most Web server packages come in either a publishing or a commerce version. The publishing version supports content and interactive information in an unsecured form. The commerce-based Web server software supports the SSL or S-HTTP protocols that form the basis of encryption between Web browsers and Web servers. The use of encryption of communications allows your business to work with sensitive information, such as credit card numbers, across the Internet.

To activate a secure Web server, the Web server software must support SSL or S-HTTP. SSL (secure socket layer) and S-HTTP (Secure-HTTP) are the leading security protocols supported by Web browsers. SSL is currently more popular because it's supported by the dominant browser Netscape Navigator. S-HTTP, developed by NCSA and supported by Mosaic, is not in widespread use yet. Most packages support SSL, and some support both SSL and S-HTTP. The support for these protocols provides the foundation for adding encryption capabilities via digital certificates, which is explained in more detail later.

Secure Web server software allows all the same kinds of publishing features inherent in the publishing-only packages. In fact, you can operate the commerce-enabled Web server programs as publishing servers without invoking the security. Although most publishing-only Web server software programs are cheaper than secure versions, the commerce version is the way to go. Even if you don't plan to implement a secure system immediately, you'll ultimately want your site to handle the full range of publishing, secure communications, and transaction processing.

Common Features of Web Server Software

Web server software coordinates the distribution of documents. A common term for a Web server is HTTP server, which refers to the hypertext transport protocol that forms the basis of the Web. The following sections describe common features used by Web servers.

Directory Indexing

When a Web browser opens a URL on a Web server, a directory mapping takes place. For example, if a user enters the URL http://www.netgen.com, the server returns the contents of a default index file called index.htm or index.html. This file is located in a directory called a Document Root. If no index file is available, the server generates a directory index that resembles an FTP directory listing. The index file can also be named default.htm or home.htm.

Aliased Directories

An aliased or virtual directory is a URL that is mapped to a defined directory.

Port Numbers

Ports, which are part of TCP/IP, have numbers on your server that identify where the application or service listens for data. Commonly known port numbers are used for specific services. HTTP uses the default port of 80; using any other port but the default requires it to be entered in the URL as in the example http://www.netgen.com:8001.

Log Files

Most Web servers generate useful log files to track every request for a file from your server as well as a variety of other information, such as the host from which the request originated, the date and time of the request, and types of requests. Most Web servers generate a log file that adheres to the Common Log Format. Utility programs let you take this log file information and generate sophisticated reports for managing your Web site effectively.

Controlling Access

Web server access control is administered at both the Windows NT and Web server software levels. Access control lets you determine who can access different levels of files and directories on the server. Security can be configured at the global or server platform level, by directory, and by file. You can also use authentication of users by username and password.

MIME Typing

MIME (mulitpurpose Internet mail extensions) is a standardized method for organizing file formats and matching them at the Web browser end to execute a helper application or be read by the Web browser's built-in capabilities.

Image Maps

Image maps are clickable graphics that appear on Web pages. For example, a home page might have a map that allows the user to point to or click on different locations to display information related to those locations. An image map is a graphical image that is then defined with hot spots that link to information via URLs.

Common Gateway Interface

Common gateway interface (CGI) is a standardized means of connecting a Web server to other executable programs. CGI programs access back-end programs, such as databases. Newer Application Programming Interfaces (APIs) are being used in Windows NT-based Web servers that work faster than CGI programs.

Warfare on the World Wide Web

Netscape and Microsoft's war on the Web is a superpower contest that's shaking up the Web server software business. Microsoft has bundled its secure Web server product, Internet Information Server with Windows NT Server, in a direct attack on Netscape's bread-and-butter Web server software. Netscape was already under assault with lost-cost Web server software packages from such vendors as the Internet factory, O'Reilly, and others. Netscape currently owns the Web browser market, with over 70% of the browsers used. However, Microsoft is just gearing up with its Internet Explorer Web browser, which it includes with Windows 95 and Windows NT Server.

Add-On Programs

Web server software acts as the simple distribution mechanism for delivering documents to Web browsers. A growing number of third-party software developers are providing software tools to extend the capabilities of Web sites. These tools include such programs as form generators and logging data analysis. Other tools integrate databases and ordering systems for handling Web transactions.

TABLE 9.1 Leading Secure Web Server Software Packages

Web Server	Publisher
Commerce Server	Netscape Communications Corporation (http://home.netscape.com/)
Internet Information Server	Microsoft Corporation (http://www.microsoft.com/)
WebSite Professional	O'Reilly & Associates (http://website.ora.com/)
Commerce Builder	The Internet Factory (http://www.aristosoft.com/)
Purveyor Encrypt WebServer	Process Software (http://www.process.com/)
Spry SafetyWeb Server	CompuServe (http://www.server.spry.com)

Windows NT-Based Commerce Server Software

Microsoft's Windows NT Server is ushering in an abundance of affordable Web server software packages. The competition is hot for Windows NT-based servers. The current leading products in the Windows NT-based secure Web server market are listed in Table 9.1.

Secure Web server software prices range from free to $1,499, which in itself represents a dramatic drop in prices. Netscape's Commerce Server, which was one of the earliest and continues to be the leading secure Web server package, has reduced its price from $5,000 to $1,295 to stay competitive. Expect even more drastic price reductions and outright elimination of many secure Web server publishers as a result of the recent actions by the sleeping giant, Microsoft. Freshly converted to the Internet, Microsoft has bundled its secure, SSL-compliant Internet Information Server with Windows NT Server.

Narrowing the Field of Web Servers

Netcraft, an Internet consultancy based in England, conducts a Web server survey (http://www.netcraft.co.uk/Survey/) once a month. The survey shows that the leading Web servers have been and continue to be NCSA, CERN, and Apache, which are available at no cost. However, they're all unsecure Unix-based servers. The Internet was by and large built on the back of the Unix operating system, so its Web server software still reigns supreme in numbers.

The two Windows NT-based Server software programs that are in the top five deployed Web servers are Netscape's Commerce Server and O'Reilly's WebSite. Netscape's Commerce Server comes in both Unix and Windows NT flavors, while O'Reilly's WebSite is Windows 95- and Windows NT-based Web server software. WebSite, the earlier unsecured predecessor to WebSite Professional, experienced a 1,400% increase, and Netscape Commerce Server experienced a 1,600% increase between September 1995 and February 1996. Microsoft's Internet Information Server was too new to show up in the statistics. However, expect to see this bundled, secure Web server software capture a large share of the Web server market.

For starters, Microsoft's Internet Information Server, Netscape's Commerce Server, and O'Reilly's WebSite Professional are reasonable bets. This doesn't mean the other secure Web server software products are inferior. Our focus on the top three selling programs has more to do with long-term survival in the extremely competitive marketplace than with quality. However, because most Web server software publishers let you take a free 60-day test drive of their product by downloading the software from their Web sites, you may certainly try any package you want. The following sections present an overview of Microsoft's Internet Information Server, Netscape's Commerce Server, and O'Reilly & Associates' Web Site Professional.

Microsoft Internet Information Server

The Microsoft Internet Information Server comes bundled with Windows NT Server, which provides the powerful tools for handling the server side of client/server computing. The NT Server lists for $700 compared to about $300 for Windows NT Workstation. The Internet Information Server supports the SSL protocol and also includes ODBC (Open DataBase Connectivity) support, which allows you to connect a database to your Web site. Internet Information Server supports multihosting, so that you can run multiple Web sites on a single PC. The Information Servers include additional server software for FTP and Gopher as well as ISAPI (Internet Server Application Programming Interface) support for connecting your Web site to external programs using Application Programming Interface (API), which improves performance over CGI. On the down side, because Internet Information Server is bundled with Windows NT, technical support for the product is available only at the expensive technical support rates of Microsoft. Fortunately, the product is relatively easy to set up and run.

Netscape Commerce Server

Netscape Commerce Server has been the leader in the commerce server market and is designed more for large-volume sites with plenty of in-house expertise. It was originally written for Unix and was ported over to NT. It supports both CGI and Netscape's API called Netscape Server Application Programming Interface (NSAPI), which, like Microsoft's API, provides better performance over CGI. Commerce Server doesn't support multihosting; Microsoft's Internet Information Server and O'Reilly's WebSite Professional do.

Commerce Server is currently the most expensive product, with a list price of $2,995. If you want any support for the product, you must sign a $495 support contract when you buy the product. You can run Commerce Server on Windows NT Workstation, which costs around $300 less than running it on Windows NT Server, but the price of Commerce Server is simply too high for many small businesses. The bet on Netscape Commerce Server has more to do with its potential for exciting new enhancements from a company that leads the way in technological advancements. As of the writing of this book, Netscape had not responded to Microsoft's bundling of a sophisticated secure Web server software package with Windows NT Server. For now, the Netscape Commerce Server is a safe bet based on its widespread deployment, technological leadership, and browser domination on the Web.

O'Reilly & Associates' WebSite Professional

WebSite Professional is the secure version of the popular WebSite publishing-only Web server software, with a design approach of WebSite Professional to offer a complete set of tools for running and building a Web site. The amount of functionality that WebSite delivers for its $1,499 price makes it a strong choice for anyone looking for a complete solution. Its well-thought-out design and attention to simplifying the entire process of setting up a Web server add to its value. It also includes support for ODBC and SQL databases, multihosting, and SSL. Besides a robust HTTP, WebSite Professional includes a host of useful Web site building tools, including the following:

- HotDog HTML Editor, a popular HTML editor.

- WebView, a graphical, hierarchical tool to visually construct your Web site. It lets you toggle among several viewing categories, including directory location, URL, title, and label. The most useful tool of all is hyperlink, whereby WebView maps all links descending from the first designated Web page. Once you navigate to where you want to be in your Web site, you can use WebView to go directly to the appropriate editor.

- WebIndex, which lets you create indexes of the entire server contents or of selected files. You can set these up as standalone Web pages (the better for users to browse through, especially at a crowded Web site) or incorporate them into other Web pages.

- WebSite's Image Map Editor that lets you create clickable image maps easily.

Making Your Web Server Secure

Buying secure Web server software doesn't automatically make your Web site ready to handle secure transactions or secure communications. First you must get your Digital ID from a certificate authority that adds the encryption technology that operates over the SSL or S-HTTP protocols. Current digital identification systems are based on proprietary technology that requires all parties to use the vendor's technology in order for a digital certificate to be approved. The Digital ID market is currently dominated by a single company, RSA, whose VeriSign division handles its Digital ID business. If you plan to operate a secure Web server, you will need to obtain a VeriSign Digital ID, called a certificate, for your system. Once you complete all the paperwork, it can take anywhere from five working days to two months for RSA to issue your certificate. For the server side the cost is around $300 for the first year and $75 per year thereafter. Users must also apply for digital certificates, which range in cost from $6 to $24 per year.

Note: *Because any organization can become a certificate authority, expect to see other companies enter the digital ID marketplace. Standards and competition will make the process of getting a digital ID less complex and less expensive.*

VeriSign as a division of RSA owns the public key encryption algorithms upon which much of public key encryption is based, and RSA provides the central certificate authority for most secure servers. Public key algorithms use a pair of keys—a public key and a private key—to encrypt and decrypt messages. Anyone can use your public key to encrypt data meant for your eyes only. When you receive the encrypted data, you use your private key to decrypt it, and your private key always remains secret. When you want to send confidential data to someone else, you use that person's public key to encrypt it, and the receiver uses a private key for decryption.

The following sections explain the current procedures for getting your secure certificate from VeriSign. Keep in mind that different secure Web server software packages include built-in support for signing up for your digital certificate and implementing it once you receive your keypairs.

VeriSign Client Digital IDs

Beyond securing your Web server, Digital IDs must be issued for use with Web browsers. VeriSign issues and manages several classes of Digital IDs, differentiated by the associated level of assurance or trust, which depends on the degree of rigor or due diligence VeriSign applies to establishing a binding

VeriSign Online

At the time of this book's writing, VeriSign announced an online system for getting digital certificates. The unnamed issuing system will enable users to receive digital certificates for identification purposes for sending and receiving secure messages and accessing secure Web servers. The system lays the groundwork for VeriSign to provide users with digital certificates that will mimic traditional credit cards and ATM bank cards for doing purchases over the Internet, eliminating the need for users to reenter credit-card numbers when conducting a transaction. Both the ID certificate and the electronic payment certificate will be integrated with Web browsers to interact with a Web server transparently. Netscape's Web browser will support this system.

between individuals or entities and their public keys. The registration for all classes of Digital IDs is completed online to ensure a fast response. The four classes of Digital IDs currently issued by VeriSign are explained below.

Class 1 Digital IDs ensure uniqueness of name or e-mail address only, providing a low level of assurance for secure e-mail and casual Web browsing. Noncommercial and evaluation versions are offered free, with a VeriSign-supported commercial version for $6 per year.

Class 2 Digital IDs provide a higher level of assurance regarding a person's identity by involving third-party verification of the name, address, and other personal information provided in the registration process. These IDs support intracompany e-mail, online purchasing from electronic malls, and online subscriptions and are used for access to advanced Web sites. The cost is $12 for one year.

Class 3 Digital IDs provide yet a higher level of identity assurance by involving personal presence or registered credentials. Typical applications might include intercompany e-mail, electronic banking, higher-value purchases from electronic malls, and membership-based online subscription and information services. The cost is $24 for one year.

Class 4 Digital IDs involve personal presence plus a more thorough investigation of the individuals and/or the organizations they represent. This maximum level of identity assurance, for high-end financial transactions and trades, is issued based on information provided by a third-party credit reporting agency, such as TRW or Equifax. It uses application-specific pricing.

As soon as a Web browser, such as Netscape Navigator, is Digital ID enabled, users will be able to create their digital identities by getting an online Digital ID from VeriSign. With a Digital ID, Navigator users will be able to communicate via secure electronic mail, positively identify other, be authorized to access information, ensure privacy, and enable digital signatures. VeriSign's Digital IDs prove a user's online identity, acting much like an Internet driver license.

How To Tells If Security Is in Effect

Netscape Navigator identifies secure documents in several ways, one of which is in the URL field. If the URL begins with https:// instead of http://, the document comes from a secure server. You need to use https:// for HTTP URLs with SSL and http:// for HTTP URLs without SSL.

You can also verify the security of a document by examining the security icon in the bottom left corner of the Netscape Navigator window and the colorbar across the top of the content area. A doorkey on a blue background shows secure documents, and a broken doorkey on a gray background means insecure documents. The colorbar across the top of the content area is blue for secure and gray for insecure.

A document containing both secure and insecure information is displayed as secure with insecure information replaced by a mixed-security icon. Some servers may permit you to access documents securely using http://, permitting you to view mixed documents without icon substitution. More detailed security information can be found under the File|Document Information menu item in Netscape's Navigator. Several configurable notification dialog boxes inform you when you are entering or leaving a secure space, viewing a secure document that contains insecure information, and using an insecure submission process. You'll always be warned if a secure URL is redirected to an insecure location, or if you're submitting via a secure form using an insecure submission process.

The Document Information dialog box displays a document's title, location (URL), date of last modification, character set encoding, and security status. Secure documents specify the type of encryption protecting the document and the version, serial number, issuer, and server subject of the certificate backing the document.

The Encryption Key states the type of public key supported. For example, the high-grade encryption key for U.S. domestic use only (RC4, 128-bit) refers to the 128-bit key size for the RC4 stream encryption algorithm.

The certification request process requires that each server administrator supply an e-mail address and certain identifying information, which may include:

- Country (C): two-character country code
- State or Province (ST): unabbreviated state/province name
- Organization (O): legal, registered organization name
- Organizational Unit (OU): Optional department name
- Locality (L): city in which the organization resides or is registered
- Common Name (CN): the server's fully qualified host name

The Issuer (certifier id) identifies the certificate authority responsible for issuing the certification using the same abbreviations as those used to identify the server.

Document Your Web Server

Before a Digital ID is issued to your organization's Web server, certain procedures must be followed to maintain the integrity of the Secure Server Digital ID hierarchy that you are about to join. VeriSign Digital ID Services require a letter from your organization, which may be put together by the Webmaster, but must also be signed by the properly authorized representative of your organization. The purpose of this letter is to do the following:

1. Identify the Webmaster(s) of your organization.
2. State the formal name of your organization.
3. Present proof of the right to use the proposed name contained in the Organization field of the Server Name request form. Proper forms of documentation for this right are as follows:
   - For state level: articles of incorporation or partnership papers
   - For city/locality level: business license or partnership papers
   - For universities: notarized letter from office of the dean
   - For government organizations: notarized letter from a properly authorized person.

Once you have completed the requirements outlined below, fax the information on your organization's letterhead, including all supporting documents to VeriSign at (415) 508-1121. Specify Digital ID Services as the recipient. You must also mail an original copy to VeriSign Inc., P.O. Box 2004, Belmont, CA 94002. Here is the boilerplate text for your letter to VeriSign:

Our Server Name (Common Name) is [host and domain name].

Our billing method is [purchase order or check number here].

I, [name of authorized representative], hereby attest that the following individuals are employees of [name of organization]. I further attest that they are authorized to operate the software referred to as [name of secure server software].

[Insert table of Webmaster(s) information, including name, address, e-mail address.]

I understand that this software may conduct business over the Internet on behalf of [name of organization], and that the organization is solely liable for the products and services it offers through [name of secure Web server software].

[Name of organization] hereby certifies to VeriSign Inc. that it has the right to use the name presented in the Organization field within the Server Name. The proof of right to use the name is based on registering the respective organization name with the state, county, or city that the [name of secure Web server software] will be operated in. I have included this legal paperwork with this letter.

[Name and signature of authorized representative]

[letter affixed with company seal/letterhead]

Apply for VeriSign Digital ID and Make Your Payment

Based on the distinguished name you have chosen, generate an RSA Key Pair and an associated Digital ID request using your secure Web server software.

An e-mail message is generated and sent to VeriSign. You will be sent an acknowledgment when your Digital ID request has been received by VeriSign.

When submitting your request you must fax or mail a signed authorized letter including the company Visa/MasterCard number, card expiration date, and name of the cardholder or you must provide a facsimile copy of a purchase order that includes the date, purchase order number, company name, amount, product, and authorization number. Mail the original purchase order to VeriSign Inc., 100 Marine Parkway, Suite 525, Redwood City, CA 94065. Your Digital ID request can then be processed.

Install Your Digital ID

If no changes are requested by VeriSign and you have documented your server as required, you should receive an approved Digital ID from VeriSign to install in your secure Web server software. Each Web server handles the installation of keypairs differently, so check your Web server software documentation to find out how to set up the Web server for handling secure communications.

Chapter 10

Test Driving Microsoft's Internet Information Server

Microsoft is a late bloomer in the Web server software business. However, bundling a complete secure Web server package with its popular Windows NT Server should make the company move ahead quickly. This chapter takes you through the process of installing, configuring, and running Microsoft Internet Information Server.

Installing Microsoft Internet Information Server

Installing Microsoft Internet Information Server is relatively simple. If you already have the necessary Internet connection, you can accept all the default settings during setup and then add your HTML content files to the \Wwwroot directory. Your files will be immediately available to Internet users. The default setup configurations are suitable for many publishing and commerce scenarios without any further modifications. Before you install the Microsoft's Internet Information Server you must have the following:

- A computer with the configuration to support Windows NT Server

- Windows NT version 3.51 or higher

- Transmission control protocol/Internet protocol (TCP/IP) running on your NT Server

- A CD-ROM drive supported by Windows NT

- A hard disk partition formatted with the Windows NT File System (NTFS)

- An Internet connection and Internet protocol (IP) address for your machine from your Internet service provider

- A domain name system (DNS) registration for your IP address, which is supplied by your Internet service provider

- A network adapter card suitable for your connection to the Internet or remote access service installed

To install the Internet Information Server services, you must be logged on with administrator privileges or as a member of the administrators group and follow these steps:

1. Insert the Microsoft Internet Information Server CD into the appropriate CD-ROM drive.

2. In the File Manager prompt, change to the drive containing the CD. Double-click the SETUP.EXE in the root directory of the CD.

3. If you have not installed Service Pack 3 for Windows NT version 3.51, a dialog box will appear and offer to install the service pack automatically at the conclusion of Setup. Microsoft Internet Information Server will not operate without Service Pack 3 installed. Choose the Yes button to install Service Pack 3.

4. The Microsoft Internet Information Server Setup dialog box appears. Choose the OK button. A second dialog box appears, displaying the installation options listed in Table 10.1. By default all the options are selected for installation. If you do not want to install a particular item, click the box next to it to clear it.

TABLE 10.1 Installation Options

Item	Description
Internet Service Manager	Installs the administration program for managing the services.
World Wide Web Service	Creates a WWW publishing and commerce server.
Gopher Service	Creates a Gopher publishing server.
FTP Service	Creates an FTP server.
ODBC Drivers and Administration	Installs Open Data Base Connectivity (ODBC) drivers. These are required for logging to ODBC files and for enabling ODBC access from the WWW service. If you want to provide access to databases through the Microsoft Internet Information Server, you will need to set up the ODBC drivers and data sources by using the ODBC applet in Control Panel.
Help and Sample files	Installs online help and sample hypertext markup language (HTML) files.
Microsoft Internet Explorer	Installs the Web browser.

5. Accept the default installation directory C:\Intersrv and choose the OK button. A message box appears telling you that the directory doesn't exist. Click on the Yes button to create the directory. The Publishing Directories dialog box appears. Accept the default directories for the publishing services you have installed. Choose the OK button.

6. When prompted to create the service directories (Wwwroot, Ghophroot, and Ftproot by default), click Yes. The Create Internet Account dialog box appears. This is the account used for all anonymous access to the Internet Information Server.

7. Enter a password and confirm the password for this account. Choose OK. Set up copies of all remaining Internet Information Server files.

8. If the ODBC Drivers and Administration option box was selected, the Install Drivers dialog box appears. To install the SQL Server driver, select the SQL Server driver from the Available ODBC Drivers list box and choose the OK button. Setup completes copying files.

9. The Setup completion dialog box appears. Click the OK button to complete setup.

10. If during Setup you were prompted to install the Service Pack 3 update and you answered Yes, the Service Pack 3 update program will start automatically after setup. Choose the Restart button. After Microsoft Internet Server is installed, the Microsoft Internet Server group window appears, as shown in Figure 10.1.

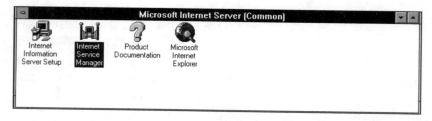

FIGURE 10.1 The Microsoft Internet Server group window.

Testing Your Server

Now that Microsoft Internet Information Server is installed and running, you are ready to publish on the Internet. If your files are in HTML format, just add them to WWW service root directory Wwwroot using the File Manager. Dial up to your Internet service provider using Windows NT Remote Access Service, then use the Internet Explorer from the Microsoft Internet Server group or use any Web browser. Type in the URL for the home directory of your new server; your home page should appear on the screen. The browser and server can be operating from the same computer.

Configuring and Managing Internet Information Server

Once you have completed setup and tested your installation, you can use Microsoft Internet Service Manager to configure features of the Internet Information Server and enhance the configuration and performance of your server. The Internet Service Manager in the Microsoft Internet Information Server group lets you configure and monitor all the Internet services running on your Windows NT Server. Double-clicking on the Internet Service Manager icon displays the Microsoft Internet Service Manager window, as shown in Figure 10.2. This default Report view alphabetically lists the selected computers, with each installed service shown on a separate line. You can also choose the Servers or Services view from the View menu. The Servers view displays services running on network servers by computer name. The Services view lists the services on every selected computer grouped by service name.

Double-clicking on the WWW service entry in the Internet Service manager window displays the WWW Service Properties dialog box (Figure 10.3), which includes the Service, Directories, Logging, and Advanced property sheets. Click the tab at the top of each property sheet to display the properties for that category.

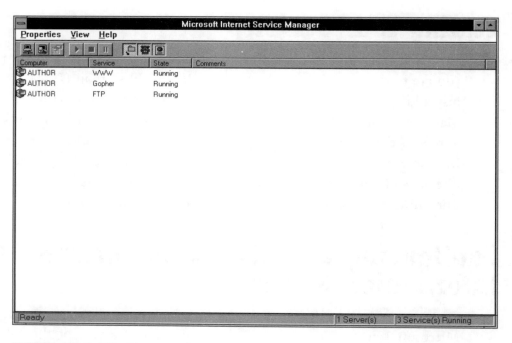

FIGURE 10.2 The Report view.

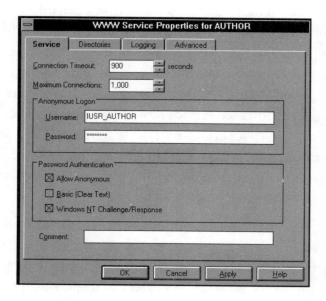

FIGURE 10.3 The WWW Service Properties dialog box.

The Service Property Sheet

You use the Service property sheet to control who can use your server and specify the account used for anonymous client requests to log on to the computer. If you allow anonymous logons, as most Internet sites do, all user permissions for the user, such as permission to access information, will use the IUSR_*computername* account, where *computername* is the name of the computer running Internet Information Server. By default, all requests use anonymous access through the IUSR_*computername* user account created during Internet Information Server setup. The following describes the settings in the Service property sheet:

- **Connection Timeout** sets the length of time before the server disconnects an inactive user.

- **Anonymous Logon** sets the Windows NT user account to use for permissions of all anonymous connections. By default, Internet Information Server creates and uses the account IUSR_*computername*. The password field pertains only to logons within Windows NT, not Web server logons. If you are allowing anonymous logon, first ensure that computerwide User Rights (in the User Manager Policies menu) do not allow the *IUSR_computername* account, the Guests group, or the Everyone group any right other than to "Log on Locally." Next, ensure that the file permissions set in the Windows NT File Manager are appropriate for all content directories used by Microsoft Internet Information Server.

- **Password Authentication** specifies the authentication process to use if anonymous access is disallowed or the remote user requests authentication. Basic authentication is encoded and is typically used in conjunction with SSL to ensure that usernames and passwords are encrypted before transmission. Windows NT Challenge/Response automatically encrypts usernames and passwords from Microsoft's Internet Explorer 2.0.

- **Comment** specifies the comment displayed in the Internet Service Manager's window.

The Directories Property Sheet

The Directories property sheet (Figure 10.4) lists directories available to users. The default document and directory browsing settings in the Directories property sheet are used to set up default displays that will appear if the remote user does not specify a particular file. Directory browsing means that users are presented with a hypertext listing of the directories and files so that they can navigate through your directory structure. You can place a default document in each directory so that when a remote user does not specify a specific file, the default document in that directory is displayed. A hypertext directory listing is sent to the user if directory browsing is enabled and no default document is provided.

Note: *Unless it is part of your strategy, you should disable directory browsing on the Directories property sheet. Directory browsing exposes the entire file structure; if it is not configured correctly, you run the risk of exposing program files or other files to unauthorized access.*

FIGURE 10.4 The Directories property sheet.

For each service Internet Server provides a default home directory, which for the WWW service is \Wwwroot. The HTML and other files that you place in the home directory of Internet Information Server and its subdirectories are available to remote Web browsers. You can change the location of the default home directory and add other directories outside the home directory that will appear to browsers as subdirectories of the home directory. That is, you can publish from other directories and have those directories appear to reside within the home directory. These are called virtual directories.

The Directory listing box shows the directories used by the WWW service and includes the following information:

- **Directory.** Lists the path of directories used by the WWW service.
- **Alias.** Lists the path for service users for virtual directories.
- **Address.** Lists the IP addresses using that directory.
- **Error.** Indicates system errors.
- **Add**, **Remove**, and **Edit Properties.** Let you manage entries in the Directory listing box. The Add button lets you add a directory, and the Remove button removes the selected directory. The Edit Properties button lets you edit directory entries.
- **Enable, Default, Document,** and **Directory Browsing.** Set up default displays that will appear if a remote user does not specify a particular file. Directory browsing means that users are presented with a hypertext listing of the directories and files so that they can navigate through your directory structure. You can place a default document in each directory so that when a remote user does not specify a specific file, the default document is displayed. A hypertext directory listing is sent to the user if directory browsing is enabled and no default document is in the specified document.

Table 10.2 describes the available permissions for your WWW service from the Edit Properties button.

TABLE 10.2 WWW Service Directory Permissions

Permission	Description
Read	Allows users to view files contained in a directory.
Execute	Allows users to start applications or scripts. All Internet Server API (ISAPI) applications and Common Gateway (CGI) scripts must be placed into the default \Scripts directory or into a directory configured with Execute permission. Execute permission must be set in both Internet Service Manager and File Manager when you install applications and scripts on an NTFS drive. Install server applications into a directory that is configured for Execute in Internet Service Manager and is *not* configured for Write permission on an NTFS drive. This will prevent malicious users from copying programs to your computer that could damage it when run.
Require Secure SSL Channel	Allows users to send information to the server in encrypted format, ensuring data privacy.

Note: *On NTFS drives you must ensure that permissions similar to those for your WWW service from the Edit Properties button are set on directories.*

The Logging Property Sheet

The Logging property sheet (Figure 10.5) lets you configure the Internet Information Server logging feature, which provides valuable information about how a server is used. You can send log data to files or an ODBC-supported database. If you want to log a file, you can specify how often to create new logs and which directory to put the log files in. If you log to an ODBC data source, you must specify the ODBC data source name (DSN), table, and valid user name and password to the database. If you have multiple servers or services on a network, you can log all their activity to a single

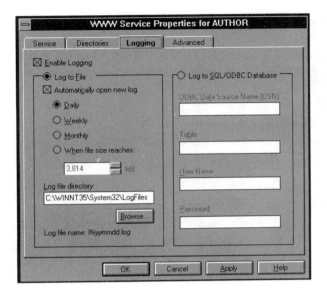

FIGURE 10.5 The Logging property sheet.

file or database on any network computer. The Logging property sheet includes the following settings:

- **Enable Logging.** Select this box to start or stop logging.
- **Log to File.** Choose this option to log to a text file.
- **Automatically open new log.** Select this box to generate new logs using the specified frequency.
- **Log file directory.** This shows the path to the directory containing all log files. To change directories, click Browse and select a different directory.
- **Log file filename.** This names the log file. The yy will be replaced with the year, mm will be replaced with the month, and dd will be replaced by the day.
- **Log to SQL/ODBC Database.** Choose to log to any ODBC data source. Set the Datasource name and Table name (not the filename of the table), and specify a user name and password that is valid for

the computer on which the database resides. You must also use the ODBC applet in the Control Panel to create a system data source.

The Advanced Property Sheet

The Advanced property sheet (Figure 10.6) lets you set access by specific IP address to block individuals or groups from gaining access to your server. You also set the maximum network bandwidth for outbound traffic to control the amount of data traffic on your server. If you choose to grant access to all users by default, you can then specify the computers to be denied access. For example, if you have a form on your Web server and a particular user on the Internet is entering multiple forms with fictitious information, you can prevent the computer at that IP address from connecting to your site. Conversely, if you choose to deny access to all users by default, you can then specify which computers are allowed access.

The source IP address of every packet received is checked against the Internet Information Server settings in the Advanced property sheet. Microsoft

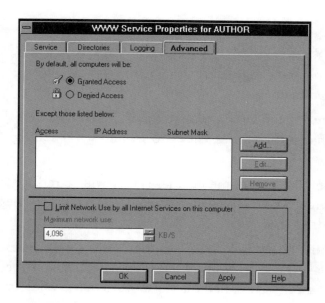

FIGURE 10.6 The Advanced properties sheet.

Internet Information Server can be configured to grant or deny access to specific IP addresses. For example, you can exclude a harassing individual by denying access to your server from a particular IP address or prevent entire networks from accessing your server. Conversely, you can choose to enable only specific sites to have access to your service. The following sections explain how to control access.

Denied Access

To deny access to your server by specific IP addresses, choose the Denied Access option, then click on the Add button to list computers that will be denied access. Choose Single Computer and provide the IP address to exclude a single computer. Choose Group of Computers and provide an IP address and subnet mask to exclude a group of computers.

Granted Access

To allow access to your server by specific IP addresses, choose the Granted Access option, then click on the Add button to list computers that will be granted access. Choose Single Computer and provide the IP address to include a single computer. Choose Group of Computers and provide an IP address and subnet mask to include a group of computers.

Limit Network Use by All Internet Services

You can control your Internet services by limiting the network bandwidth allowed for Internet services on the server. Set the maximum kilobytes of outbound traffic permitted on your server computer.

Planning Your Content Directories and Virtual Servers

If your hypertext markup language (HTML) content files are contained under one directory tree, all you need to do is copy them to the default World Wide Web (WWW) home directory (\Wwwroot) or change the home directory to refer to the location containing your files. However, if your files reside in multiple directories, or even multiple computers on your network, you will need to create virtual directories to make those files available.

Setting the Default Document and Directory Browsing

If a remote user sends a request without a specific file name (for example, http://www.microsoft.com/), the WWW service will return the specified default document if it exists in that directory. You can place a file with the specified default document filename in each subdirectory. If no default document is available, the server will return an error, unless directory browser is enabled, in which case, a directory listing containing links to the files and directories in that directory will appear.

A default document can be included in all WWW directories. In the Directories property sheet for the service, change the Default Document entry to the default file name you will use on your system. Often the default document is set to be an index file (Index.htm) for the contents of that directory (or of the entire server). The default file name used is Default.htm. If the user does not specify a file for a particular directory, a hypertext file and directory listing will be returned. Directory browsing on the WWW service is very similar to browsing in file transfer protocol (FTP). Directory browsing is useful if you have a lot of files that you want to share quickly without converting them to HTML format.

Creating Virtual Servers

By convention each domain name, such as www.company.com, represents an individual computer. However, it is possible to use a single computer and make it appear to be not only a primary server (for example, named www.company.com), but also multiple servers for different departments of your company (for example, marketing.company.com, sales.company.com).

You can create "virtual servers" for these departments with Microsoft Internet Information Server without a different computer for each domain name.

To do this, you must obtain IP addresses from your Internet Service Provider (ISP) for the primary server and for each virtual server you want to create. For example, you assign the first IP address (10.212.56.184) in the DNS as www.company.com (your primary server) and assign C:\Wwwroot as its content home directory. You register the second IP address (10.212.56.185) in DNS as marketing.company.com and assign a different drive or directory as its content home directory. Thus, it appears to users on the Internet that there are two computers when in fact the same computer is running one copy of the service. If you create a home directory without specifying an IP address, that home directory will be used for all requests containing server IP addresses not specified in other home directories. If you have assigned more than one IP address to your server, when you create a directory, you must specify which IP address has access to that directory. If no IP address is specified, that directory will be visible to all virtual servers. To specify the fully qualified path for the directory to use for the selected virtual server, choose the Add button and type the path in the Directory box of the Directory Properties dialog box or use the Browse button to pick the directory to use.

You use the Network applet in the Windows NT Control Panel to bind the additional IP addresses to your network adapter card. After the IP address is assigned to the network adapter card, you must assign a home content directory to that IP address. In the Directories property sheet, select the Virtual Server box and enter its IP address. You can also restrict virtual directories (directories that are not home directories) to one virtual server by assigning an IP address to them. To create more than five virtual servers you must change a Windows NT Registry entry.

——**Note:** *The default directories created during setup do not specify an IP address. You may need to specify IP addresses for the default directories when you add virtual servers.*

Home and Virtual Directories

Every server must have a home directory for content files that is` the "root" directory for that service. As a root directory it does not have a name. By default, the home directory and all subdirectories are available to users. For example, if you want to provide three different product catalogs, virtual directories can be used to present three separate drives as three subdirectories. To browsers, virtual directories appear as subdirectories off the root home directory. You must provide the name (alias) that browsers will use to specify that directory. You can create an almost unlimited number of virtual directories for your service, although it is wise to use them only as required because performance may suffer if you create too many.

——**Note:** *To browse virtual directories, the user must specify the URL for the virtual directory by clicking a hypertext link containing the URL or by typing the URL in the Location box of the browser.*

Monitoring Your Server with Performance Monitor

Internet Information Server automatically installs Windows NT Performance Monitor counters. With the HTTP service and Internet Services Performance Summary objects, you can use the Windows NT Performance Monitor for real-time measurement of your Internet service use. Similar counters for the Gopher and FTP services are also available. The WWW service object provides counters, including the following, to monitor the WWW service:

Microsoft Internet Information Server automatically logs all activity on your server. You can use this information to analyze traffic to your site and identify possible problems. This section explains how to configure logging, read file logs, view logs in databases, and convert log files to other formats.

Bytes Sent/sec

Bytes Total/sec

CGI Requests

Connection Attempts

Connections/sec

Current Anonymous Users

Current ISAPI Requests

Current CGI Requests

Current Connections

Current Non-Anonymous Users

Files Received

Files Sent

Files Total

Get Requests

Head Requests

Logon Attempts

Maximum Anonymous Users

Maximum ISAPI Requests

Maximum CGI Requests

Maximum Connections

Maximum NonAnonymous Users

Not Found Errors

Other Request Methods

Post Requests

Total Anonymous Users

Total Non-Anonymous Users

Configuring Logging

When you set up Internet Information Server, you enable logging to see who has been using the server and how many times your online information was accessed. In Internet Service Manager, double-click the service to display its property sheets. The Logging property sheet sets logging for the selected information service. To configure logging, you determine in which directory the logs will be stored, specify how often logs are to be collected (every day, every week, every month, and so on), and select the log tools you want to use to analyze the logs your server collects. The maximum total log line is 1200 bytes, and each field is limited to 150 bytes. When you use ODBC for logging, each field is limited to 200 bytes.

Reading Log Files

You can use any ODBC-supported database to log server activity. Logging to a database allows you to direct the logging of all Internet Information Server services to a single source. You can use any ODBC-compliant application to view the log data in your database. In addition, you can use the Internet Database Connector to view log data in a Web browser. The Microsoft Internet Log Converter converts Microsoft Internet Server log files to either European Microsoft Windows NT Academic Centre (EMWAC) log file format or the Common Log Format. Convlog.exe is located in the \Inetsrv\Admin directory. At the command prompt, type convlog without parameters to see syntax and examples, or see Help.

Securing Data Transmissions with SSL

Microsoft Internet Information Server provides users with a secure communication channel through support for secure sockets layer (SSL) and RSA encryption. The SSL protocol provides secure data communication through data encryption and decryption. An SSL-enabled server can send and receive private communication across the Internet to SSL-enabled Web browsers. SSL, a protocol layer between the TCP/IP layer and the application layer (HTTP), provides server authentication, encryption, and data integrity. Authentication assures the client that data is being sent to the correct server and that the server is secure. Encryption ensures that the data cannot be read by anyone other than the secure target server. Data integrity ensures that the data being transferred has not been altered. Enabling SSL security on a Microsoft Internet Information Server involves the following steps:

1. Generate a key pair file and a request file.
2. Request a certificate from a certification authority.
3. Install the certificate on your server.
4. Activate SSL security on a service directory.

Keep in mind the following points when enabling SSL security:

- You can enable SSL security on the root of your Web home directory (\Wwwroot by default) or on one or more virtual directories.

- Once SSL security is enabled and properly configured, only SSL-enabled clients will be able to communicate with the SSL-enabled directories.

- URLs that point to documents on a SSL-enabled WWW directory must use https:// instead of http:// in the URL. Any links using http:// in the URL will not work on a secure directory.

- You enable and disable SSL security by using Internet Service Manager.

How to Acquire an SSL Digital Certificate

The following procedure details the entire SSL configuration process, including how to obtain an SSL digital certificate. You must consult the certificate authority before performing the following steps:

1. Change directories to C:\Inetsrv\Server (or the directory in which you installed Internet Information Server). This is where the key and certificate utilities (Keygen.exe and Setkey.exe) are contained.

2. Use Keygen.exe to create two files. The first file is a key file containing the key pair; the second file is a certificate request file. (Type keygen with no arguments to see command syntax and an example.)

The following example creates the key file named Keypair.key and the certificate request file named Request.req for a server named www.netgenesis.com. The files are generated in the current directory, C:\Inetsrv\Server.

```
C:\Inetsrv\server>keygen MyPassword1 keypair.key request.req "C-US,
S-Massachusetts, L-Cambridge, O-Example, OU-Marketing, CN-www.netge-
nesis.com"
PCT/SSL Key generation utility, Version 1.0
Copyright (c) 1995 Microsoft Corporation
Generating key pair of length 1024 bits...
Completed.
Send the generated request file. Request.req, to your Certificate
Authority for signing.
```

By default Keygenexe generates a key pair 1024 bits long. You can use the -bits parameter to specify keys that are 512 or 768 bits in length.

The argument in quotation marks in the Keygen.exe command line (C=US, S=Massachusetts, L=Cambridge, O=Example, OU=Marketing, CN=www.netgenesis.com) specifies several fields for the certificate request related to your organization and server.

Note: *Do not use commas in any field because they are interpreted as the end of that field and will generate a bad request without warning.*

The valid field types follow:

C = Two-letter ISO country designations (for example, US, FR, AU, UK, DE)

S = State or province (for example, Massachusetts, Alberta, California—do not abbreviate)

L = Locality (for example, Cambridge, Calgary, Redwood City)

O = Organization (preferably ISO-registered top-level organization or company name)

OU = Organizational unit

CN = Common name (domain name of server, such as www.netgenesis.com)

If you run Keygen.exe more than once, note that it does not overwrite existing files; instead, it returns an error 80, meaning that the file already exists. Be sure to delete any existing files created by Keygen.exe if you need to run it more than once.

3. E-mail your request to your certificate authority for signing. It is best to include the Keygen.exe command line used, followed by the text from your request file (Request.req). Be sure to remove your password from the command line sent to your certificate authority. For example:

```
From:    webmaster@netgenesis.com
To:      certificates@authority.com
Subject: Certificate Request
```

```
C:\Inetsrv\server>keygen <be sure to remove your password> keypair.key
request.req "C-US, S-Massachusetts, L-Cambridge, O-Example, OU-Marketing, CN-
www.netgenesis.com"
--- BEGIN NEW CERTIFICATE REQUEST ---

MIIBSzCBEOIBADAOMQwwCgYDVOOGEwNVUOEwgZ8wDQYJKoZIhvcNAQEBBOADgYOA  MIGJAoG-
Bal7nOitueTDEChJJTyOpKPSIDbtRDRouhCei5SWw2t5fxc7Vs46kPTF9
1J9UuwpM5TtzqDbBDn7PkpqfV5Cea6LYaAp5UIOdBs+IAAqOlRivVfgaz3M8cDUB
eEBbdcWS70a2X9/R44ploXODwUnuOnGVW3rha00gpFOi85bAVvMRAgMBAAEwDOYJ  KoZIhvc-
NAQEEBOADgYEAicID2qfNkttpx3zagtEEoDgDi5VQfA7bSIJXQORNtKKr
MBa3tsqqNOUdABKY4Abb7Yr9nFrJf3emSgJ2QcE2NxnEX59NS+JEbLkBTVRt/Twr
3xJUBwq3sBMuy/9ReozxGWTWQBORXyhDpJyOncwuSo/N8GUWAB2ddUm6+d+LraA-

--- END NEW CERTIFICATE REQUEST---
```

4. After completing all documentation requirements from your certificate authority and sending the e-mail in the previous step, you will probably receive an e-mail response containing a signed certificate from your certificate authority. For example:

```
From:     certificate@authority.com
To:       webmaster@netgenesis.com
Subject: Certificate Response
--- BEGIN CERTIFICATE ---

ZIICUJCCAb8CBQJyAAL3MAOGCSqGSIb3DQEBAgUAMF8xCzAJBgNVBAYTAIVTMSAwHsYDVOOKExd-
SUOEgRGFOYSBTZWN1cmIOeSwgSWSJLJEuMCwGAlUECxM1U2VJdXJl          IFNIcnZlciB-
DZXJOaWZpY2FOaW9uIEFIdGhvcmIOeTAeFwO5NTA5MTkwMDAwMDBa
FwZaNJAzMJAyMzU5NTlaMIGFMOswCOYDVQQGEwJVUzETMBEGA1UECBMKV2FzaGluZ3RvbJEOMA4G
AlUEBxMHUmVkbW9uZDEeMBwGAIUEChMVTWlJcm9zb2Z@IENvcnBvcmFOaW9uM08wDOYDVOOLEwZ-
ibGRnMJYxHJAcBgNVBAMUFUtleU51dCoubWlJcm9zb2ZOXCVvbTCBnTANBgkqhkiG9wOBAQE-
FAAOBiwAwgYcCgYEAvp3ba@pkrNNBtJ4q
3ngFdfVMF+Jonem6zwsyBMOWmxVbEaIarmFAKIMAaRro9qvqH2LFRdWHHdgb8dhp  h5mzYMtEo-
RiLnY/saoUDulVMBloUpVhlErbkNtdVDXoQvwq+IJ5df7y2rQTezf55  uVDNOSkmcJYDBkAXN-
SZQbEknpOUCAOMwDQYJKoZIhvcNAQECBQADfgAdT6fQntzx
YXzMsL78qaQheMk+Mb6CKc1zLBCYOwKSOGZBWFuhpLbOkMoBCV3u37UcK/RxLSzp
XIMU5aDWP6gvSXUraDXIWhEA83fBPdHKOE81nKpcVJiR53UkLGTIJLATYnoCdx9a  HOyCVVSmb-
syFKMX405PXoOAYdIfOUA-

--- END CERTIFICATE ---
```

5. Copy the text to a file by using Notepad or another text editor and save it (for example, as Certif.txt).

6. Use Setkey.exe to install your signed certificate on the server; for example:

```
setkey MyPassword1 keypair.key certif.txt
```

——**Note:** *If you do not specify an IP address, the same certificate will be applied to all virtual servers on the system that are confined to use a secure SSL channel for communication. Specify the IP address of a virtual server if the certificate should apply only to that IP address or domain name. For example:*

```
setkey MyPassword1 keypair.key certif.txt 10.191.28.45
```

7. Use Internet Service Manager to set the Require Secure SSL Channel option for directories that you want to protect by using SSL. For example, the configuration in the preceding graphic shows the SSL-protected directory C:\Www\Secure-content for the virtual server on IP address 10.191.28.45. To gain access to this content, a client would specify https://www.netgensis.com/storefront (note the "https" rather than http"). Clients must then use the https:// syntax to access any content in the \Storefront directory. Links to content in the \Storefront directory should be changed to use "https" as well. Standard requests (for example, http:www.netgenesis.com/storefront) will fail.

Use Separate Content Directories for Secure and Public Content

Microsoft recommends that you use separate content directories for secure and public content (for example, C:\Inetsrv\Wwwroot\Secure-Content and C:\InetsrvWwwroot\Public-Content). It is important to avoid having a server directory not protected by SSL as a parent for a secure directory. It is suggested that you save your key file (Keypair.key) in a safe place in case you need it in the future and store Keypair.key on a floppy disk and remove it from the local system after completing all setup steps. Do not forget the password you assigned to the keypair file in step 2.

Publishing Information and Applications

Internet Information Server can publish both information and applications, so your server can contain anything from static pages of information to interactive applications. You can also find and extract information from and insert information into databases. This section explains how to prepare your server and your information for publishing, install and use interactive applications on your server, and publish using an ODBC-compliant database source.

Publishing HTML and Other File Formats

Most Web pages are formatted in HTML as simple ASCII text files with codes embedded to indicate formatting and hypertext links. HTML specifications are changing constantly. You should probably review the HTML specifications (available on the Internet) to fully plan your HTML pages.

You can use any text editor to create and edit your files, but you will probably find an HTML editor, such as Internet Assistant for Microsoft Word, easier to use. You use the HTML editor or other system to create HTML files, which can include hyperlinks to other files on your system. If you want to include images or sound, you will also need appropriate software to create and edit those files.

When your files include images and sound, you can create links to Microsoft Office files or to almost any other file format, but remote users must have the correct viewing application to view non-HTML files. For example, if you know that all remote users will have Microsoft Word, you can include links to Microsoft Word .doc files. A user can click the link to have the document appear in Word on the user's computer. Once you have created your information in HTML or other formats, you can either copy the information to the default directory \Inetsrv\Wwwroot or change the default home directory to the directory containing your information.

MIME Type Configuration

If your server provides files that are in multiple formats, it must have a multi-purpose Internet mail extension (MIME) mapping for each file type. If MIME mapping on the server is not set up for a specific file type, browsers may not be able to retrieve the file. See the Windows NT Registry for the default MIME mappings.

To configure additional MIME mappings start Regedt32.exe and open:

```
HKEY_LOCAL_MACHINE\CurrentControlSet\Services\InetInfo\Parameters\MimeMap
```

Add the value for the MIME mapping required for your server with the following syntax:

```
<mime type>,<filename extension>,<unused parameter>,<gopher type>
```

For example:

```
text/html,htm,/unused,1
image/jpeg,jpeg./unused,5
```

The default entry with the filename extension specified as an asterisk (*) is the default MIME type uses when a MIME mapping does not exist. For example, to handle a request for the file Current.vgr when the filename extension vgr is not mapped to a MIME type, the server will use the MIME type specified for the asterisk extension, which is the type used for binary data. Usually, this will cause browsers to save the file to disk.

Including Other Files with the Include Statement

You can insert repetitive information into an file just before sending the file to a user. This feature is handy for including the same text on each HTML page, such as copyright information or a link to the home page.

The format of the include statement is:

```
<!--#include file='value"-->
```

The value must contain the full path from the home directory of your WWW service.

For example, to include a link to your home page in each HTML document:

1. Create the file linkhome.htm, which contains the HTML codes you want to repeat. For example, for a button to your home page, the file would contain an HTML that looks similar to this:

```
<A HREF-'"homepage.htm"><IMG SRC="/images/button_h.gif"></A>
```

2. Use the filename extension .stm (rather than .htm or html) when you create your Web pages.

3. In each .stm file, use an include file statement where you want the repeated information to appear. For example:

```
You can return to: <!--#include file="/linkhome.htm"> at any time
```

Note: *All paths are relative to the WWW home directory and can include virtual roots.*

Publishing Dynamic Applications

One of the most exciting features of Microsoft Internet Information Server is its ability to run applications or scripts that remote users start by clicking HTML links or by filling in and sending an HTML form. Using programming languages such as C or Perl, you can create applications or scripts that communicate with the user in dynamic HTML pages.

Interactive applications or scripts can be written in almost any 32-bit programming language, such as C or Perl, or as Windows NT batch files (.bat or.cmd). When you write your applications or script, you can use one of two supported interfaces, the Microsoft Internet Server Application Programming Interface (ISAPI) or the Common Gateway Interface (CGI). Documentation for ISAPI is available from Microsoft via subscription to the Microsoft Developer Network (MSDN). Documentation for CGI is available on the Internet. Batch files can issue any command valid at the command prompt.

Applications that use ISAPI are compiled as Dynamic-Link Libraries (DLLs) that are loaded by the WWW service at startup. Because the programs are resident in memory, ISAPI programs are significantly faster than applications written to the CGI specification.

Internet Server API

ISAPI for Windows NT can be used to write applications that Web users can activate by filling out an HTML form or clicking a link in an HTML page on your Web server. The remote application can then take the user-supplied information and do almost anything with it that can be programmed and then return the results in an HTML page or post the information in a database.

ISAPI can be used to create applications that run as DLLs on your Web server. If you have used CGI scripts before, you will find that the ISAPI applications have much better performance because your applications are loaded into memory at server run time. They require less overhead because each request does not start a separate process.

Another feature of ISAPI allows preprocessing of requests and postprocessing of responses, permitting a site-specific handling of HTTP requests and responses. ISAPI filters can be used for applications such as customized authentication, access or logging. You can create very complex sites by using both ISAPI filters and applications. ISAPI extensions can also be combined with the Internet Database Connector to create highly interactive sites.

Common Gateway Interface

The Common Gateway Interface (CGI) is a standard interface used to write applications that remote users can start by filling out an HTML form or clicking a link in an HTML page on your Web server. As with ISAPI, the remote application can then take the user-supplied information and do almost anything that can be programmed, then return the results of the application in an HTML page or post the information in a database. Because simple CGI applications are often written scripting languages such as Perl, CGI applications are sometimes referred to as scripts.

Most 32-bit applications that run on Windows NT and conform to the CGI specifications can be used by Microsoft Internet Information Server. For information about how to convert existing CGI programs or scripts from Unix, see Help. For more information about the CGI specifications, consult the CGI specifications widely available on the Internet.

Installing and Running an Application

You place any application or script in the /Scripts directory, a virtual directory for applications. You must also ensure that every process started by your application is running by using an account with adequate permissions. If your application interacts with other files, the account you assign to your program must have the right permissions to use those files. By default, applications run using the IUSR_computername account.

If your application doesn't require data from the user, you will typically create a link to your application in a simple HTML fileand probably use an HTML form. In other instances you can just sent a URL, usually containing data parameters, to invoke a program. An HTML link to an application that does not require input from the user might look like the following:

```
http://www.company.com/scripts/catalog.exe?
```

In this example, \scripts is the virtual directory for interactive applications. If you are creating an application that requires input from the user, you will need to understand HTML forms and how to use the forms with ISAPI or CGI. This information is widely available on the Internet.

Because you have the flexibility to create applications in almost any programming language, Internet Information Server uses filename extension to determine which interpreter to invoke for each application. The default Interpreter associations are listed in Table 10.3. You can use the Registry Editor to create additional associations.

TABLE 10.3 Default Interpreter Associations

Extension	Default Interpreter
.exe, .com, .bat, .cmd	Cmd.exe
.idc	Httpodbc.dll. (an ISAPI DLL that uses ODBC to gain access to databases)

When you allow remote users to run applications on your computer, you run the risk of hackers attempting to break into your system. Microsoft Internet Information Server is configured by default to reduce the risk of malicious intrusion in two important ways. First, the virtual directory \Scripts contains your applications and is marked as an application directory. Only an administrator can add programs to such a directory, so unauthorized users cannot copy a malicious application and then run it on your computer without first gaining administrator access.

Second, if you have configured the WWW service to allow only anonymous logons, all requests from remote users will use the IUSR_computername account. By default, the IUSR_computername account is unable to delete or change files by using the Windows NT File System (NTFS) unless specifically granted access by an administrator. Thus, even if a malicious program were copied to your computer, it would be unable to cause much damage to your content because it would have only IUSR_computername access to your computer and files.

Publishing Information Using a Database

With the WWW service and the ODBC drivers provided with Internet Information Server, you can do the following:

- Create Web pages with information contained in a database
- Insert, update, and delete information in the database based on user input from a Web page
- Perform other Structured Query Language (SQL) commands

Database access is performed by Internet Information Server when Web browsers submit requests to the Internet server by using HTTP. The Internet server responds with a document formatted in HTML. Access to databases is accomplished through a component of Internet Information Server called the Internet Database Connector. The Internet Database Connector Httpodbc.dll is an ISAPI DLL that uses ODBC to gain access to databases.

The Httpodbc.dll uses two types of files to control how the database is accessed and how the output Web page is constructed. These files are Internet Database Connector (.idc) files and HTML extension (.htx) files. The Internet Database Connector files contain the necessary information to connect to the appropriate ODBC data source and execute the SQL statement. An Internet Database Connector file also contains the name and location of the HTML extension file. The extension file is the template for the actual HTML document that will be returned to the Web browser after the database information has been merged into it by Httpodbc.dll.

Note: *In order to provide access to an SQL database from your Web page, you will need to create an Internet Database Connector file and an HTML extension file. For more information on creating these files, see Help.*

When the ODBC option is selected during setup, ODBC version 2.5 components are installed. This version of ODBC supports System DSNs (data source names) and is required for using ODBC with Microsoft Internet Information Server. System DSNs were introduced in ODBC version 2.5 to allow Windows NT services to use ODBC.

To install the ODBC drivers follow these steps:

1. If you did not install the ODBC Drivers and Administration option, run Setup again by double-clicking on the Internet Information Server Setup icon in the Microsoft Internet Server program group of Program Manager. You will need the Internet Information Server CD or a network installation directory of the complete contents of the CD.

2. Choose the OK button.

3. Choose the Add/Remove button.

4. Choose the OK button.

5. Select the ODBC Drivers and Administration option.

6. Choose the OK button. The Install Drivers dialog box appears.

7. To install the SQL Server driver, select the SQL Server driver from the Available ODBC Drivers list box and choose the OK button. Setup completes copying files.

To create the system data sources do the following:

1. Double-click the Control Panel icon in the Main program group of Program Manager.

2. Double-click the ODBC icon. The ODBC Data Sources dialog box appears. You may see other data sources in the list if you previously installed other ODBC drivers.

3. Choose the System DSN button. The System Data Sources dialog box appears.

Note: *Be sure to click the System DSN button. The Internet Database Connector will work only with System DSNs.*

4. Choose the Add button. The Add Data Source dialog box appears.

5. Select SQL Server from the list box and click OK. The ODBC SQL Server Setup dialog box will appear.

6. Enter the name of the data source.

The data source name is a logical name used by ODBC to refer to the SQL Server driver and the actual server name on which SQL Server is running. You can also use the server name "(local)" if SQL Server is on this computer. The data source name is used in Internet Database Connector files to tell Internet Information Server where to access the data. The server name, network address, and network library are specific to your installation. If you do not know what to enter in these controls, accept the defaults. To find out the details, click the Help button and find the section that describes your network.

7. Choose the OK button. The System Data Sources dialog box will be displayed again, but now it will have the name of the data source displayed.

8. Choose the Close button to close the System Data Sources dialog box.

9. Choose the Close button to close the Data Sources dialog box.

10. Choose the OK button to convert the ODBC and DSN setup.

Using the FTP Service

In addition to the WWW service, the Microsoft Internet Information Server includes file transfer protocol (FTP) and Gopher. In most cases, you'll have no need for Gopher services, but you may want to use FTP to deliver files to users connecting via FTP to your server.

FTP was one of the earliest protocols used on TCP/IP networks and the Internet. Using character-based programs it transfers files from one computer to another computer on the same network. A character-based program was used to log on to the remote computer, browse directories, and then transfer files. Web browsers simplify this process by automatically logging you onto the FTP server if anonymous connections are permitted. Directory listings are automatically displayed as hypertext links, permitting point-and-click simplicity in traversing directories and copying files from a server to a client. You can use any FTP client to connect to the Internet Information Server FTP service. Windows NT Workstation and Windows NT Server include a character-based FTP client (this client can be started only at the command prompt). Microsoft Internet Information Server includes Internet Explorer, which allows you to browse FTP servers. You use a URL such as ftp://ftp.microsoft.com to connect to an FTP server.

The World Wide Web has replaced most functions of FTP. However, only FTP can be used to copy files from a client computer to a server. If your remote users need to do this, they must use FTP. Also, if you have existing files that you want to make available to remote users, FTP is an extremely easy server to install and maintain. After installation, point the FTP service to your files; no additional configuration is necessary. Files made available through FTP can be in any format, such as document files, multimedia files, or application files. Clients can specify whether to copy the file or to start a helper application to immediately display or play the file. The FTP service requires that users log on to use the service. Once logged on, users can navigate the directories made available to the FTP service. On older character-based FTP clients, remote users can copy files to the server and issue other FTP commands.

Configuring FTP Logon

You use Internet Service Manager to configure logon requirements for the FTP service by double-clicking on the FTP service entry. If the FTP service is configured for anonymous logon, clients can log on with the user name "anonymous." Traditionally, anonymous FTP users log on using their e-mail addresses as passwords. Most browsers automatically log on anonymously to FTP servers that permit anonymous logon. FTP clients are also permitted, by default, to log on with a Windows NT username and password permitted to use that computer. As a result, you can control every user's access permissions and file access on Windows NTFS drives.

You can configure the number of simultaneous connections allowed and the amount of time allowed for connections. Because users are logged on until they log off or break the connection, you can use the Connected Users button in the Service property sheet to keep track of which users are currently connected. Select the Allow anonymous only check box to prevent users from logging on with usernames. With this check box enabled, any account other than "anonymous" cannot logon. This feature is useful for security because only one account, that assigned for anonymous logon, is permitted access; intruders cannot attempt to gain access with the administrator account.

Configuring FTP Directories

By default, all subdirectories are available in the home directory. You should place all your FTP files in the home directory. You may also add virtual directories, just as with the service; however, FTP is an older protocol, and because of its technical limitations, virtual directories are not visible to users. Users can enter a virtual directory only if they know its alias. Some browsers require that the FTP listing be styled in Unix format, so you should set the FTP listing style to Unix format for maximum compatibility with browsers.

Setting Read and Write Permission

Read permissions are set to all directories by default. You may remove the Read permission and set a Write permission to create a dedicated directory to which users can copy files, but cannot see any files left by others. Setting Write permission will allow users to leave files on your computer. You must set Read and Write permissions by using Internet Service Manager. On NTFS drives you must also set matching permissions by using File Manager.

Creating Annotation Files

Each directory can contain an annotation file, which can be used to summarize the information that the directory contains. This summary appears automatically to remote browsers. You can add directory descriptions to show FTP users the contents of a particular directory on the server by creating a file called ~ftpsvc.ckm in that directory. Usually you want to make this a hidden file so that directory listings do not display it.

Special Directories in the Home Directory

You can add special directories to the home directories to control the root directory displayed to FTP users. These directories must be physical subdirectories; you cannot specify them by using virtual directories. Username directories are directories in the home directory with names that match a username. If a user logs on with a username that has a matching directory in the home directory, that directory is used as the root. You can use FTP senate directories to control the root directory presented to users. FTP username directories are not created by default during setup.

The Anonymous directory is in the home directory named "Anonymous." If a user logs on using the password Anonymous, the directory name Anonymous is used as the root. You can use FTP username directories to control the root directory presented to users. FTP username directories are not created by default during setup.

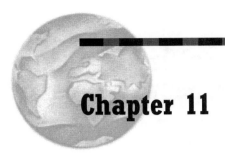

Chapter 11

Test Driving Netscape's Commerce Server

Netscape Commerce Server is the leader in the commerce server market. Originally written for Unix, it was ported over to NT and can run on Windows NT Workstation. It supports the SSL security protocol and both CGI and NSAPI (Netscape Server Application Programming Interface). This chapter takes you on a test drive of the Netscape Commerce Server.

Before Installing Netscape Commerce Server

Before you install Netscape Commerce Server, you need to make sure you have some information and networking pieces in place. However, out of the items listed below, the only one required for installation is the port number.

Make Sure DNS Is Up and Running

When you install the Commerce Server, some items on the installation forms request either a hostname or an IP address as input. A hostname for a specific computer is in the form of machine.subdomain.domain, which is translated into a dotted IP address by a Domain Name Service (DNS). Also make sure your DNS is up and running properly via your Internet service provider. Your server must have an entry in a DNS server: you cannot simply configure your Windows NT machine with a host name by entering a host name and domain name in the Network configuration utility in the Control Panel.

Create a Home Page

If you already have a home page, you can specify it during the installation process. If you don't have a home page, you can either create one before installation or use the one the installation process creates. You can edit it after installing the server.

Create an Alias for Your Web Server

Your Internet service provider should set up a DNS CNAME record or an alias that points to the actual server machine. Later, should the need arise, you can change the actual hostname or IP address of the server machine without having to change all of your URLs. For example, you might call the server myserver.anycompany.com and then use an alias like www.any company.com. Thus, the URLs to documents on your server would use the www alias instead of myserver.

Create a User Account

You should create a user account for the Web server to give the server restricted access to your system resources. Use your administrator account in Windows NT. The installation process uses the LocalSystem account, which has a limited set of privileges. You can change the user account for the server after the installation process and then configure that user account to have permissions to get files on another machine, which lets your server access files that are mounted from another machine.

Choose Port Numbers

You need two port numbers to install Netscape Commerce server: one for the administration server and one for the commerce server. The administration server is a separate utility that lets you manage multiple servers from a single forms-based interface. The standard port number is 80 for HTTP and 443 for secure HTTP, but you can install the server to any port. You should choose a random number, such as 777, for the administration server to make it harder for anyone to breach your server's security. When you access the administration forms, you use the administration server's port number.

Installing Netscape Commerce Server

Installing Commerce Server consists of two processes: copying files from the CD-ROM to your hard disk, then configuring and starting the server. To install Commerce Server, do the following:

1. In Windows NT Program manager, choose File|Run.

2. Type D: \i386\SETUP, where D: is the drive letter for your CD ROM drive. Press Enter.

3. A dialog box appears asking you for the directory in which you want to install the server. The default is C:\NETSCAPE, the server root directory where you install all servers, but you can type another drive and directory. Click Continue. The installation program copies files to the specified directory.

4. A dialog box appears asking if your machine has a DNS entry in a DNS server. If you choose DNS Configured, the installation process assumes you want to use host names (you can still use IP addresses if you like). If you choose no DNS Entry, the installation process uses only IP addresses. If your machine doesn't have access to a DNS server that can do DNS lookups or if your machine doesn't have an entry in the DNA map of the DNS server, you must click No DNS Entry and use IP addresses throughout installation. Also, if your machine has an entry in the DNS server but your machine isn't configured to do DNS lookups on the DNS server, you should click No DNS Entry. This means clients can access your server using a hostname, but your server will use IP addresses instead of DNS hostnames.

5. The installation program goes to your computer's Registry and determines your host name or IP address. It displays a dialog box asking you to confirm the entry or change it in the dialog box, then click Continue. A dialog box appears telling you the installation of Netscape Commerce Server was successful. Click OK.

6. The Netscape Navigator appears with a form to start your configuration of the Commerce Server. Scroll to the bottom of the form, then click on the Start the Installation! button. Netscape Navigator appears displaying the Installation Overview form shown in Figure 11.1.

Working with Commerce Server Configuration

The Installation Overview form is the starting page for configuring all aspects of the Netscape Commerce Server. The following three buttons display forms to complete for configuring your server:

- The **Server Config** button takes you through a series of forms that configure the server.

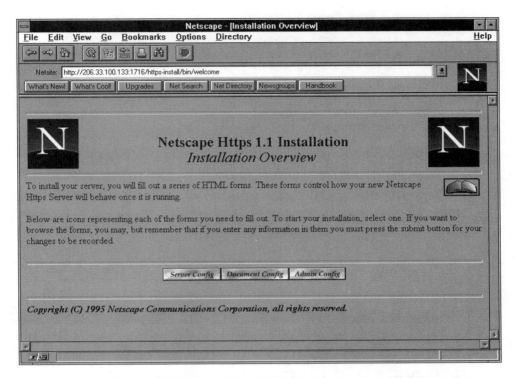

FIGURE 11.1 The Installation Overview form for configuring Netscape Commerce Server.

- The **Document Config** button displays a form for configuring the document root directory and the types of documents your server can send to clients.

- The **Admin Config** button displays a form for configuring the administration server. You can specify which users have permission to use the administration forms to configure all of your installed servers.

Each of these buttons displays a page of configuration options. To systematically configure Netscape Commerce Server, start with the Server Config button. After you complete the settings in the Server Configuration page, click the Make These Changes button at the bottom of the form. The Install program automatically displays the Document Configuration page until you click on Make These Changes at the end of the Administrative Configuration page. The installation program then displays a summary page of your configuration options, as shown in Figure 11.2. If all the setting are correct, click on the Go for it! button at the bottom of the Configuration Summary page. You can also make changes at any time.

After you click on the Go for it! button, Netscape installs all the files on your hard disk. Then the Welcome to the World Wide Web page appears, as shown in Figure 11.3. From this page, you can choose to access your server as a client, administer your server, generate a secure key, or register your server with Netscape Communications Corporation.

The installation process creates a Netscape server group with three icons, as shown in Figure 11.4.

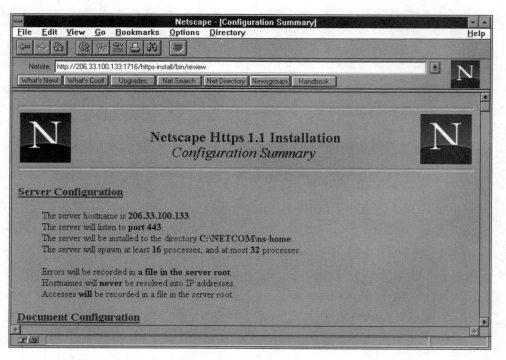

FIGURE 11.2 The Configuration Summary form.

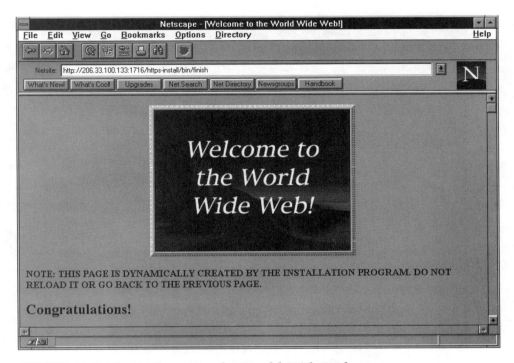

FIGURE 11.3 The Welcome to the World Wide Web page.

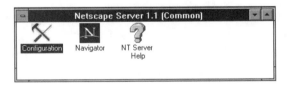

FIGURE 11.4 Netscape Server program group.

Server Configuration

Clicking on the Server Config button displays the Server Configuration form (Figure 11.5). Use this page to access configuration forms for your server name, server port number, server location, and number of threads. The following sections explain each of these settings. After making your configuration settings or using the default settings, choose Make These Changes at the bottom of the form.

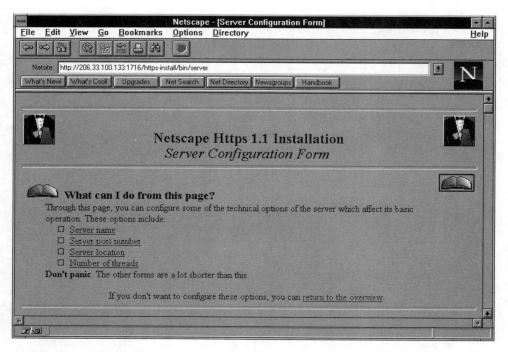

FIGURE 11.5 The Server Configuration form.

Server Name

Your server uses the name you give it in the Server Name field in the Server Configuration form. It's the central URL for your Web site. For example, it could be www.netgen.com. The server name is built from the domain name, netgen.com, and the name of the server, which in this example would be www. In other words, the Server name includes your domain name as well as the machine name. Remember that if you activate security on your server, the URL that refers to your server will become https://www.yourdomain.com/ instead of just http. If you specified IP address No DNS Entry during installation, the entry in the Server Name field is the IP address of your machine.

Server Port

The machine on which your server runs has a number of ports it uses to differentiate requests through different protocols. The standard HTTP port number is 80, and the standard HTTPS port is 443. You can choose another port (from 1 to 65535), but you need to make sure that the port you choose is not already in use. If you choose a port other than the default port, the URL used to access your home page will change. For example, if you choose port 8080, the URL to your home page will be http://www.netgen.com:8080/. If you decide to activate security on your server, remember that the default port for HTTPS is 443. In most cases, you'll want to use the default port 80 for unsecured Web serving and port 443 for secure Web serving.

Server Location

The directory you specify in the Server Location field will contain all the Netscape server files you will install after finishing the configuration. By default, the directory specified is C:\Netscape\ns-home. If you want to run two servers on two different ports or on different IP addresses, you should specify the same server location for both of them. The installer program will recognize the two servers and create a new configuration directory for the second sever, which allows them to share common programs.

Number of Threads

When your server machine starts up, the server creates a number of threads that take turns answering requests. You can set the number of threads to achieve a balance between system load and request response time as determined by the number of requests you expect and the speed of the hardware on which your system runs. On a low-demand system, the server may need only 5 or 10 threads. On a high-demand system, you may want to use as many as 30 threads. The default settings are 16 minimum threads and 32 maximum threads.

Hostname Resolution

When a Web browser connects to the Commerce Server, the server knows only the client's IP address. It does not know that this IP address is actually the host name, such as www.netgen.com. For certain operations like CGI, error reporting, and access logging, the server will resolve the user's IP address into a host name. However, as your server becomes busier, this process adds a load to the DNS server. The default setting for this control is Never attempt to resolve IP addresses into host names, which is what you should use. If you want to activate resolving IP addresses into hostnames, choose the Always attempt to resolve IP addresses into host names.

Access Logging

Every time a Web browser contacts your server, the server keeps a record of the IP address or hostname. Along with this information, it records what document was accessed, whether the access was successful or not, which user the browser authenticated as, and how many bytes were transferred. By default, this setting is activated via the Log all accesses to the server in the common format. You can shut this off by choosing the Do not log setting.

Document Configuration

After you click on the Make These Changes button in the Server Configuration form, the installation program displays the Document Configuration Form (Figure 11.6). This form sets up the initial document configuration for Netscape server, including establishing the document root directory, setting up directory index filenames, choosing a form of automatic indexing, and telling the server what home page to use. When you finish making all your changes, click on the Make These Changes button.

Document Root

By creating a root directory for all your documents, you can keep them in one location and let the server handle the URLs. This way, any incoming request for a document automatically gets redirected to the document root directory you name in this setting. Full file system pathnames are not used and are not displayed on any Web browser, thus the file system is kept safe from outsiders who won't be able to get information about the rest of your system. Using a

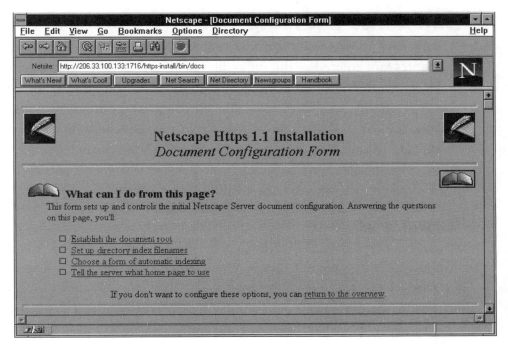

FIGURE 11.6 The Document Configuration form.

central document root directory also lets you move your documents to a larger disk as your service grows and expands, without having to change your URLs. The default document root directory is C:\NETSCAPE\ns-home\docs, which appears in the Document Root field.

Index Files

When you reference a directory on your server, it's useful to have an index file in it that tells people what's in the directory. When Web users follow the URL that points to a directory, the server finds this file and uses it to display a catalog of what's inside. By entering a name in the Index files setting, you can standardize directory index filenames. A popular name is index.html. If you want to use more than one name, separate the names with commas. The server sends back the first one it finds. The default entries in the Index files field are index.html, and home.html.

Automatic Indexing

When a user accesses a directory that doesn't have an index file with one of the names you entered in the Index files field, the server creates an index of directory contents automatically. These automatic indexes come in two flavors: a simple index displays a list of the directory contents by name only, and a fancy index displays file and directory names, icons, file sizes, and last modification dates. The default setting is Use fancy directory indexing, which is the better of the two options. Showing the size of files is useful for Web users to determine downloading time.

Home Page

When users first navigate to your server, they usually start with a URL like http://www.netgen.com/, which displays your server's home page. To set your home page, you can do one of two things: create an index file in your document root or specify the name of a file in the document root to use. In most cases, you'll enter an HTML document filename in the Web server's root directory that is your home page. If you don't enter any home page file, the Commerce Server creates an automatic index of the root directory. You can also reference a pathname to another filesystem.

Administrative Configuration

After you click on the Make These Changes button in the Document Configuration form, the installation program displays the Administrative Configuration form (Figure 11.7). This form sets up the initial server administrative configuration, which includes choosing a username and password for administering the Commerce Server, establishing which hosts have administrative access to your server, establishing a port for your administrative server, and assigning a user for the administration server to run as.

Administrative Username and Password

To get access to the administrative forms, use a URL similar to http://your server.yourdomain.com:11111, using your server name and your administra-

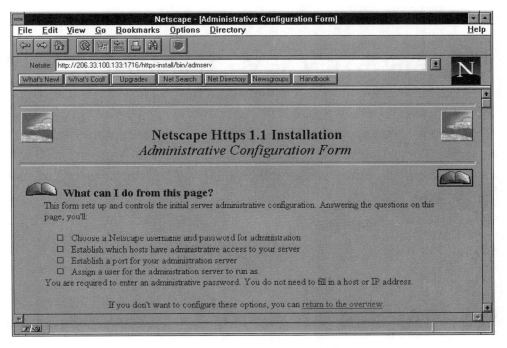

FIGURE 11.7 The Administrative Configuration form.

tive port instead. When you access your server's administrative forms, your Web browser will ask you to enter a username and password. Give it the user name you entered in the Username and Password fields. The default username is admin. Enter a password in the Password field, then enter it again in the Password field.

Administrative Access Control

Once the server is installed, you administer and manage it using any Web browser. Obviously, you don't want off-site people changing your server, and you want only authorized people to administer your server. You need to indicate in the Administrative Access Control fields which hosts are allowed administrative access. All others will get an error message if they attempt access. You can specify a host name as either a DNS entry or an IP address. If you want access only from the machine running the Web server, enter its host name or IP address.

——Caution: *If you leave this setting blank, anyone can administer your server.*

Administrative Server Configuration

When you configure and administrate your server, you will access not the server itself but a separate HTTP server called an administrative. This server is run separately to give you more control over when administration is done. The port you select here does not affect your regular server's URLs. Rather, it's the port number that will be used in the URL you use to configure your server.

——Caution: *The port you use for the administrative server should be different from the port on which you install your HTTP server.*

Starting and Stopping Commerce Server

Once installed, the server runs constantly, listening to and accepting requests. If your machine crashes or is taken offline, the server stops, and any requests it was servicing are lost. There are three ways to restart the server:

- Use the Administration Manager to restart any server.
- Use the NT Control Panel Services to restart any server.
- Use the Control Panel Services to configure the operating system to restart the server each time the machine is rebooted.

Restarting Commerce Server with Control Panel

To configure the operating system to restart the server each time the machine is started or rebooted or to start the administration server, use the following procedure:

1. In the Main group, double-click the Control Panel icon.
2. Double-click the Services icon.

3. Scroll through the list of services and select the service called Netscape Httpd or Netscape Https if you have the Commerce server configured to use SSL security.

4. Click the StartUp button. The Service dialog box appears.

5. Check Automatic to have your computer start the server each time the computer starts or reboots.

6. Click OK.

Using the Server Manager

After you install your server, you'll need to do periodic maintenance. This includes infrequent configurations such as changing the server's name and port number to daily tasks such as adding, changing, and removing users in user database files. Once in the Server Manager, you click links to configure parts of the server. Most links go to forms that configure the entire server. Some links go to forms that can configure the entire server or files or directories the server maintains.

The Configuration icon in the Netscape Server group window is your gateway to the Netscape Commerce Server's Server Manager. The Server Manager is a set of forms you use to change options and control your server. You can view the Server Manager immediately after installation (there is a link to it). You can use the Server Manager from any remote machine—you don't need to use the machine the server is installed on.

To view the Server Manager at any time, do the following:

1. Double-click the Administrator icon in the Netscape Server group if you're making changes directly on the Web server machine. For remote access, use a forms-capable Web browser to point to the URL: http://[servernamel.[yourdomainl.ldomainl:[port]/ For example, type http: //www. netscape.com: 13579.

2. You'll be prompted for a user name and password, which are the administration user name and password you specified during the

installation process. The Administration Manager appears listing all the servers you have installed on the machine.

3. Click the link for the server you want to configure. The Server Manager appears as shown in Figure 11.8.

Note: *You must restart the server for your changes to take place.*

Changing the User Account

After you install the server, you might want to change the user account the server uses. By default, the user account is LocalSystem. To change it after installation, do the following:

1. Go to the Administration Manager and click the link for System Specifics.

2. Type the name of the server user account you want to use.

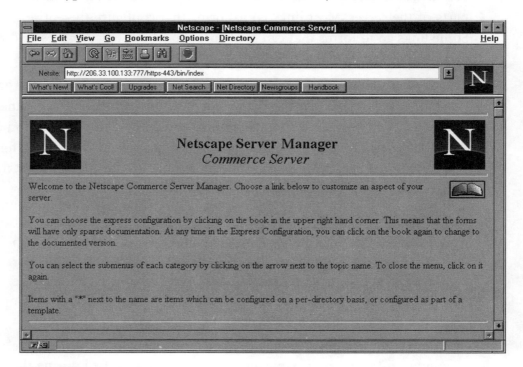

FIGURE 11.8 The Netscape Server Manager.

3. Scroll down the form and click on Make These Changes.

4. Go to the Control Panel and double-click on the Services icon.

5. Select the server name (this is either Netscape Httpd or Netscape Https).

6. Click on the StartUp button.

7. In the Logon section, type the account name you want to use.

8. Type the password for that account, then type it again to confirm it.

9. Click OK.

10. Restart the server using either the Services program or the Administration Manager.

Securing Your Commerce Server

The Netscape Commerce Server uses the secure sockets layer (SSL) protocol to provide advanced security features for secure data communications. This means the server can send and receive private information across the public Internet to SSL-enabled browsers without the data being compromised during transfer. Before you can activate SSL on the Netscape Commerce Server, you need to acquire a digital certificate for your server from a certification authority (CA). The signed digital certificate contains two groups of information. First is information on the certificate itself, including the name of the server, its public key, the certificate's validity dates, and the name of the CA. The second piece is the digital signature, which cannot be forged. This entire message is digitally signed by a CA who is known to many servers and who can verify the relationship between a server and its public key. The procedure for installing security on your Netscape Commerce Server is straightforward:

Caution: *Make sure you've read the section on getting a digital certificate in Chapter 9 and have prepared all the information before you begin this process!*

1. Use a form to generate a private and public key pair.

2. Request a certificate from a certification authority.

3. When the certificate is transmitted back to you from the CA, install it using another form.

4. Configure and activate security for the server.

Generating a Keypair File

Your server needs to generate a keypair file that holds the *public* and *private* keys that are used during secure communications. The private key is stored in encrypted form using a password you specify. A public key is usually used to exchange session keys. It is also used to verify the authenticity of digital signatures and to encrypt data. A private key is usually used to decrypt session keys that were encrypted with the matching public key. You always keep your private key private. The Commerce Server keyfile password protects this key, but for additional security you shouldn't keep the key file in a directory where people have access to it. The private key is also used to create a digital signature when you first request a certificate.

To generate a keypair file, do the following:

1. Start the Server Manager and click the Security Configuration link called Generate a key.

2. In the form that appears, type a path (relative or absolute) where you want to store the key file. This directory should be safe from other users. For example, use a directory to which only you have read and write access to.

3. Type a password for the key file. Make sure you memorize this password (and don't write it down). The security of your server is only as good as the security of the key file and its password. Any time secure servers are restarted, this password is required to decrypt the key file and extract the public and private keys. The password must be eight characters in length and have at least one non-alphabetical character (a number or punctuation mark) somewhere in the middle. You shouldn't administer security using

a remote connection because anyone on your network could potentially intercept your password.

4. Click the Make These Changes button. The server generates the keypair file and places it in the directory you specified.

Note: *You should periodically change your key file password using the Security Configuration link called Change your key file pair password. If you forget your password, you will have to regenerate your keypair file. This means you must also obtain another certificate (usually at an additional cost).*

Requesting a Certificate

Before you can request a certificate, you must contact a certification authority regarding the specific format of the information required. (See Chapter 9 for more information.) To request a security certificate, do the following:

1. From the Server Manager, click the link called Request or renew a certificate.

2. In the form that appears, type the e-mail address for the CA you have chosen.

3. Specify if this is a new certificate or a renewal. Certificates are generally good for six months to a year. Some CAs will automatically send you a renewal.

4. Type the location and password for your key file.

5. Type the information for your distinguished name. The format of this information varies by CA. This usually isn't required for a renewal.

6. Type your phone number. Be sure to include your area code and any international codes as applicable. The CA uses this to contact you regarding your request for a certificate.

7. Double-check your work to ensure accuracy. The more accurate the information, the faster your certificate is likely to be approved. Click the Make These Changes button when the information is correct.

The server composes an e-mail to the CA that includes your information and has a digital signature created with your private key. The digital signature is used by the CA to verify that the e-mail wasn't tampered with during routing from your server machine to the CA. In the rare event that the e-mail is tampered with, the CA will contact you by phone. You can't continue installing security until your request for a certificate is approved and a confirmation is sent to you via e-mail.

Installing the Certificate

When you get an e-mail from the CA that contains your certificate, you need to decode the certificate from the e-mail. You can either save it somewhere accessible to the server or copy the text of the mail and be ready to paste the text in the form. The information in the e-mail is encrypted, but you should take every protection to prevent unauthorized access to the certificate file. To install the certificate, do the following:

1. From the Server Manager, click the link called Install a certificate.

2. Either type the full pathname to the saved e-mail or paste the e-mail text in the space provided.

3. Specify a destination directory for the certificate. You can enter the name as a relative path or as an absolute path. The default name and location is [ServerRootl\https-443\config\Servercert.der. Remember where you put this file! It should not appear in your document root directory or any generally available directory.

4. Click the Make These Changes button. The server extracts the certificate from the e-mail and saves it to the directory you specified.

5. Continue by activating security and specifying ciphers, as explained in the next section.

Activating Security and Specifying Ciphers

Most of the time, you want your server to run with security enabled. At other times, you might want to disable security temporarily, but make sure you enable it again before processing transactions that require encryption, authentication, or data integrity. Also remove any private files from public access.

Ciphers define how a document is encrypted. Generally, the more bits used during encryption, the harder it is to decrypt the data. To activate security and specify ciphers, do the following:

1. From the Server Manager, click the link called Activate security and specify ciphers.

2. Check the radio button to enable security. You can always return to this form and disable security.

3. Specify a new port number. The standard HTTP port is 80, and the standard secure HTTP port is 443. You should always use 443 with the secure server.

4. Type the path to the key file. This is used when the server needs to encrypt or decrypt messages and digital signatures.

5. Type the path for the certificate file. The server uses the certificate to let clients verify the server's identity (server authentication).

6. Activate any ciphers by checking them. These ciphers are used when the client and server try to agree on the encryption method they should use.

   You should check all the ciphers and let the browser and server decide the method. However, you might want to uncheck some ciphers to exclude some transactions. For example, some ciphers are used only for data transfer outside the United States. If you uncheck these, you're basically restricting access to browsers who use the checked ciphers (for example, U.S. versions of Netscape Navigator). The ciphers are as follows:

   - RC4 cipher with 128-bit encryption
   - RC4 cipher with 40-bit encryption
   - RC2 cipher with 128-bit encryption
   - RC2 cipher with 40-bit encryption
   - IDEA cipher with 128-bit encryption

- DES encryption, 64 bits
- DES encryption with EDE 3, 192 bits

7. Click the Make These Changes button. You'll need to restart the server before using any secure features.

Effects of Running a Secure Server

You need to keep a few things in mind once security is enabled for your Netscape Commerce Server. This section describes what effects you need to know about running a secure server versus running an unsecured server.

Secure URLs are constructed with https instead of simply http. URLs that point to documents on a secure Commerce Server have the format:

```
https://[servername].[domain].[dom]/[pathname]/[document]
```

Once security is installed and enabled on a Netscape Commerce Server, all communications between the server and SSL-enabled browsers are private and authenticated. This means that any document sent to a user with an SSL-enabled browser is automatically encrypted. Browsers not enabled with SSL won't work with a secure Commerce Server because they can't decrypt the data. (They will work if the Commerce server doesn't enable SSL security.)

Once security is enabled, a new log, called secure, is created in the normal log directory. Entries in the log look like this:

```
198.93.92.99: (02/Nov/1994:23:51:46 -0800) using keysize 40
```

where the IP address is first, followed by the date and time of access, and then the key size. The key size represents a level of security. Generally, the bigger the key size, the higher the level of security.

Server Control Configuration

You can configure the server's basic functions with the forms under Server Control in the Server Manager. The following describes the configuration options available in the Server Control group of links in the Server Manager.

System Specifics

With system specifics, you can configure the server's technical options, including its location, the user account it uses, and the threads the server spawns.

Changing the Server's Location

For various reasons, you might need to move the server from one directory to another. To do this, change the location the server references—it needs to know where the binary files are. Then shut down the server and copy the server files and subdirectories to a new location.

Changing the Server's User Account

Server User specifies a user account that the server uses. By using a specific user account (other than LocalSystem), you can restrict or enable system features for the server. For example, you can use a user account that can mount files from another machine.

Server Threads

Whenever people use the server, the server uses background threads to service their requests. You can specify the minimum number of threads dedicated to the server. These threads are spawned when the server starts, and they remain idle until needed. The maximum number sets a limit on the number of threads your server can use. The actual number of threads fluctuates between the minimum and maximum numbers.

Domain Name Service

The server can be configured never to use Domain Name Service (DNS) lookups during normal operation. Even though DNS lookups are useful tools, they can be expensive in terms of performance. Don't use DNS lookups if your server machine doesn't have an entry in a DNS server or isn't configured to use DNS lookups. Be aware of the consequences of turning off DNS on your server: hostname restrictions won't work, and hostnames won't appear in your log files.

Stopping and Restarting the Server

You can stop, start, or restart the server from the Server Manager. Sometimes you'll need to do a stop and start, such as if you change the port number or enable security. Stop shuts down the server completely, interrupting service until it is restarted. You can configure the server to restart when the system starts.

Rotating Log Files

The server uses several log files, logging accesses to the server and any errors that occur. At times you'll want to archive the log files and have the server create new log files. When you rotate log files, the server renames the existing log files and then creates new log files with the original names. This lets you back up or archive (or simply delete) the old logs. The old log file is saved with the name of the file combined with the date the file was rotated.

URL Configuration

URL configuration group in the Server Manager lets you change elements that affect the URLs to documents on your server. You can change the server name and port number and the directories to your documents, and you can map URLs for one directory to another. The general structure for URLs is:

```
http://servername.domain.dom[:portnum]/directory/filename
```

You can also map URLs to another server or directory. This is useful when you move files and directories among file systems.

The Global URL config link configures the structure of all the URLs for your server. The server name is the final hostname of your server machine. When clients access your server, they use this name. The format for the Server Name is machinename. yourdomain. domain. If your system administrator has set up a DNS alias for your server, you should use that alias here. If not, you should use the machine's name combined with your domain to construct the full host name.

The Server Port Number specifies the TCP port the server listens to. The port number you choose can affect your users—if you use a nonstandard port, anyone accessing your server must specify a server name and port number in the URL. For example, if you use port 777, the URL would look like this:

```
http://www.netscape.com:777
```

The standard HTTP port number is 80, and the standard secure HTTPS port is 443. Technically, the port number can be any port from 1 to 65535.

Document Configuration

The Document config link configures how the server deals with URLs. These configuration settings include document root, directory indexing, server home page, default MIME types settings, and URL mapping.

Document Root

For a public server, you probably don't want to make all the files on your file system available to remote clients. The easiest way to limit them is to keep all your server's documents in a central location known as a document root. Another benefit of the document root is that you can move your documents to a new directory (perhaps on a different disk) without changing any of your URLs because the paths specified in the URL are relative to the document root directory.

For example, if your document root is \user\htmldocs, a request such as http:www.acme.com/products/info.htmi tells the server to look for the file in \user\htmldocs\products\info. html. If you change the document root (that is, you move all the files and subdirectories), you have to change only the document root directory that the server uses instead of mapping all URLs to the new directory or somehow telling all your users to look in the new directory. You can choose not to use a document root, but it isn't recommended because the server assumes C:\ as the document root, which means users have access to all files on your server.

Directory Indexing

In your document root directory you'll probably have several subdirectories. For example, you might create a directory called products and another called people. It's often helpful to let clients access an overview (or index) of these directories. There are two ways the server can do this:

- It first searches the directory for an index file called index. html, which is a file you create and maintain as an overview of the directory's contents. You can specify any file as an index file for a directory. This means you can also use CGI programs to configure pages. You can specify two or more files by separating them with commas.

- If an index files isn't found, the server generates an index file that lists all the files in the document root. The generated index has two formats: fancy directory indexing is fairly detailed and includes a graphic that represents the type of file, the date the file was last modified, the file size, and a description. Simple directory indexing is less detailed but takes less time to generate.

Server Home Page

When users first access your server, they usually use a URL such as http://www.acme.com/. When the server receives a request for this document, it returns a special document called a home page. Usually this file has general information about your server and links to other documents. Either you can specify a file in the document root as the home page or the server will create an index file instead.

Default MIME type

When a document is sent to a client, the server includes a section that identifies the document's type so that the client knows what to do with the document. However, sometimes the server can't determine the proper type for the document. In those cases, a default value is sent. The default is usually text/plain, but it should reflect the most common type of file stored in your server. Some common types are as follows:

text/richtext

text/plain

text/html

image/tiff

imagejpeg

image/gif

application/x-tar

application/postscript

application/x-gzip

audio/basic

audio/x-wav

cal directory

URL Mapping

URL mappings let you map URLs to another server or directory. You specify a URL prefix to map and where to map it. When a client accesses the server with a mapped URL, the server gets the requests from the mapped server or directory. URL mappings are used to point to documents in directories outside the document root directory. Most of the time, you keep all your documents in the document root, but when you want to refer to a directory outside your document root, you can do it through directory mapping.

First, you choose the URL prefix to map, the one users send to the server when they want documents in the mapped directory (this is seamless to the user). For example, a mapped URL could be http:// www.acme.com/ products/index.html where products/ is the prefix you specify. Next you specify the directory to map those URLs to. For example, the directory could be called \ sales \ tools \products. It should be a full system path. Finally, you might want to use a template to specify how this directory should be configured. You can choose an existing template or choose cgi to specify that all files in this directory are CGI programs. If you don't specify a drive letter, the server uses the drive it is installed on, so the path is relative to the root directory on that drive.

To map a URL to another server, you must first specify the URL prefix you want the server to redirect. For example, if the URL you want to map is http://www.netscape.com/info/movies, you'd type /in f o/ movies as the prefix to redirect. Next, you choose which URL you want to redirect them to. You have two choices:

- Specify a single complete URL (host name, directory, and file name). For example, type http:// w3.acme.com/new-files/info/movies.

- Specify a URL prefix if the directory on the new server is the same as in the mapped URL. For example, you type only the new server name http://w3.acme.com/.

You can view all URL mappings on a server and then use links to edit and remove any URL mappings. Each URL mapping is listed with a pair of links next to it for editing and removing the URL mapping. The Edit link takes you to the same page you used to add the mappings, except you can change the values in the form. The Remove link immediately and permanently removes the mapping from your server.

User Databases Configuration

User databases, which are lists of users who can access the server, to control who has access to which documents through the server. The server stores its user files in a .pfw file where the format for each line is username:encrypted-password, and it stores its databases in the directory \userdb in the serve root. When specifying a database, use only the name. not the full path.

Creating and Removing a User Database

To create a user database for your server, do the following:

1. Click the Server Manager link to create a user database.

2. Type a name for the database, but don't type a path because all databases are stored in \userdb. The database name can be up to 256 characters long.

3. Check the type of database you want to create. A DBM file stores the passwords encrypted. An NCSA-style database encrypts the passwords, and each line has the format user: password.

4. Type a password for this database. The password can contain up to eight characters. Retype the password to ensure accuracy. When you click the Make These Changes button, the server creates the database, then lets you jump to the page where you can add users to the new database.

To remove a user database, follow these steps:

1. Click the Server Manager link to remove a user database.

2. In the form that appears, choose the database you want to remove.

3. Type the password for the database. You can't remove the file unless you have the password.

4. Click the Make These Changes button. The user database is permanently removed from the server.

Adding, Editing, and Removing Users in a Database

To add a user to a database, do the following:

1. Choose the database and type the password for the database.

2. Type a user name of up to 254 characters. This is the name the user types when authenticating with the server.

3. Type a password for the user of up to eight characters. Type it twice to ensure accuracy. The user types this password when authenticating with the server.

4. Click the Make These Changes button. The user name and password are added to the database. You can continue adding names to the database, or you can return to the Server Manager.

If you want to change a user's name, you need to remove then add the user with the new name. You can change a user's password in a database, as follows:

1. Click the link to edit users.

2. Choose the database that contains the user whose password you want to edit.

3. Type the password for the database file.

4. Type the user name you want to edit.

5. Type the new password.

6. Click the Make These Changes button. You can continue removing users or return to the Server Manager.

To remove users from a database, follow these steps:

1. Click the link to remove users.

2. Choose the database that contains the user name that you want to remove.

3. Type the password for the database file.

4. Type the user name you want to delete.

5. Click the Make These Changes button. You can continue removing users or return to the Server Manager.

Converting a Text File to a User Database

The server stores its databases in the server root, in the directory \userdb. The text file to convert can reside anywhere for the conversion, but the converted file is stored in \userdb. The format of the file to convert looks like the following:

userl:passwordl

user2:password2

user3:password3

user4:password4

If the file is an NCSA file, the passwords will already be encrypted. If the passwords aren't encrypted, you can have the converter encrypt the passwords for you. You need to choose a name for the converted file, but you don't need to type a full path name because all user databases are kept in \userdb. Sometimes, a user name is entered twice into a database. You can choose how the converter behaves under this circumstance: either it can overwrite the existing user or it can leave the user unchanged and keep track of the user's activity. You also need to specify a password for the user database; type it twice to ensure accuracy. You need this password to add, remove, or edit users.

Changing a Database Password

You can change the administrative password for a database by typing the name of the database whose password you want to change. Type its current password, then type the new password twice (to ensure accuracy). Click the Make These Changes button. The server stores the new password.

Removing an Existing Database

You can remove a database from the \userdb directory, deleting the file from the directory. Type the name of the database you want to delete, then type the password for the database. Click the Make These Changes button. The server deletes the file from the file system.

Access Control Configuration

The Access Control links let you restrict access to a resource according to the client's hostname or IP address. You can either protect your entire server or select a resource to apply it to.

Restricting through User Authorization

To restrict access to your entire server or a particular section of it (files or directories) by using HTTP user authorization, you need a user database that provides the server with a list of users. Be sure to choose the section of the server you want to restrict! When a user accesses a port of the server that uses user authorization, the client application asks the user for a name or password before continuing. After the user enters this information, the server checks the information and then either allows or denies the user. If you have the Commerce server configured to use SSL, the user name and password are send encrypted.

To set up user authorization, choose the database the server uses to look up user names and passwords. Next, type a wildcard pattern to tell the server which users from the database are allowed access. For example, if your database contained Bob, Fred, Mary, and Joe but you wanted only Bob and Mary to have access to this section, you could use a wildcard pattern of (Bob I Mary). If you leave this entry blank, all users from the database are allowed access. Finally, you create a realm that describes the part of the server on which you're using access control. This is a text string that helps users know what part of the server they are trying to access. For example, if you were restricting access to a directory of product schedules, you might name the realm Confidential products schedules.

Restricting by Hostname and IP Address

You can restrict access to pages on your server by hostname or IP address, limiting access to only the sites that you want to have access to various parts of your server. Address restriction is an easy way to get better control over who is seeing your documents. When a request comes in for a document, the server knows the IP address that the request is coming from. Once it has this address. it uses DNS to look up the hostname that corresponds to that IP address. Then, it checks its address restriction.

Note: *If your server machine doesn't have DNS or if it has an entry in a DNS server but the machine isn't configured to do DNS lookups, you must restrict users by using only IP addresses. If you try to use hostnames without DNS, you'll get errors.*

The address restriction is done in two steps: first, the server tries to match the incoming host name with the restriction host name. If the client passes, the document is served. If the client fails the test, the server checks its IP address against the restriction IP addresses. If it passes, the document is served, and if it fails, the server takes appropriate action.

First, choose what files or directories inside this resource you want to protect. This is simply a way to be more specific about what the server should apply restriction to. For example, if you choose the directory \user\html-docs\inf as the resource you want to edit, you could specify "No additional specification—protects everything in this resource with hostname restrictions." A wildcard pattern, such as *.gif, would match only certain files. Note that by using this specification you can protect many different things in the same directory with different address restrictions for all of them.

Enter a wildcard pattern of hosts to allow, restricting access by hostname or by IP address. Restricting by hostname is more flexible because if a machine's IP address changes, you won't have to update your server. On the other hand, restricting by IP address is more reliable because if a DNS lookup fails for a connected client, hostname restriction cannot be used.

Remember that the hostname and IP addresses should be specified with either a wildcard pattern or a comma separated list, but not both. Also be sure your wildcard pattern is not recursive; there should be only one level of parentheses in the expression.

Finally, specify what should happen when a client is denied access. Normally, the server sends Not Found, which is the same thing that happens when a client requests a document that does not exist. However, sometimes you want to let users know what they are missing. In those cases, you can specify a file that the server sends back. The file name should be an absolute path.

Dynamic Configuration

Web server content is seldom managed entirely by one person. Many times different parts of a web server are written by different people. For example, each employee might maintain a home page in his or her directory. When these users need to configure something, it is unrealistic for you as the administrator to allow all of them access to the Netscape Server Manager. Rather, it is useful to allow them a subset of configuration options so that they can control only what they need to.

With this feature, you can give users the ability to control more about their home pages in their directories. You can allow them to apply access control or customize error messages without allowing them to use CGI or parsed HTML. The format and capability of these dynamic configuration files is described in the following section.

When a request is made for a resource in which dynamic configuration is enabled, the server must search for the configuration files in one or more directories of that resource. This search can be an expensive operation in terms of performance, so the server lets you configure the amount of flexibility you need, weighing it against the efficiency cost. You provide a base directory to the server from which it will starts its search for configuration files. Alternatively, you may provide no base directory, in which case the server attempts to infer the base directory from the URL. That is, if the requested URL is going to be serviced with a file from the document root, it will start searching from the document root. The same applies to URL mappings and CGI mappings.

You also specify the name of the configuration file for which to search in the base directory. Normally, you will want to centralize all of your configuration information for the subdirectories of the base directory into the configuration file in the base directory. This makes the server more efficient, because it does not have to waste time searching for configuration files in each of the subdirectories. However, for convenience you will sometimes want to tell the server to search the subdirectories. For example, if you have selected the base directory inferred from URL translation and selected .nsconfig for your configuration file name, when a user requests the file system path \ns-home\docs icons \ logo.gi f, instead of just searching for \ns-home\docs\.nsconfig, you want the server to Search all subdirectories:

\ns-home\docs\.nsconfig

\ns-home\docs\gfx\.nsconfig

\ns-home\docs\gfx\icons\.nsconfig

Finally, you would enter a wildcard pattern of file types you want to absolutely disable in directories where dynamic configuration is enabled. For example, to disable CGI programs and server-parsed HTML, use *(cgi|exe|parsed-html).

Configuration Templates

Configuration templates make it easy to apply a set of options to specific files or directories that your server maintains. For example, you can create a template that configures access logging and apply that template to the files and directories you want to log. This saves you having to individually configure access logging for all the files and directories.

To create a template, do the following:

1. Click the link called Create a template.

2. In the form that appears, type the name you want to give the template.

3. Click the Make These Changes button. The template is created as a named object in obj.conf.

4. When you return to the Server Manager, configure the attributes for your template and then click on Apply a template to part of

your server link to apply the template to files or documents in your server. When configuring attributes for a template, the forms list the template name at the top of the form.

Not all links in the Server Manager apply to templates. The links you can use for templates are listed here for your reference (a graphic also appears next to the link in the Server Manager page).

You can apply templates to files or directories in your server by either specifically choosing files and directories or specifying wildcard patterns (such as *.gif). To apply a template, do the following:

1. Click on Apply a template to part of your server link.

2. In the form that appears, click a button to choose the resources to which you want to apply the template. The buttons are described as follows:

   - Choose Entire Server applies the template to every document the server maintains.

   - Browse files applies the template to specific files or directories. You can view files or directories and you can specify whether or not to view files that are symlinks to files in other directories.

   - Choose Wildcard Patterns lets you apply the template to files or directories you specify with wildcard patterns. This is an easy way of specifying lots of files in different directories (such as *.gif) or many subdirectories (such as \publ ic*).

   - Choose a template is what you would normally use to choose templates when configuring other aspects of the server. Use the template dropdown list instead of clicking this button to apply a template.

3. Select the template you want to apply. The None template can be applied to files or directories to remove any templates previously applied to the resource.

4. Click the Make These Changes button. The template is applied to the resources. You'll need to restart the server for the template to take effect.

When you remove a template, it is deleted from the obj.conf file (it was stored as a named object). The template isn't applied from any resources you have applied it to so before you remove a template, you should apply the None template to any files or directories first. You can also remove a template and then search and replace all instances of the template in obj.conf. If you don't remove these entries, you'll get a server misconfiguration error when anyone accesses the files or directories that had the template. To remove a template, follow these steps:

1. Click the link called Remove a template.

2. In the form that appears, select the template you want to remove.

3. Click the Make These Changes button. The template is removed.

Error Handling Configuration

The error handling section lets you view the error log file and customize error messages sent to clients. Click the View error log link to see a list of all errors the server has encountered since the log file was started (you can rotate log files to save the current log file and then start adding entries to a new log file). You can limit the number of errors you see by typing ?nn at the end of the URL in the Locations box in Netscape Navigator. The question mark specifies a query, and nn represents the number of errors you want to view. After you type the query at the end of the URL, press Enter. The page redraws, showing you the most recent errors.

You can specify a custom error response that sends a detailed message to users when they encounter errors from your server, and you can specify a file to send or a CGI script to run. You may want to change the way a directory behaves when it gets an error. Instead of sending back the default file, you could send a custom error response. For example, if a user tried and failed to repeatedly to connect to a section of your server protected by access control, you could have the error file returned with information on how to get an account.

You can customize the server's response to several different kinds of errors:

- **Unauthorized.** This error occurs when a user who does not have permission tries to access a document that is protected by access control. You might send information on how the user can get access.

- **Forbidden.** This error occurs when the server doesn't have file system permissions to read something or is not permitted to follow symbolic links.

- **Not Found.** This error occurs when the server can't find a document or when it has been instructed to deny the existence of a document.

- **Server Error.** This error occurs when the server is misconfigured or when a catastrophic error occurs, such as the system running out of memory or a core dump.

Before you can set up the response, you need to either write the HTML file to send or create the CGI program to run. After you do this, jump to the customizing error response form and select the error response you want to customize. Type the absolute pathname to the file or script you want to return for that error code. Check if the file is a CGI program that you want to run. Do this for each of the errors you want to customize, then click the Make These Changes button. To remove a customization, return to the form and delete the file name from the text box next to the error code.

Logging Configuration

You can customize access logging to any resource by specifying whether to log accesses, from whom not to record accesses, and whether the server should spend time looking up the domain names of clients when they access a resource. You need to decide if you want to use access logging for this resource in the server. If you do, the server records in common logfile format many specifics about the request, including the client's address, how long the transfer took, the response the server made, how many bytes were transferred, and whether or not the user was authenticated. You also need to choose a name and location for the access log file. If you specify a partial path name here, the server assumes the path is placed in the server root in the directory logs. This means you create a log file for each resource you want to log.

You also have the option of recording the IP addresses of only incoming requests. DNS lookups can turn an IP address into a hostname, but this can be quite costly in terms of performance. You can also choose to have the server not log accesses from certain addresses, such as those within your own company. Type a wildcard pattern of hosts from which the server should not record accesses; for example, *.netscape. com doesn't log access from people with the domain netscape.com. You type wildcard patterns for either host names or IP addresses or both.

Chapter 12

Test Driving O'Reilly's WebSite Professional

WebSite Professional is designed as a complete solution for running and building a secure Web server. The amount of functionality that WebSite delivers makes it a strong choice for anyone looking for a complete solution. WebSite's strength lies in its well-thought-out design and attention to simplifying the entire process of setting up a Web server. It includes support for ODBC and SQL databases, multihoming, and SSL. Beside a robust HTTP, WebSite Professional includes a host of useful Web site building tools, including an HTML editor, a visual Web site management tool, an indexing program, an image map editor, and a performance monitor.

Before You Start

Before you install WebSite, make sure your PC system is running Windows NT Workstation or Windows NT Server. WebSite requires that your system have a TCP/IP stack installed and running. If you don't have TCP/IP running, you must first set it up through the Network option of the Control Panel. (See Chapter 7 for more information.) The most important piece of information you need to know about your TCP/IP setup is the IP address for your computer. To test your server, you must have a physical connection to a TCP/IP network.

During installation WebSite requests the Internet e-mail address for the WebSite server administrator. The e-mail address can be for any location, not necessarily the system on which the WebSite server resides. You must also have a domain name, which includes the full hierarchical name of the computer. WebSite uses the term Fully Qualified Domain Name (FQDN). An FQDN is written from the most specific address (a hostname) to the least specific address (a top-level domain). Your Internet service provider maintains the DNS server for your Web site.

Installing WebSite Professional

Once you have your Windows NT platform and Internet requirements in place, you're ready to install WebSite. If your computer and network are properly prepared, installing WebSite is a fairly simple job handled by the WebSite setup utility. During installation, WebSite takes the information you provide and gathers other information from your system's configuration to set basic parameters for the server. To install WebSite, do the following:

1. Start your computer and log on to Windows NT. If you are installing WebSite as a service, you must be an Administrator or member of either the Administrator or Backup group.

2. Insert the CD into your CD-ROM drive and choose File|Run in the Windows NT Program Manager.

3. Type D:\SETUP and click OK.

4. Click on the Install button in the WebSite Setup Utility window.

5. Accept or change the default installation path in the Installation Directory

6. Enter the Fully Qualified Domain Name in the first field of the Server Configuration window. If you don't have one, make one up because the field cannot be left blank.

7. Enter the Internet e-mail address of the WebSite server administrator in the second field. WebSite uses this name and address for creating mailto URLs in automatic directory indexes. The e-mail address can be any Internet address, not necessarily an address on the computer on which you are installing WebSite.

8. Accept the defaults for the document root and home page in the Home Page window and click on the OK button. As the installation finishes, one or two Command Windows may open and close on your screen. This is a normal part of setup.

9. When Setup is complete, a final dialog appears with some suggestions for what to do next with your WebSite server. Press OK to close Setup.

10. On exiting Setup, the WebSite server is launched as a desktop icon, and the WebSite program group is displayed on your desktop, as shown in Figure 12.1.

Overview of WebSite

Within the WebSite Professional program group is a collection of icons representing several applications that together make up WebSite. The following describes the function of each of these programs.

FIGURE 12.1 The WebSite Professional Program Group for Windows NT.

WebSite Server

The heart of WebSite, the server handles requests from clients (browsers) for documents, whether they be text, graphic, multimedia, or virtual. The WebSite server is a 32-bit HTTP server that runs under Windows NT (or Windows 95). Under NT, the server can run as an application or as a service. Usually the server appears as an icon on your screen with the status shown as either idle or busy. Configuring the server is the job of the Server Admin application.

Server Admin

Server Admin lets you configure the WebSite server to meet the needs of your environment. Although the setup utility handles the basic configuration, you will probably want to enhance your server by changing some settings.

WebView

WebView works on any web to help you build and manage your web by graphically depicting it. It shows all hypertext links between and within documents—internal or external, broken or complete—and lets you not only see your web from a bird's-eye view, but also edit individual files. In WebView you can launch an appropriate application based on the file's type, or you can drag a file into the desired application using WebView's drag-and-drop capability. If you're building a new web, start with WebView. If you are managing an existing web, use WebView to make improvements and fix problems. To track activity on your web, WebView includes a way to see current logging data.

WebIndex

WebIndex and WebFind work together to provide full-text search capability for users of your web. WebIndex appears as an icon in the WebSite program group while WebFind is a CGI program. WebIndex lets you create the index used in WebFind searches. Before WebFind can work, you must run the WebIndex program and indicate which portion of your Web is to be searchable. WebFind is a powerful tool for users of your Web. If you use WebFind, make it a prominent feature of your web, perhaps with an iconified link. WebFind first displays a search form for the user to complete and then executes the search.

Enhanced NCSA Mosaic

Enhanced NCSA Mosaic, also referred to as EMosaic or simply Mosaic, is supplied with WebSite to give you a fully featured Web graphical browser. Other browsers are available; some are distributed freely over the Internet while others are sold commercially. Since the display of web documents depends on how the browser interprets HTML, we recommend you view your web using different browsers just to see what others might see.

Image Map Editor

The Image Map Editor lets you graphically build clickable image maps by defining hotspot shapes and then assigning those shapes to target URLs. WebSite registers clickable image maps internally, eliminating the linked sets of cryptic configuration files used by other servers to create clickable image maps. Clickable image maps work by mapping a set of coordinates in an image to a particular URL. On WebSite, this coordinate mapping is registered internally, with no external configuration files required.

Uninstall WebSite

The Uninstall WebSite program automatically uninstalls WebSite from your system.

Monitor Server

Performance Monitor is a graphical tool for measuring the performance of the computer running as a Web server. It lets you view a variety of performance indicators, such as processor, memory, cache, threads, and processes.

HotDog HTML Editor

HotDog HTML Editor is a full-featured HTML editor for creating your Web document. It supports Netscape Extensions and proposed HTML 3 elements.

Note: *WebSite Professional will also include support for ODBC-compliant databases.*

Managing Your WebSite via Server Admin

During installation, the WebSite Setup utility puts specific information about your server in the Server Admin application. To view the general information, launch the Server Admin icon from the WebSite program group. The General property sheet page appears (Figure 12.2.). The Server Admin program includes nine property sheets for managing your WebSite server. When you make a change to Server Admin, it does not take effect until you close the program. A few seconds after you close it, you will hear the computer beep, indicating the server's configuration has been updated. If the server is not running, you will not hear a beep, but the configuration is in effect the next time you start the server.

General Property Page

The General property page includes general controls for setting up your WebSite server. The Server group includes the following control settings:

- **Working Dir.** indicates where WebSite is installed. This directory is also called the server root.

FIGURE 12.2 The General property page.

- **CGI Temp Dir.** is where WebSite stores the temporary spool files used for exchanging data between the server and CGI programs.

- **Administrator Adr.** shows the complete e-mail address of the WebSite server administrator. Notice that the address is the Internet address you entered during setup. You can change the address here by typing in a new one.

- **Run Mode.** specifies how WebSite will run the next time it is started. For Windows NT, the pulldown field has three choices: desktop application, system service with icon, and system service without icon. If you want to run WebSite as a service, you must first select a new run mode here and then restart the server as a service using the Services program in NT's Control Panel.

The Network group includes the following settings:

- **Normal Port** tells the server what port number to use for HTTP. The standard TCP/IP port is 80. Unless you know what you are doing, don't change this number, and never use a port below 1024.

- **SSL Port** tells the server what port number to use for secure HTTP using SSL. The default port is 443.

- **Timeouts (receive and send)** are fairly standard settings. You may need to increase timeouts if you are on a slow link or if users complain that your server seems slow or cuts off documents. Increase the timeouts to 60 seconds for a PPP connection.

- **Max Simultaneous Connects** limits the number of simultaneous connections that the server will accept. For 28.8Kbps connections use 40. For ISDN (2B channels) use 150.

- **Hold connections open for reuse** lets you support browsers that support keep-alive connections, which keep a connection open for faster processing of multiple requests from the Web server.

- **Winsock Vendor Information** lists the valid Winsock programs detected on your system. WebSite uses Microsoft Winsock Version 1.1. You cannot change this field.

Identity Property Page

The Identity property page (Figure 12.3) controls the server's Internet host-name or multiple hostnames, Web mappings, and logfile assignments. When you click on the Identity tab, Server Admin displays an information box telling you that changes made on this property page take effect immediately. Click on OK. The following describes the settings in the Identity property page:

- **Multiple Identities** lets you share settings across multiple IP address identities.

- **IP Address** selects the IP address for which subsequent settings apply. Select an IP address, then change the settings as needed or use the Identity Wizard. You must click on the Update button after entering a new IP address.

- **Server Name** shows the fully qualified domain name (FQDN) of the server, which you entered during setup. The server's FQDN is not necessarily the same as the computer's name.

FIGURE 12.3 The Identity property page.

- **URL Prefix** is inserted at the beginning of all URL paths received on the selected IP address, then passed to the mapper for URL to file resolution.

- **Access Log** specifies the access logfile to be used with the specified IP address.

- **Certificate** selects the digital certificate for use with the specific IP address. Clicking on the Certs button displays the WebSite Certificate Manager.

Mapping Property Page

The Mapping property page (Figure 12.4) controls URL mapping, content type mapping, and directory listing icon mapping. The List Selector group defines the settings for this property page. For example, choosing Content Types displays a different collection of relevant settings, as shown in Figure 12.5. The following describes each of the List Selector settings:

FIGURE 12.4 The Mapping property page displaying the default Documents List Selector.

FIGURE 12.5 The Content Types setting in the Mapping property sheet.

- **Documents.** Document mapping provides a way to map document URL paths into physical directory paths and allows you to place parts of your Web site on any drive or shared drive using the Universal Naming Convention (UNC).

- **Redirect.** Redirect mapping causes a reference to one URL to be redirected to another URL located on the local system or a remote system.

- **Windows CGI.** Windows CGI mapping provides a way to map Windows executable CGI script URL paths into physical directory path and to place Windows CGI programs on any drive or remote system.

- **Standard CGI.** This mapping provides a way to map standard CGI scripts via URL paths into physical directory paths and to place standard CGI programs on any drive or remote system.

- **DOS CGI.** This mapping provides a way to map DOS CGI scripts via URL paths into physical directory paths and to place DOS CGI programs on any drive or remote system.

- **Content Types.** The content types map defines the Web standard MIME content type for a document, given the document's file's extension (for example, image/gif).

- **Directory Icons.** This setting provides a way to map icons displayed in a server-generated directory listing to the content types of the files listed.

The Dir Listing Property Page

The Dir property page (Figure 12.6) controls the server's automatic HTML directory listing feature. If no default document (index.html) is present in the directory, the server will generate an HTML format listing of the files in the directory. The following briefly describes the functions of each group in the Dir property page:

- The **Features** group of settings controls the level of detail for server-generated directory listings.

- The **Special Documents** group controls the filenames for the special documents used by the server's automatic directory listing feature.

- The **Ignore Patterns** group permits files to be excluded from a server-generated directory listing based on a pattern match. Files matching items in the Ignore Patterns list box are excluded from the listing.

- The **Special Icons** group of settings controls the filenames for the special icons used by the server's extended directory listing feature.

The Users, Groups, and Access Control Property Pages

The Users, Groups, and Access Control property pages all deal with restricting access to your Web site. The Users property page (Figure 12.7) is used to control user accounts, and to control realms that contain separate sets of users and groups. The Groups page (Figure 12.8) is used to control groups of

FIGURE 12.6 The Dir property page.

FIGURE 12.7 The Users property page.

users and realms that contain separate sets of users and groups. The Access Control property page (Figure 12.9) controls access restrictions by user authentication, IP address filtering, and hostname filtering. Access control can be applied to any URL path, but not on an individual document. If applied, it affects the URL path and all subpaths below it.

The Logging Property Page

The Logging property page (Figure 12.10) controls the server's logging and diagnostic tracing features. It shows the names of the three WebSite log files as well as the location of the log directory. The Logging property page also includes the options that affect logging, reverse DNS lookup, and tracing options for the server log.

The CGI Property Page

The CGI property page (Figure 12.11) controls the low-level operation of the three CGI interfaces in the server: Windows CGI, Standard CGI, and DOS CGI. Don't mess around with these interfaces unless you're familiar with the operation of the CGI interfaces in WebSite.

FIGURE 12.8 The Groups property page.

FIGURE 12.9 The Access Control property page.

FIGURE 12.10 The Logging property page.

FIGURE 12.11 The CGI property page.

Activating the Administrative Account

WebSite comes with a default user account called Admin, which is dormant, meaning it has no password and belongs to no groups. To activate the account, you must assign a password and add it to at least one group. The Admin account is useful for restricting certain URLs and server functions to a single account and for remotely administrating WebSite. To activate the administrator account, first select a password, then complete the following steps:

1. Launch the Server Admin icon from the WebSite program group and click on the Users tab to display the Users property sheet.

2. In the User field, select the user Admin and click on the Password button. The change password dialog box appears.

3. Place the cursor in the New Password field and type in the new password. Press Tab and type in the new password again.

4. In the Group Membership section of the property sheet, highlight Administrators and click on the Add button.

5. Press OK to update the server and finish the activation. If the server is running, wait for it to beep before trying to use the new account.

Running WebSite as a Service

To run WebSite as a service rather than a desktop application under Windows NT requires a few quick steps. By default, WebSite runs as a desktop application, so it isn't available as a Web server. To run WebSite as a Web server service, you need to start it as a service via the Windows NT Service icon in the Control Panel. Complete the following steps to run WebSite as a service under Windows NT:

1. Exit the WebSite server if it is running.

2. Double-click on the Server Admin icon in the WebSite group window.

3. In the General property page, change the server's Run Mode from Desktop Application to System Service, either with or without an icon. Click on the OK button.

4. In the Windows NT Control Panel, open the Services icon. The Services dialog box appears, as shown in Figure 12.12.

5. Scroll through the listed services until you come to Web Server entry.

6. Highlight Web Server entry and click on the Start button.

7. If you want WebSite to start automatically whenever the system starts, press Startup on the Services window and complete the necessary information.

Note: *To return WebSite to a desktop application, simply stop the service, reset the Run Mode in Server Admin, and launch the server as an application.*

Testing Your WebSite Server

After installing WebSite, you need to test the server to verify that it is installed and operating properly. The test involves viewing a WebSite document from the local computer, viewing a WebSite document from a remote computer,

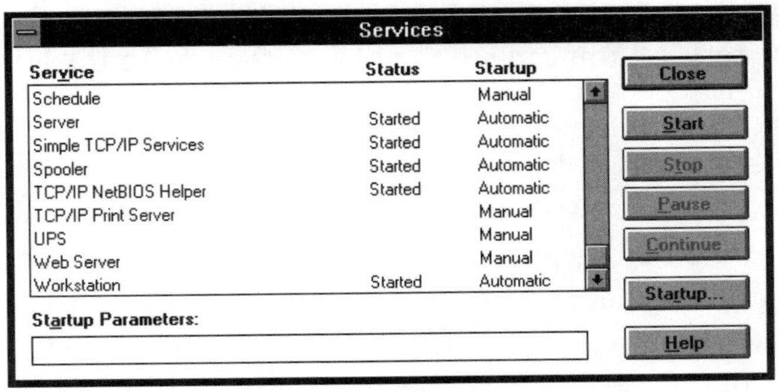

FIGURE 12.12 The Windows NT Services dialog box.

and running the server self-test. When you exit the Setup utility, the WebSite server is launched and minimized to a desktop icon. If you can see the icon on your screen, the server has passed the first test—it's running. The icon title indicates the server's status as idle or busy.

To become familiar with the WebSite components, double-click on the WebSite icon to display the WebSite Server window. The only action you can execute from the Control menu is to exit the server. The easiest way to test if your computer and WebSite are set up correctly is to launch a Web browser (for example, EMosaic in the WebSite program group) and specify the URL for your server. Follow these steps:

1. Make sure your WebSite server is running (the icon is visible on the desktop).

2. Make sure your TCP/IP connection is open. If you are on a TCP/IP network or have a dedicated connection to the Internet, this is probably transparent to you. If you are on a standalone computer and get your TCP/IP connectivity with a dial-up SLIP or PPP account, make sure that the connection is up and clear. The WebSite server and browser require an open TCP/IP socket to work.

3. Double-click on the Enhanced Mosaic icon in the WebSite program group. This icon launches Mosaic and displays the ReadMe file. However, displaying this document does not verify that the server is working because the browser did not find it by contacting the server. (You can see the file's pathname in the URL field.)

4. Click on the hypertext link homepage. The link is for the URL http://localhost/. The browser sends out the request for this URL, which is interpreted by the browser and server as the home page file on the local computer. (Note that using localhost in a URL won't work when you try to reach your server from another computer.) If the server and computer are set up correctly, the temporary WebSite home page appears in the browser window.

5. Test the server using the IP address. Select Open URL from the Mosaic File menu, and type in the URL for your server, using the following format: http://your.IP address/, where your.IP.address is the IP address of your server, such as 198.112.209.138. Don't forget the final slash.

6. If your server's domain name is registered with DNS, reset the server using the domain name. Type in the URL for your server, using the following format: http://your.server.name/, where your.server.name is the FQDN of your server.

The next step in testing the server is to view a document on your WebSite server from a different computer, either one on your internal network or one connected to the Internet. To complete this test you must have access to another computer that has a Web browser. Obviously, if that computer is on your network, it must also be configured for TCP/IP. To test the WebSite server from another computer, follow these steps:

1. Make sure your WebSite server is running.

2. Make sure your computer's TCP/IP connection is open.

3. From the other computer, launch a Web browser such as Mosaic.

4. Specify the URL for your server, using the following format: http://your.IP.address/, where your.IP.address is the IP address of your server. Don't forget the final slash. The browser uses the URL to locate your WebSite server. If everything is set up correctly, you will see the WebSite default home page.

5. If your server's domain name is registered with DNS, test the server specifying the URL again, using the following format: http://.your.server.name/, where your.server.name is the FQDN of your server. Don't forget the final slash. If everything is set up correctly, you will see the WebSite default home page.

If you performed this test from a computer on your local network and it does not work, make sure the server is running and then check the TCP/IP configuration of the computer and the network. If you conducted this test from a computer connected to the Internet and it failed, try again. Sometimes heavy traffic on the Internet can cause connections to timeout. If after several tries you still cannot reach the server, recheck the TCP/IP connections on both computers. Also make sure that your server's name is a fully qualified domain name and that it is registered with DNS. If you continue to have difficulties, consult your Internet service provider.

Mapping WebSite

Think of mapping as a behind-the-scenes direction finder for your web. When a browser requests a URL, the WebSite server first compares the URL to several Server Admin tables to see how that URL should be translated on your Web site. The WebSite server supports four types of mapping:

- Document mapping, which maps a logical URL to a physical location on your system

- Redirection mapping, which maps one URL to another URL, often on another server and generally only temporarily

- Executable or CGI mapping, which maps URLs for CGI programs to the location of the specific type of CGI program (Standard, Windows, or DOS) and tells the server to execute the CGI program rather than display it

- Content type mapping, which maps the type of document (as defined by the file extension) to a standard MIME (multipurpose Internet mail extensions) protocol type, used by the web browser to correctly display the document.

The WebSite default mapping is probably sufficient for your web, especially in its early stages. As your web grows and becomes more sophisticated, mapping will become an important tool for making your Web site flexible and extending its capabilities.

Adding, Changing, and Deleting Mapping Values

To work with the mapping page, you must launch the Server Admin application from the WebSite program group or from WebView. Click on the Mapping tab to display the Mapping property page. The top section of the page shows the current mapping in two columns, which change according to the mapping type being displayed. HTDOCS is the default document root of the server (which you may have changed during installation). \wsdocs\ is the location of documents shipped with WebSite, such as the server self-test and release notes. Because this location is owned by the server, you may want to add access control to it at some point.

You can add, change, or delete mapping values using the two fields and buttons in the lower right of the page. To add a value, do the following:

1. Put the cursor in the first of the two edit fields and type in the value to be mapped.

2. Press Tab to move the cursor to the second field.

3. Type in the value being mapped to.

4. Press Add.

To change a value:

1. Highlight the value to be changed in the box at the top of the page. The values appear in the two edit fields.

2. Edit one or both of the values as necessary in these fields.

3. Press Replace.

To delete a value, highlight the value to be deleted in the box at the top of the page. The values appear in the two edit fields. Press Delete.

After you have made all the changes to the mapping type, press Apply Now. You may select another mapping type to modify or update the WebSite server by pressing Close. Changes made on any Server Admin page are not in effect until you close the application. After exiting Server Admin, wait for the server to beep to ensure the registry is updated. If the server is not running, the updates are in effect the next time you start the server.

Selecting Other Mapping Types

In the List Selector box of the Mapping page, you will see the other types of mapping available for the server. To see the values for another mapping type, click on the button in front of the type. For each type, the mapping values change, as listed in Table 12.1.

Document Mapping

Document mapping lets you assign logical pieces of your web (as defined by URLs) to physical locations on your system or any other system on your network. This capability means that the actual files that make up your web can be in a variety of locations, but all are reachable from a single URL hier-

TABLE 12.1 Mapping Types in WebSite

Mapping Type	Value Being Mapped	Mapped Value
Documents	Document URL Path	Directory (full or document-relative)
Redirect	Original URL	Redirected URL
Windows CGI	Win CGI URL Path	Directory (full or server-relative)
Standard CGI	Standard CGI URL Path	Directory (full or server-relative)
DOS CGI	DOS CGI URL Path	Directory (full or server-relative)
Content Types	File Extension (class)	MIME Content Type
Directory Icons	MIME Content Type	Icon File for Directory Listing

archy. The URL hierarchy includes the protocol, hostname, and server root (for example, http://localhost/), and any directory and/or file names added to that URL. In document mapping, the URL path can include directories, but not filenames. The tree starts at the document root (/), which is off the server root. The default server root is C:\WEBSITE, so the default document root is C:\WEBSITE\HTDOCS\. You may have changed the server and/or document root during installation. You can find the server root on the General page of Server Admin (in the Server Working Directory field).

If you accepted index.html as the default home page when you installed WebSite, the server looks for that document. If you changed the default, the server looks for a file by the new name. If no default file exists and automatic directory indexing is on, WebSite creates an automatic directory index. If directory indexing is disabled, the user receives a forbidden message.

Redirect Mapping

WebSite lets you temporarily assign a URL on your web to another URL— usually a URL on another server—through redirect mapping. When the server receives a request for a redirected URL, it automatically sends the browser to the new URL. The redirection is transparent to the user. WebSite includes no default-redirected URLs. The original URL is entered as a URL path for your server. If the new URL is on another server, the redirected URL must be a full URL (including protocol and/or hostname and path). If the new URL is on the same server, the redirected URL can be entered as either a full URL or a relative URL. You might find redirect mapping useful for your web under the following conditions:

- If a portion of your web is undergoing heavy revision and you don't want users to see it under construction, you can redirect the URL for that portion of the web to a document explaining the current situation. If you do so, include an expected Grand Reopening date for your web and a teaser to encourage users to come back to the new web; otherwise, people may never visit it again.

- If your web is mirrored on other servers in various locations, you can redirect the URL for one server to the URL for another server. You may want to do this when you are revamping the web or when a network problem for a mirrored site is slowing response time.

To implement redirect mapping, follow the steps described in Adding, Changing, and Deleting Mapping Values, described earlier in this chapter.

CGI Mapping

WebSite mapping includes three types of CGI (Common Gateway Interface) mapping for the three types of CGI programs WebSite supports: Windows CGI, Standard CGI, and DOS CGI. CGI mapping accomplishes two things:

- It identifies a URL as a program, and thus the response to the browser will be to execute an object rather than return a document.

- It specifies what types of CGI programs are in the URL and where those programs are located on the web.

In general, the default CGI mapping in WebSite should be sufficient for your web. The directory paths for CGI mapping are relative to the server root, not to the document root as in document mapping. If you change or add entries for CGI mapping, use full pathnames. To edit the CGI mapping tables, follow the steps described in Adding, Changing, and Deleting Mapping Values explained earlier in this chapter.

Content Type Mapping

One of the HTTP standards for a Web server is that it includes a content type with every document returned to a browser. A Web browser must be able to identify the content type and display the document appropriately for the type. For example, if a browser requests an HTML document, the server not only returns the document, but also includes the content type in the header information. The browser reads the header information first, knows that it can display an HTML document without an external viewer, and then does so.

If the content type requires an external viewer (such as for an audio file), the browser tries to launch the appropriate viewer. Content types can also be defined for applications (such as Microsoft Word or Adobe Acrobat), in which case the browser would launch the appropriate application. These content types are also called MIME types. The standard format of a MIME content type includes a main type and subtype, separated by a slash (/). The MIME content type for HTML is text/html.

In mapping content types, you assign a particular class of document to a particular content type. Because the file extension is the most common and consistent way of identifying particular classes of documents, WebSite uses file extensions for mapping to content types. For example, an HTML file has the extension html or htm, which is by default mapped to the content type text/html. When the server returns a document with the extension html, it sends the text/html content type in the header, and the browser knows how to display it.

Many content types exist, including *audio/basic, image/gif, and video/mpeg.* In addition to the standard content types, you can create new content types as necessary. Content types known to the server must also be defined in the user's Web browser to correctly display documents. Several Web browsers refer to this task as setting up Helpers.

WebSite includes 34 predefined content types that are listed in the Mapping property page, which shows the beginning of the list with the file extension in the left column and the content type (in the form type/subtype*)* in the right column. Note that the file extensions may be any number of characters because you are running WebSite on a file system with long filenames enabled. However, since many legacy documents exist from the MS-DOS and Windows environment, several default WebSite content types are defined for both short and long file extensions. For example:

.htm text/html

.html text/html

.mpe video/mpeg

.mpegvideo/mpeg

.mpg video/mpeg

WebSite includes five standard content types (with multiple subtypes) and one custom content type, as listed in Table 12.2.

Adding a New Content Type

Before you add a new content type, make sure that the class of files uses consistent filename extensions (and that you know what they are). These extensions must not conflict with extensions used by other content types known to your server (or users' browsers). Decide what you are going to call the content type. To add the new content type, follow these steps:

1. Launch Server Admin from the WebSite program group and select the Mapping tab. Make sure the List Selector is on Content Types.

2. Place the cursor in the File Extension (class) field and type in the first file extension.

3. Press Tab to move to the MIME Content Type field and type in the new content type, such as *application/format.*

TABLE 12.2: The Six Content Types Used by WebSite

Content Type	Description
text	For ASCII text documents such as HTML files
image	For full-color images to be displayed apart from the document (that is, not as inline graphics), such as JPEG files.
video	For video clips such as MPEG files
audio	For audio clips such as WAVE files
application	For specific applications such as MS Word (defined by .doc)
wwwserver	For specific use on the WebSite server

4. Press Add.

5. Repeat steps 2 through 4 for the second file extension up.

6. Press Close to update the server. Don't forget that you must let users know the new content type application/format so that they can update their browsers.

You can also map MIME extensions to icons used in automatic directory indexes and map files to unique icons that are used in automatic directory indexing. When the server creates an automatic directory index, it looks at the content type, then looks at this table, and includes the appropriate icon for the type of file.

Controlling Access to Your Web Site

Applying access restrictions to all or part of your web is an important tool in the server administrator's toolbag. WebSite complies with the HTTPD standard of Basic Authentication and makes setting up, applying, and managing access control easy through a graphical user interface. Access to your web is controlled either by authenticating users or by restricting certain classes of connections through IP address filtering or hostname filtering. Access control can be applied either to the whole web or to a specific URL path in the web. A URL path is a directory and any files or subdirectories beneath it. Thus, when you restrict a URL path, you are protecting an entire directory, not a single file.

When you are applying access control, remember two rules that govern how the server handles access control along a URL path. A restriction on a URL path restricts that directory and all subdirectories unless another restriction exists below it in the path (that is, at a URL that is a subdirectory of the current URL). When restrictions are applied, the server refers to them as control points. The deepest access control point determines the access restrictions at a particular level. In other words, the server starts at the current level and works up levels until it finds a control point. The server applies the restrictions at that point and stops. You should keep these principles in mind as you apply access control restrictions to URLs in your web.

User Authentication

When you control access by user authentication, users must prove to the server that they are allowed to view a certain part of the web. The server must know who the user is and that the username and password are valid for that URL path. Here's how user authentication works. When someone requests a restricted URL, the server sends an error message to the browser, indicating that authentication is required before it can return the document. The browser responds to that message by presenting an authentication dialog to the user. When the user enters a name and password, the browser resubmits the same request with the accompanying authentication data. If the user is authenticated, the server returns the document. Otherwise, the process starts over again with the server sending the error message. There is no limit on the number of times users may attempt to authenticate themselves to the server.

Once a user is authenticated, the server remembers the authentication information and supplies it the next time user authentication is required. If that user is allowed access, the server automatically returns the document and does not again query the user. However, if that user is not allowed access to a restricted area, the server sends the authentication required error message again.

Two standard groups included in WebSite are Users and Administrators. In fact, all users added to WebSite are automatically members of the Users group and may not be removed from it. You can also create groups that make sense for your web, such as a group of people all working on the same project or in the same department. WebSite users and groups are completely separate from users and groups set up under Windows NT.

A realm is a collection of specific users and groups that lets you segregate users and groups when applying access controls to portions of your web. WebSite is shipped with a default realm, Web Server, and a realm used for the server self-test, Examples. Members of this realm have access to certain URLs in the server self-test that no members of the realm Web Server can reach. Once you have an established realm of users and/or groups, you can attach the realm to any URL path in your web. Attaching a realm does not automatically apply access control. You must now select users and/or groups from the realm who are authorized to have access to the URL.

IP Address Filtering and Hostname Filtering

IP address filtering and hostname filtering—generically called class restrictions—control access to the server by preventing certain Internet nodes from connecting to the server. For each request from a browser, the server can either deny or allow access based on the Internet node of the requester. When a browser requests a URL from the WebSite server, the server first looks at the IP address or hostname of the request and the URL. The server then checks to see what IP address or hostname restrictions apply for that URL. The restriction may be either to allow or to deny access to the URL, and the server responds accordingly by returning the document or sending an access not allowed message.

IP address and hostname filtering are helpful for quickly limiting access without creating groups and adding usernames. In WebSite, setting up class restrictions requires selecting a URL path to be restricted, identifying the IP address or hostname, and then specifying whether you are allowing or denying access to that address.

Using WebSite to Control Access

The Users, Groups, and Access Control property sheets are used for defining realms, users, and groups, and attaching them to specific URL paths.

Defining User Restrictions

Choose the Users tab to display the Users property sheet. The Users page includes the three sections described below.

Authentication Realm

In the Authentication realm you can select an existing realm to use (such as Web Server), create a new realm, or delete an existing realm. Your web can have one realm or multiple realms, although we recommend you start with only one realm until your web demands multiple realms. When you create a new realm, it has no users. The realm you select here is the one affected by any users you add or change.

User

You can select an existing user in the User realm, change a user's password, add a new user and password, or delete a user. The default Web Server realm has an Admin user; part of the installation process was to add this user to the Administrators and Users group (if you didn't do so then, you should now).

Group Membership

You can view and change the group membership status for the selected user. Every realm has an Administrators and a Users group. All users in a realm are part of the Users group and cannot be deleted from it, unless of course you delete them altogether. In the preceding example, we could remove Admin from the Administrators group but not from the Users group. If you plan to add users to a realm and put them in new groups, create the groups first and then add the users. That way you can place the users in the new group as you add them rather than add them one at a time later. WebSite does not allow you to add multiple users to a group simultaneously.

Defining Group Restrictions

To see the Groups property page, click on the Groups tab. The Groups page has basically the same three sections as the Users page.

Authentication Realm

With Authentication realm, you can select an existing realm to use (such as Web Server), create a new realm, or delete an existing realm. Your web can have one realm or multiple realms, although we recommend you start with only one realm unless your web demands multiple realms. The realm you select here is the one affected by any groups you add or change.

Group

You can select an existing group in the Group realm, add a new group, or delete a group. Every realm automatically has an Administrators and a Users group, which have no members when first created. All users in a realm are part of the Users group and cannot be removed.

Group Membership

You can view and change the selected group's membership list. In the preceding example, the Administrators group includes the user Admin but not the user Susan. We can add Susan to the group or remove Admin from the group. If we had selected the Users group, all users in the realm would be listed in the members box and none could be removed.

Note: *WebSite users and groups are completely separate from users and groups established on your server. WebSite users and groups are for restricting access to your web and have no connection with the system at large. If you want to restrict access to your web, you must add users and groups to the WebSite server.*

Access Control

To see the Access Control page, click on the Access Control tab. On this page, you can apply restrictions for user authentication and/or IP address/hostname filtering. The three sections of the Access Control property sheet are discussed below.

URL Path or Special Function

You can select, add, or delete a URL path or special function. A URL path is the directory portion of a full URL and cannot specify a file, only a directory. For that reason, a URL path includes all files and/or subdirectories under that directory. You can select an existing URL path from the pulldown list to view or change the access control. You can also add new URL paths to protect. Note that when you do so, all files and subdirectories off that path will have the same protection. You can also delete a URL path from the list; however, deleting the URL path only deletes the access restrictions, not the actual URL from the web.

All the special-function URLs in WebSite are on the Access Control list, although only those that cause the server to do something are protected. When you add a URL path or special function, you attach a realm to it. The groups and users in that realm are the only ones for which you can add user authentication to the URL path or special function. By default, any new URL path or special function you add is in the Web Server realm; you can select a different realm, but only one realm per path. If you delete access control for a special function, that function is *completely disabled* for the server. No one, not even the administrator, can activate it. You can re-enable the special function by adding it back into the access control list.

Authorized Users and Groups

You can view or change the users and/or groups authorized for the selected URL path or special function. The realm for this URL is shown first. If no users or groups are shown in this box, the URL has no user authentication restrictions. You can add or delete other members of the realm Examples to the authorized list.

Class Restrictions

User authentication and class restrictions work together to provide access control for your web. The server first checks the class restrictions settings and determines whether or not to accept the connection. If the class restriction test is met, the server looks to see if the URL path requires user authentication. If so, the server sends an error message to the browser, causing it to present a user authentication form to the requester. The server checks the browser's response against the authorized list and returns either the requested document or the same error message.

Managing Your Web Site's Content Using WebView

As you build and manage your web, you will find WebView an invaluable tool. WebView is a meta-authoring environment that lets you author your entire Web, jumping from bird's-eye view down to document links. WebView uses the tree metaphor to visually present the relationships between links in a web. You can expand and collapse the tree and open multiple trees at once. You can also view the elements in the tree from different perspectives. Figure 12.13 shows what WebView displays when you first start it.

WebView presents you with a graphical representation of your entire Web site, showing all links to all documents, whether they are on the same server or an external one, and the type of document each link is: HTML, text, graphic, audio, video, or virtual. WebView indicates broken links, which are links to nonexistent documents, and it provides access control, mapping,

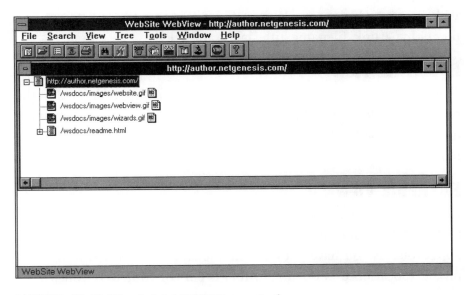

FIGURE 12.13 The initial WebView window.

diagnostics, and logging information about Web documents. However, its greatest value is that it also lets you manipulate the objects that make up your web. For example, WebView will launch an appropriate application to edit an HTML or graphics file, or you can use one of WebView's wizards to create a typical HTML home page or What's New document. You can also use WebView to change access control on a URL. WebView has a search feature to locate specific components of your web. From WebView you can launch several other WebSite applications including Server Admin, Image Map Editor, WebIndex, and a Web browser.

WebView uses icons to identify file types as well as link types. The graphical representation includes not only the physical links shown by the tree, but also informative icons. If your web has many external links and you don't want WebView to verify them all, you can turn off the Verify External Links feature in the Preferences dialog by selecting Preferences from the File menu.

The Different Views of Web View

WebView can depict your Web in five different ways as listed on the Views menu: hyperlink, filename, title, label, and URL.

Hyperlink View

The hyperlink view shows you the exact way the link is defined in the document. Useful for seeing the relative structure in the current web and the way links are defined in the documents, this view is a quick way to spot inconsistencies or wrong hypertext links.

Filename View

Filename view gives the local filename for each document in the web. The pathnames include the disk drive, directory, subdirectory, and filename, if applicable. As you have guessed, the filename view is useful for finding the physical location of a document that is part of your web. You will probably use this view in conjunction with the other views for locating specific links you wish to edit.

Title View

Title view gives the title of each document in the web. The title is defined by the HTML tag <TITLE> and is typically used by Web browsers for building hotlists and displaying in the browser window with the document's URL. Not all documents are required to have titles; in fact, only HTML files can have them. WebView looks at each file and pulls out the title text for this view. If no title is found, WebView displays the title [none]. Since document titles are used by browsers, they are often what users recall when they want to revisit your server. Take care to create titles that have clarity and meaning, and then use them consistently.

Label View

The label view gives the anchor- or label-text that accompanies each HREF link in the web. Not all links have labels; only those created with the HTML anchor tag (<A>). WebView pulls the words Return to WebSite Read Me from the anchor tag and puts them in the label view. If there is no anchor, WebView displays [none]. The label view is useful for seeing the choices presented to users of your web. You can compare labels in various portions of your web and use consistent references. You can also edit out overuse of vague references, such as Click here, and add text where none exists, if necessary.

URL View

The URL, or Uniform Resource Locator, is the full address for the document on the Internet. The URL view includes the protocol used for reaching a document (http), the server name (localhost), and URL directory path on the server (with or without filename). The URL view is particularly useful for giving you an absolute picture of the relationships among documents in a web. It is also helpful for identifying links to other types of Internet servers, such as *ftp*. In a URL to an FTP site, the URL would start with ftp rather than *http*.

Editing and Displaying with WebView

WebView makes editing your documents easy. You can open any file on the web with an appropriate editor and make changes. The WebView tree is instantly updated when you close the files. The editor that WebView uses for a document is determined by the application associated with the file type by the operating system. Under Windows NT, associations are made in the File Manager. WebView also supports drag and drop of files into open applications. WebView lets you also examine and change certain properties of the documents on your Web site.

WebView lets you display information about each document on your web. For example, for HTML documents, WebView shows four properties: general, access control, diagnostics, and activity. The following sections briefly describe each of these properties.

General

General, an informational page that allows no editing, is divided into two sections: Link Properties and Document Properties. You'll recognize much of the information about these properties from the different WebView tree views. This page also includes the document's content type (for this document it is *text*/html). The size and date last modified are also given for the document. The icons that appear with a document in a WebView tree also appear on this page.

Access Control

This page shows the current access control setting for all URL paths of which this document is a member. All web documents are in the URL root directory, which is indicated by the / (since this example uses the server's default home page, the URL is the document root). Other URL paths for the document are listed in the pulldown URL Path field. If access to this URL path is limited, the Access page lists authorized users and groups; otherwise, this box is blank (as in the example above).

The Class Restrictions field shows if and how access is restricted by allowing and/or denying predefined classes of users. Class restrictions invoke IP address and hostname filtering. In the above example all classes of users are allowed. In short, this URL has no access restrictions. You can change the access control of a URL path by making changes on this page, which is the same as the Access Control page of Server Admin, except it is focused on the specific document. You can change the access control on this page for any URL path of which this document is a member. Note that access can be limited only by URL directory, not by specific document. Access control is a powerful tool for securing your web.

Diagnostics

Diagnostics are available for HTML files only. This page is informational and allows no editing. WebView generates these diagnostics by comparing the document's HTML coding against the current standard for such coding, the HTML 2.0 DTD (document type definition). Diagnostics are divided into three classes, which indicate their level of severity and what action you might want to take:

- Error messages mean that the coding is not up to the standard, and documents may not display correctly. You should fix errors or at least view the documents in a variety of browsers to make sure the error does not affect the display.

- Warning messages mean that the coding is not completely up to the standard, but it should not affect the display of the document.

- Information messages mean that the coding is within the acceptable range allowed by the specification.

Activity

The Activity page shows the access activity for the document based on information from the server's access log. The information includes the IP address of the user who browsed the file, the date and time of the request, and the status of the request. The Activity page helps you determine how much traffic a specific document receives and where that traffic comes from. To view multiple days, enter a new number in the Days field.

Indexing Documents with WebIndex

A convenient way for a user to sort through large amounts of information is through a free-text keyword search. WebSite makes keyword searches easy by providing the two tools. The WebIndex application (Figure 12.14) lets you select the directories in your document area containing files you want included in the keyword search. The WebFind CGI program accepts a keyword and searches through the index created by WebIndex for all instances of that word. Keyword searches on WebSite have been streamlined with the process divided into two parts: requiring the WebSite document manager to create an index manually, and then having users search the index instead of the files themselves. This separation makes searches more efficient; since all the keywords are already indexed, you don't have to wait while each file is opened.

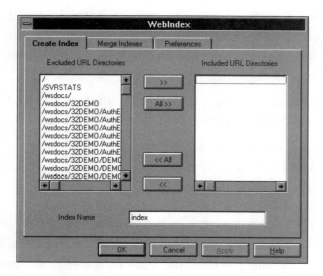

FIGURE 12.14 The WebIndex dialog box.

Logging

WebSite's logs collect information on the server's activity that you can use to monitor traffic and troubleshoot problems. The logs are also helpful for technical support in diagnosing server problems. WebSite has three main logs: access, error , and server. The access log records each request to the server and the server's response. For a short summary of access log data, use the Quick-Stats feature in WebView. The error log records access errors, such as failed user authentication. The server log is a temporary log maintained while the server is running. A variety of tracing options tell the server log to collect more or less detailed information. The contents of the server log are used primarily for troubleshooting and debugging. Every time the server restarts, the server log is cleared and started over.

The first section on the Logging page in the WebSite Admin Server dialog box shows the current names of the log files. The default names are set during installation, but you may change them at any time. For example, you may want to identify the logs with a specific system or network name so as not to confuse them with other logs. Since these are WebSite logs, let's add WS to each name.

By default, WebSite keeps the logs in a directory called *logs,* which is a subdirectory of the server root. If you installed WebSite on drive C, the path for the logs directory is C:\WEBSITE\LOGS. The logs directory can be placed anywhere on the system or on the network. You can move the WebSite logs to any location by changing the logging directory path on the Logging page of Server Admin.

WebSite's Handy Certificate Manager

WebSite Professional includes a friendly dialog box that you fill out to apply for a digital certificate so that you can add encryption to your Web server. To access the WebSite Certificate Manager, follow these steps:

1. Open the WebSite Server Admin icon and select the Identity tab.

2. Enter the name you want to use for the certificate in the Certificate field.

3. Click on the Certs button. A dialog box appears prompting you to enter a password.

4. Enter a password and click on OK. The WebSite Certificate Manager appears, as shown in Figure 12.15. (See Chapter 9 for more information on filling out this form.)

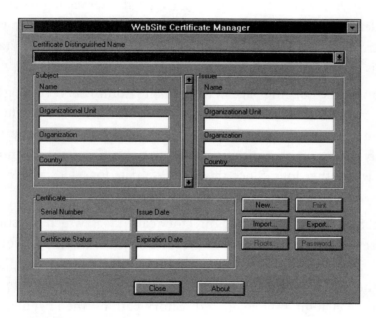

FIGURE 12.15 The WebSite Certificate Manager.

Part Four

Constructing and Managing Contact

Chapter 13

Essential Web Commerce Server Tools

Beyond the basic Web server functions inherent in HTTP is a growing number of enhancement tools for managing your Web site. Three essential programs track Web site usage, generate automatic forms, and create online conferences. Together these form the foundation for your Web site's functionality. This chapter presents an overview of these three tools.

The Big Three Tools

Setting up your site for conducting commerce requires a triad of core tools that form the site's foundation. Web site usage tracking software lets you track your Web site activity, generating valuable management information. As in any business activity, you need to know what's happening with your investment. Form and database connectivity software lets your Web site interact with customers using on-screen forms. The information from these forms is then fed to a database program for processing. The forms let you solicit input from users for everything from surveys to orders. Establishing online discussion groups lets your company interact with your customers or enhance internal communications. This type of add-on software creates a network newsgroup system delivered via friendly Web documents.

Web Site Tracking

Taking the pulse of your Web site is one of the most essential Web site management tasks because tracking usage lets you generate powerful reports about what users are visiting your site, where they came from, when they're connecting, and what they're doing. As a Webmaster, you need to know the strengths and weaknesses of your Web site. The more you know about the usage of your Web site, the more you can pinpoint trouble spots and hone your Web development efforts. With Web tracking software, you can determine the following:

- How many individual users have visited your site
- Whether Web site changes increase or decrease site traffic
- Which Internet advertising vehicles are most effective for your Web site
- Which areas of your site interest your visitors the most
- What are the busiest times for your Web site

Currently available Web tracking software for the Windows NT platform includes net.Genesis's net.Analysis (http://www.netgen.com/) and, e.g. Software's WebTrends (http://webtrends.com/). Figure 13.1 shows a sample usage report.

How Web Site Usage Tracking Works

All site analysis is based on the information contained in your Web servers access logs. Whenever a visitor comes to your site and requests a document, a record of this request is written into a log by your server. Most servers support the Common Log Format (CLF), and many support the Extended Log Format. The Common Log Format was derived from the first NCSA Web server, which kept only simple request information. It was not designed with

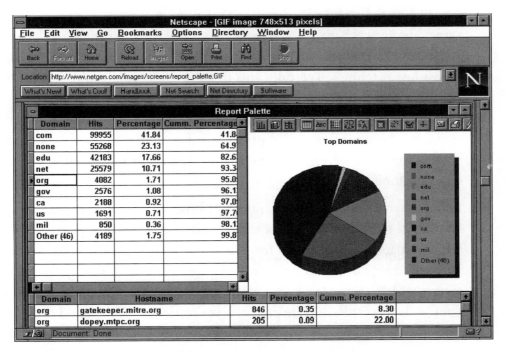

FIGURE 13.1 A sample Web site usage report.

in-depth site analysis in mind and thus lacks much of the information that is desirable from a Web site management perspective. In fact, the CLF contains only the visitor's hostname (e.g., www.netgen.com), the date and time, the actual low-level request to your server (which contains the URL), a return code for the request (e.g., the infamous 404 for nonexistent URLs), and the file size of the item requested. Extended Log Formats vary, but usually include the name of the browser the visitor is using and possibly a referrer field to indicate how the visitor got to your site.

Data Distortions in Web Site Tracking

At first glance, getting the hostnames of your site's visitors may appear to be a safe indicator of where your visitors are coming from. In fact, there are several distortions that occur because of the way the IP addressing works. First, if a hostname is recorded in the form of an IP address (e.g., 206.33.100.2) there's no guarantee that users from this address will be the same ones for each visit. Many Internet service providers employ dynamic IP addressing, a method of spreading a large user demand for IP addresses across few machines. Typically, this practice affects dial-up users and means that one day a user may come from 232.18.9.10 and the next day from 18.237.0.32. Another problem with hostname data is that in larger institutions, machines are generally not devoted to individual users, so multiple visitors to your site from the same hostname may be interested in completely different topics.

A more serious problem in compiling hostname data is the use of proxy servers on the Internet. One of the primary functions of a proxy server is to act as a trusted go-between from inside a security firewall to the outside networked world. All requests from inside the firewall first go to the proxy server, which then makes the actual request to the external Internet (e.g., your Web server) itself. The proxy server retrieves the data and then returns it to the originally requesting computer inside the firewall. In large companies, hundreds of computers may have made requests to your site, but only the hostname of the proxy server will appear in your log file.

Another related problem arises in tracking users as they move through your site. When a user requests an HTML page from a Web server, a connection from the user's browser to the server is established and the HTML document is retrieved. The connection is then terminated. If the HTML page contains an image on the same server, a new connection is created, the image is retrieved, and the new connection is again terminated. If an HTML document has many images in it, they are retrieved in the same manner, one at a time, each using a new connection. This is why HTTP (the protocol for using the Web) is sometimes referred to as connectionless or stateless. The server will log these requests independently, with no information describing how one request is related to another. If a server is highly trafficked, it's more than likely that the individual requests won't even be logged sequentially to the log file.

Data's Better with Cookies

Some recent developments partially address the problem of tracking users at a web site. One is Netscape's client side "cookies." Cookies (the name has no known significance) are identifiers that Netscape browsers use to keep persistent information about a user's interaction with a Web site over multiple requests. When a user requests something from a CGI script, the script may return a cookie to the browser. This cookie contains any information the CGI script wishes to keep persistent over multiple requests as well as a "domain" for the cookie.

The domain tells the browser which URLs the cookie should be sent back with. The next time the user wants a URL in the cookie's domain, the previously received cookie is sent back to the server with the request. Cookies are commonly used for marketplace interfaces in which a user has a "shopping basket" of goods. The returned cookie might contain all the items currently in the user's shopping basket. On the client side, cookies have been available since Netscape v1.1, but they're not supported on most Web servers. And most servers do not write cookie information to their logs.

Thus, there isn't much more you can do to track users as they move around your site than to apply some simple heuristics. A heuristic might be to look at all document requests from the same hostname. If the requests occur within short intervals, the user is probably moving around your site. When a request from a particular hostname has not been received in some threshold amount of time (say 20 minutes), you could make the assumption that the user has left your site. Data gleaned through heuristics should be analyzed conservatively.

Assuming your heuristics work out reasonably, you're still faced with the challenge of determining where users are coming from. This is a major problem because there is still no tool that can tell you every hyperlink on the Web that points to your site, based on the Common Log Format. This is where Extended Logs can help you. Many extended logs write a referrer field into their log entries. These entries come from Web browsers that send, along with your requested URL, the URL that contained the link they followed to your server. With this information, you can tell where users are coming from, as well as the path they are taking to get to your site, by following the trail of referrer fields. The referrer field is possibly the most valuable extension to the log formats, and it's beginning to be widely supported by both browsers and servers.

The Proxy Curse Continues

Proxy servers cause other problems in Web site analysis. A common use of proxy servers is to cache documents. On the client side, the user goes through the proxy to get to the external Internet. Frequently requested documents are stored locally on the proxy machine. When users request any of these documents, the proxy just returns the copy it has on disk, and no request is ever made to the Web server from where it originated. Thus, someone has requested a URL on your site and received the document, but you have no log file entry to show for it. On the server side, with the proxy sitting in front of a Web server, a similar problem arises where frequently requested documents from your Web server are cached on your proxy. When a user requests one of these common documents, the proxy returns it to the user rather than asking your Web server for the document. This can take a lot of the load off your server, but once again, you have no log file entry to show for it.

Data Mining Help

In spite of the problems collecting and analyzing usage data for a Web site, the good news is that some new analysis tools can help you get a better picture of what's going on at your Web site. These products can directly extract or interpret your log file data into several key categories. Commonly available data includes hits for each page, breakdowns of requests based on hostname or IP address, server load and performance statistics, average time that each page is looked at, paths that visitors take through your site, URLs that users came from, and a number of correlations between these data categories.

You can log analysis either off-site or on site. Both methods have their benefits and drawbacks. The off-site analysis option, such as the I/Pro (http://www.ipro.com) solution, saves you time and system resources. It eliminates the task of having to maintain a database on site with its large disk space consumption. Off-site analysis also provides a measure of platform independence because the generated log files are text files, which can be sent to any off-site platform for processing.

The on-site analysis software solution, such as net.Analysis from net.Genesis, makes the analysis of your Web site available on demand. Having the databases online allows you to reuse older log data for looking at trends going on at your Web site. On-site analysis can also be faster because it eliminates the added third-party intervention in the process. On-site analysis software must be available on a platform you use for your Web server, but you can create as many reports as you need as frequently as you want for no extra cost. However, if your site is being hosted by a content provider, you may not be able to use the on-site analysis solution.

Dressing Up Your Data for Others

Once data is mined from your Web servers log file, on-site or off-site analysis programs package it in a variety of report formats, from raw statistics to management presentation quality. What you need to determine is to whom you will deliver reports. Will reports be sent only to the Webmaster who may need just raw figures, or will you need to create beautiful reports for the marketing department with colored graphs, gorgeous tables, and multiple fonts? What options does your report generator give you about layout? Can you decide the format of your reports yourself, or do you simply fill in a stock template? What control does your report generator provide over what data is correlated, over what time frame, and with what filters (e.g., only image files or only .edu domains)? Can your analysis tool trend over multiple log files (or database archives)?

Consider also the time it takes to make a report. Trending over a year's worth of log files for a highly trafficked site can take from minutes to hours, depending on the software you use. You can also specify a variety of formats for your reports, such as HTML, Postscript, or PDF (Adobe Acrobat). Other features included in analysis products are the capability to run multiple parallel reports, import and analysis of other Internet server log files (i.e., gopher, ftp), demographic information, and automation (you may value having nightly reports mailed to your Webmaster or Internet Services administrator.)

As Web sites become mission critical, means of analyzing the way they are being used by customers and employees becomes an essential asset of any Web site management environment. Although it's valuable to realize the current technological limitations in analyzing Web site data, the new crop of analysis options provides powerful tools to stay on top of what is going on at your Web site.

Opening Up Your Web Site to Discussions

Communications to customers, vendors, salespeople, and others via your Web site is critical to conducting commerce on the Web. Web conferencing software adds threaded discussion areas to Web sites that operate much like network news. Figure 13.2 shows a threaded discussion group as it appears at the New York Times Web site. Web-based discussion areas give site users the ability to quickly and conveniently converse with each other about any topics you want on your site, ranging from entertainment to technical support questions. Threaded forums have proven to promote user interactivity and to entice users to return to sites again and again. A good discussion software tool includes a full suite of tools for delivering messages and controlling the

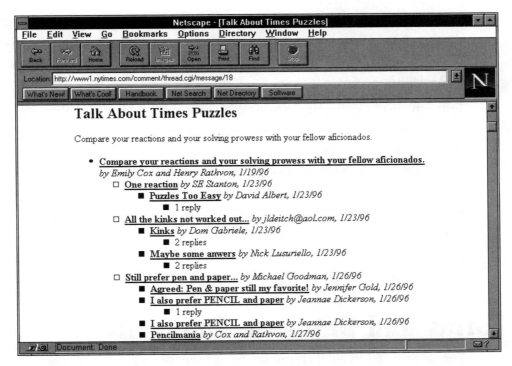

FIGURE 13.2 A threaded discussion area at the New York Times Web site.

forums on your site. Web conferencing system software products include net.Thread from net.Genesis (http://www.netgen.com/), WebBoard from O'Reilly & Associates (http://website.ora.com/), and About Groupware Server from AEX Software (http://www.aex.com/).

Web conferencing software allows you to host discussion forums accessible through a Web browser interface. In addition to providing a threaded, outline-view organization of messages within a forum, these products allow you to structure any number of forums, as well as numerous administrative functions, within a hierarchy. You can use these products for specialized discussion forums, online customer support, internal project planning, and tracking. Another key advantage of creating discussion groups is that they let you take advantage of the biggest resource for building Web content, the users themselves. Site users want to interact with each other, and their ability to do so will draw them back to the site repeatedly. Implementing discussion groups for online customer support offers customers an alternative to phone-based help and can ease the burden on telephone support personnel and telephone lines.

From the user perspective, working with discussion groups within a Web site creates a friendly and easy-to-use communications medium. Lists of threaded messages appear as hyperlinks within HTML documents. Navigating and working these discussion groups is made easy with the use of forms and buttons for point-and-click correspondence. Users can communicate with your business or with other users. These tools provide a collection of administrative tools to allow you control over the content of messages to keep out the "crazies." The friendly user interface of Web-based discussion groups enables users to easily follow and navigate online discussions.

Forms and Database Connectivity

Forms are used to elicit responses from users through a graphical user interface consisting of fill-in blanks, buttons, checkboxes, and other features. Figures 13.3 and 13.4 show examples of forms. After the user fills in form

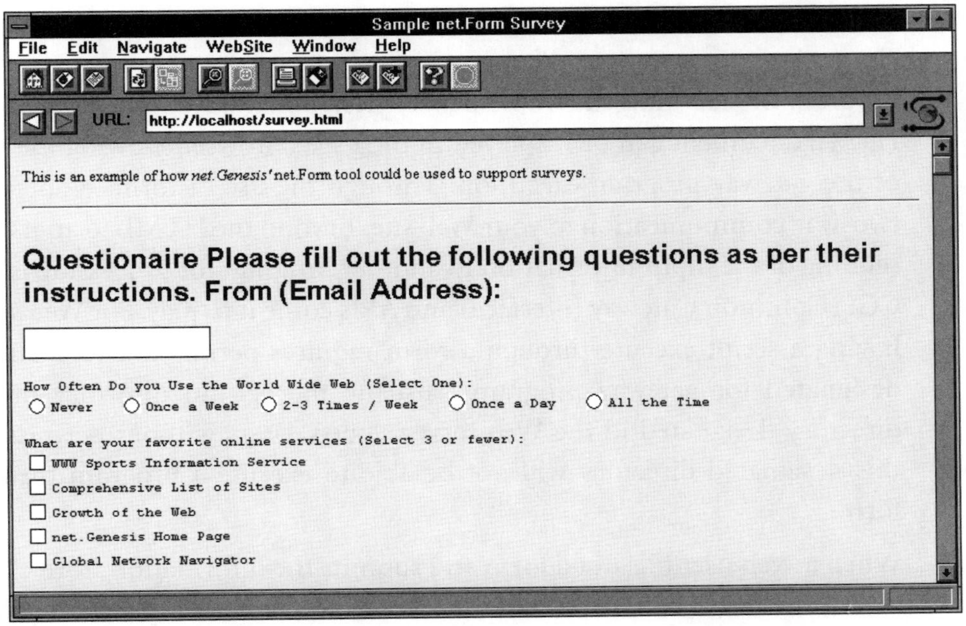

FIGURE 13.3 A sample survey form.

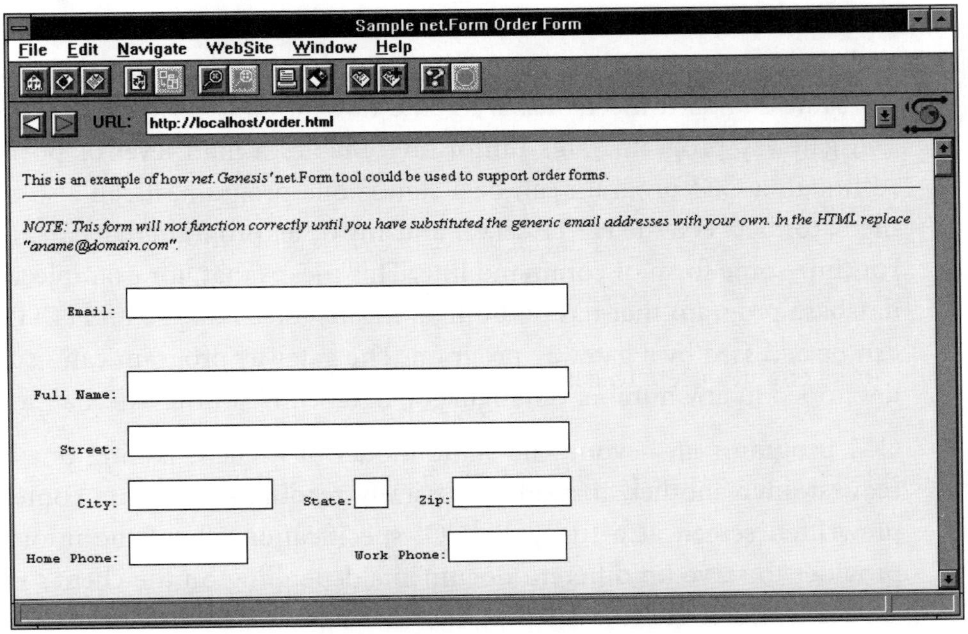

FIGURE 13.4 A sample order form.

values, the entries can be used by a script or executable (gateway) program. This gateway program can then access databases, other software, or any other program or data that the implementor designates. Based on the results, an HTML document can be displayed in the user's browser showing the results of the gateway program execution. Through the use of forms, you can add two-way communication to your Web site. Beyond the HTML form itself, the sending of the input information to another program for processing is where CGI (Common Gateway Interface) and APIs come into play. For Web servers, having a script execute through a form requires permission to a directory designated for gateway programs (usually the cgi-bin directory or other directory designated in the Web server setup). Users without permission to this designated directory will not be able to execute a program through a form.

When a Web user fills out a form and submits the information from client to server, the server receives it and then hands the request to the CGI program for execution. Output (if any) is passed back to the server then sent back to the client. The CGI is the means for the HTTP server to interact with other programs on your, or someone else's, machine. The idea is that each server and client program, regardless of the operating system platform, adheres to the same standard mechanisms for the flow of data between client, server, and gateway program. This uniformity enables a high level of portability. Although a CGI program can be a standalone program, it can also act as a mediator between the HTTP server and any other program that can accept at runtime some form of command line. This means that, for example, an SQL database program that has no built-in means for talking to an HTTP server can be accessed by a gateway program. The gateway program can usually be developed in any number of languages, irrespective of the external program.

CGI programs go beyond the static model of a client issuing one HTML request after another. Instead of passively reading server data content one prewritten screen at a time, the CGI specification allows the information provider to serve up different documents depending on the client's request. CGI also allows the gateway program to create new documents on the fly—

that is, at the time that the client makes the request. A CGI-compliant application can do almost anything with the data from the form. In particular, a CGI program can do the following:

- E-mail the response to a specific e-mail address
- Request information from a database
- Incorporate submitted data into a database
- Check the form's contents for valid information

Traditional methods for creating Web forms involve two steps. The first step is writing an HTL representation of the form using a simple HTML authoring tool. The second step is creating a CGI script to handle user input. Developing CGI scripts is a complex task requiring the time and attention of an experienced programmer familiar with both the CGI specifications and advanced scripting techniques. Additionally, whenever a form's HTML is changed, its corresponding CGI script may also need to be modified. Fortunately, there are new software tools that integrate the forms and CGI functionality into one program, so a nonprogrammer can add this functionality to a Web site.

The two leading software programs tools that integrate forms and CGI functionality into one program for nonprogrammers are net.Form from net.Genesis (http://www.netgen.com/) and Cold Fusion from Allaire (http://www.allaire.com/). Using one of these programs, you can collect information from users, seamlessly integrate access to a database, then deliver information back to the user in HTML format. The person authoring the HTML form now has the tools for creating the processing going on in the background without programming in CGI. Using a form-generating program, the Webmaster embeds special HTML tags into a basic Web document. These tags control all aspects of the form and its fields including:

- Which fields the user must fill out before the form can be successfully submitted
- What the user should be shown after submitting the form successfully

- Who should be notified by e-mail of the form's contents
- Where the data from the form's contents should be stored—in a flat file or in a database

Connecting forms to a database is ultimately where you want your Web site to go. If you use the ODBC standard-based forms generator, your site can offer seamless access to most databases on the market today.

Beyond CGI and on to API

The Common Gateway Interface (CGI) is the widely used standard that provides a mechanism for Web servers and executables to communicate with each other. But this simple, cross-platform interface isn't very efficient and can easily bog down a server's performance. Now there's a better way for integrating applications into a Web site—Web server software APIs (Application Programming Interfaces).

This new generation of Web server APIs promises to increase the flexibility of server functionality and interactivity, with several advantages over CGIs. APIs are more efficient because less memory is needed each time an API program is called and because initialization takes place only once. Another advantage is that an API application can maintain state, allowing applications to keep valuable information across client connections. APIs also enable applications to work more closely with the server's operation, giving Webmasters more sophisticated options for adding custom functionality to their server. APIs enable you to plug custom applications into the server's request-handling process, allowing Webmasters to easily insert their own authentication routines or database logging applications.

CGI has long been the standard for passing information between Web servers and executable programs. It works by executing a program when a Web browser connects to a Web server and makes a request. The Web server creates a new process each time a CGI script or program is requested by a client. After the CGI program is executed, its results are passed back to the HTTP (hypertext transport protocol) server via standard output. CGI's main drawback is the overhead of executing a process, loading it into memory, and initializing the program for each request. However, one of the major advantages of CGI applications is that they're portable across different HTTP server platforms. A specific server API is bound to that server.

Understanding APIs

Among the most popular APIs are the Netscape Application Programming Interface (NSAPI), Microsoft's Internet Server Application Programming Interface (ISAPI), and O'Reilly & Associate's WebSite Application Programming Interface (WSAPI). Netscape's Commerce and Communications Servers (http://home.netscape.com) use NSAPI, Microsoft's Internet Information Server (http://www.microsoft.com) and Process Software's Purveyor WebServer (http://www.process.com) use ISAPI, and O'Reilly & Associate's WebSite (http://www.ora.com) uses WSAPI. Given the clout of both Netscape and Microsoft, expect to see their server APIs become de facto standards among commercial servers.

These Web servers allow external programs to operate more closely with the server, streamlining many tasks that would normally be accomplished through CGI. All server applications based on any of these APIs run in the same process as the server and remain resident in memory, bypassing the overhead of executing a new process and repeating program initialization for each request.

Another important advantage of all API applications is their ability to maintain state. Because an API program remains resident in memory from one call to the next, information about the client can be stored and used the next time the client connects. This can greatly enhance applications that integrate databases with the Web. With CGI programs it is necessary to connect and disconnect from the database each time the program is requested, which is a time-consuming process with most databases. With an API application, a database connection can be held open between requests for the program because it remains in memory.

Web server API applications are developed with Dynamic-Link Libraries (DLLs) on Windows platforms. DLLs are libraries of functions stored in executable format separate from the process that actually uses them. At startup, the server is configured to recognize these libraries, which provide a common entry point into the application that the server can call. The first time the library is requested, it is loaded into the server's memory and stays resident until the server no longer needs it.

Once loaded into server memory, the DLL has access to the server's procedures and variables. From that point on, the application is resident in memory, available to service requests with minimal overhead. The server memory variables are available via generic parameter blocks. These structures contain the same variables used by the CGI standard. In some API implementations such as ISAPI extension control blocks (ECBs), the structure provides functionality to read and write from the client and redirect the client to another location. This method provides a cleaner way of interacting with a client than communicating through stdin and stdout.

Developing with APIs

There are three different methods for writing applications that link with a server's API: compile-time linking, load-time linking, and run-time linking. Compile-time and load-time programs can be used to extend the functionality of the server; while a run-time DLL can be used as a more efficient alternative to CGI. Most commercial APIs support load-time linking. ISAPI supports load-time linking with ISAPI filters and is also the main supporter of run-time linking of custom libraries.

Compile-time linking is typically supported by public domain servers because this technique requires that source code be available to the Webmaster. This type of linking is accomplished when the server is built with a statically linked library.

Load-time linking is the most widely supported method used by leading commercial server vendors. The servers are commonly referred to as NSAPI objects and ISAPI filters. This type of linking is accomplished when the server's import library is built with a custom DLL. When the server is started, the library is loaded into memory and operates as part of the server's normal processing of requests. In general, the module is called each time the server processes a request from a client.

These servers allow load-time applications to execute at various stages in the server operation. The Netscape Commerce Server (which uses NSAPI) checks a series of objects, as well as directives and functions, that are defined in configuration files in the Registry in Windows NT, and executes the appropriate functions. These plug-ins to the server make it easy to add server functionality such as custom authentication functions and more advanced tracking and logging of client transactions.

NSAPI functions can be configured to run or not run, based on certain client specifications when a set of client keys is specified. These client keys contain wildcard expressions to compare to the client hostname, allowing Webmasters to easily tailor their Web sites to the current audience. For example, you may want commercial users (*.com, *.com.*, *.co.*) to start at a different page on your site than educational users (*.edu, *.edu.*), or you may want to redirect competitors to a less revealing section of your Web site.

Run-time linking enables the initiation of DLLs via the Web. As with load-time linking, these libraries share the server's memory space and operate within the same process. Once it is loaded into the server's memory, the DLL can be accessed with minimal overhead for all requests thereafter. These applications also allow you to work more closely with the Web server because DLLs have access to the resources of the HTTP.

The main drawback of API applications is that they are currently bound to their respective Web servers, making it difficult for software developers to tailor their applications to server APIs. ISAPI currently binds the application to Microsoft Internet Information Server and Process's Purveyor WebServer, and to the Windows NT Server and NetWare platforms, although with the increasing popularity of Windows NT-based Web servers, ISAPI is sure to pick up steam. To help it along, Microsoft also plans to provide a simple wrapper for ISAPI applications that will make them CGI compliant. NSAPI applications are currently limited to Netscape, the leading commercial server used on the Web.

The wider use of APIs with Web servers will deliver a new level of capabilities for Web servers, as third-party software publishers support these APIs. By improving performance and enhancing security and logging functions, APIs will allow Webmasters access to better tools for running their Web sites.

Chapter 14

Tracking Your Web Site Activity

As a Webmaster, you have an inherent need to know how visitors are using your site, what is attracting them to it, and what is keeping them there. Collecting usage information, commonly referred to as the analysis, auditing, or reporting, is pivotal to managing and growing your Web site. The relevance of site analysis information becomes even more apparent when you start asking questions such as: Which of my pages is being requested the most? How long do visitors usually stay on my site? Where are visitors coming from externally (and to which pages)? How many visitors came to our site from our Web advertisements? How many pages, on average, did it take visitors to get to our contact page? The good news is there are a few new software products that will help you in your quest for the valuable answers to these questions and others. Not only will they generate the data, they'll let you present your findings in colorful reports laden with graphs and coupled with sophisticated trending information over the last week, month, or year.

Working with net.Analysis

net.Analysis is a powerful tool that analyzes the traffic on your World Wide Web site. It allows you to quickly create sophisticated, up-to-the-minute reports with exactly the information you want to see. net.Analysis has two components: the net.Analysis Engine and the net.Analysis Reporter. The Engine gathers detailed information about the usage of your Web site and takes this information from the access log and translates it into a database. The Reporter queries the database for information and generates reports in table or graphical format. You can use net.Analysis to accumulate weeks, months, or even years of data and to archive historic log files.

The following information is captured by your Web server's access log when users visit your site:

- User's domain
- User's subdomain
- User's hostname
- File on your site user clicked on (resource)
- Time user clicked (time the hit was generated)
- Errors, if any, returned by the server

Some servers also use other logs to record the user's browser software and the site the user came from (called a referral). Current Internet interactions don't involve information such as the user's e-mail address or other more personal information.

Generating Reports

With net.Analysis, you can quickly generate reports to analyze many different aspects of the traffic on your Web site, including the number of people visiting your site, what kind of people they are, and the most popular locations on your site. net.Analysis provides a number of standard reports, time ranges, and filters so that you can easily and quickly get the information you need. You can also create your own filters to generate reports that have a high degree of precision. To generate a report, do the following:

1. Start net.Analysis by double-clicking the net.Analysis icon in the net.Analysis group. The Report Selection window appears, as shown in Figure 14.1.

2. Select a report type from the Report Type drop-down menu.

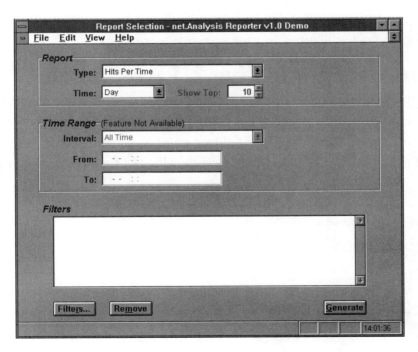

FIGURE 14.1 The Report Selection window.

3. Select an interval from the Time field or enter a number in the Show Top field. (Enter 0 in the Show Top field to show all.) If a field is inactive, it does not apply to the report type you selected.

4. Select a time range from the Interval drop-down menu or type dates and times directly into the From and To fields.

5. Click the Filters button to display the Filter Selection dialog box (Figure 14.2). Select a filter or multiple filter. If the Filters button does not appear, the report type you are using can be used with only one filter at a time.

6. From the View menu, select Options. The Report Options dialog box appears (Figure 14.3).

7. Enter a title for the report in the Report Title field and click the Close button.

8. Click the Generate button on the Report Selection dialog box. Your report will appear on the screen (Figure 14.4).

Report Types: Selecting a Presentation

net.Analysis contains several predefined report types. To select a report type, simply select one of the report types from the Report Type drop-down menu. Select an interval from the Time field or enter a number in the Show Top field. (Enter 0 in the Show Top field to show all.) If a field is inactive, it does

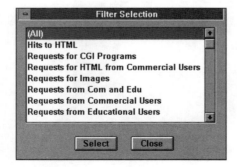

FIGURE 14.2 The Filter Selection dialog box.

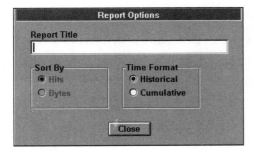

FIGURE 14.3 The Report Options dialog box.

not apply to the report type you selected. The following sections describe the types of reports available through net.Analysis.

Hits per Time

The Hits-per-Time report type shows the number of hits per time interval—minutes, hours, days, days of week, months, or years—from the domains and to the resources defined by the current filter. Use these reports with various filters to see how your site usage profile changes over time. To determine the number of users on your site, use a Sessions-per-Time report.

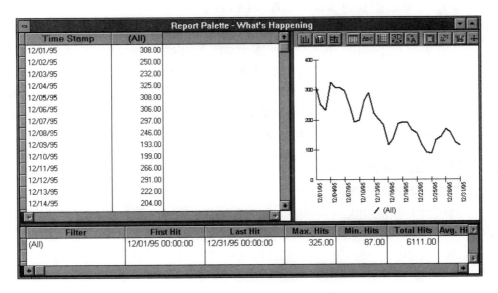

FIGURE 14.4 A sample report displayed on the screen.

Bytes per Time

The report type arranged by bytes per minute, hour, day, day of week, month, or year shows the number of bytes transferred to browsers. Use these reports with various filters to see how your site usage profile changes over time.

Sessions per Time

The session report type by minute, hour, day, day of week, month, or year shows the approximate number of people on your site. If you have extended log format, sessions are checked to see if the user came from an external referral. If so, it is considered a new session. If you do not have extended log format, the method for determining the start of a new session is less accurate: net.Analysis checks to see if the hostname or browser is different from that on the last hit. It also uses the session limit set in the configuration file to determine amount of time between hits that will create a new session. Use this report instead of one of the Hits-per-Time reports to determine the approximate number of users on your site instead of the number of hits, or requests, made by users.

Top Domains/Domain Classes

The top domains/domain classes report type shows the most common domains of people using your Web site. You can click a row in the data table generated by this report type to generate a subreport that contains the subdomains of that domain. You can click a row in the subdomain report to generate a report containing the hostnames in that subdomain. Use these reports to find out what type of user accesses your Web site most often.

Top Subdomains

The top subdomains report type shows the most common subdomains of people using your Web site. You can click a row in the data table generated by this report type to generate a subreport that contains the hostnames in that subdomain. Use this report to find out what American companies' users access your Web site most often.

Top Hostnames

In the top hostnames report type you see the most common machine names of people using your Web site. Use this report to further classify the type of users accessing your Web site.

Top Resources/Resource Classes

The top resources/resource classes report type shows the resources (such as HTML documents or images) on your Web site that receive the most hits. Use this report to find out which of your resources are the most popular with users.

Top Referrals

With a top referrals report type you see the most popular links to your site and can find out the most popular ways of getting to your site. You can generate this report type only if your net.Analysis Engine is configured to include the information in the referrer log.

Error analysis

The error analysis report displays information about the errors returned by your Web server and tells you which resources caused the problem. You can click a row in the data table to generate a subreport of the top resources that caused that error. Use this report to find out if your users are encountering errors when they use your Web site and to troubleshoot those errors if they do occur.

Selecting Time Ranges

To create a report, you must specify a time range over which you will analyze the use of your Web site. A default time interval appears with any report type you choose, but you can choose any time interval you want. To choose a time range:

1. From the Report Selection window, select a time range from the Interval drop-down menu.

2. The From and To fields will be filled in for you, or you can enter the date and time directly into the From and To fields in the

following format: Year-Month-Day-Hours-Minutes-Seconds. Hours must be expressed in the 24-hour military time format. You can modify the times that appear in the From and To fields without changing the Interval.

Filters: Selecting Data to Analyze

Filters are patterns you impose on data to sift through it for specific nuggets of useful information. By selecting a filter in net.Analysis reports, you can target your analysis to include only certain information from the access log. net.Analysis contains a number of predefined filters for you to choose from as described in Table 14.1. You can also create your own filters.

TABLE 14.1 Predefined Filters for net.Analysis

Filter	Description
All	Includes hits from all domains to all resources. Use this filter to get the most general usage patterns for your Web site.
Hits to CGI Programs	Includes hits from all domains to all the CGI programs on your Web site.
Hits to Homepage	Includes hits from all domains to your site's homepage.
Hits to Images	Includes hits from all domains to all the images on your Web site.
Hits to HTML	Includes hits from all domains to all the .htm or .html files on your Web site.
Requests from Commercial Users	Includes hits from users in the commercial domain to all the resources on your Web site.
Requests from Educational Users	Includes hits from users in the educational domain to all the resources on your Web site.

To choose one filter, go to the Report Selection window and select one of the filters from the Filter drop-down menu. The filter appears in the Filter field. To choose multiple filters, follow these steps:

1. From the Report Selection window, click the Filters button. If the Filters button does not appear, the report type you are using can be used with only one filter at a time. The Filter Selection dialog box appears.

2. Select one of the filters and click the Select button or double-click a filter. The filter appears in the Filters field on the Report Selection window. Select as many filters as you would like to include in your report.

3. Click the Close button when you are finished.

To remove filters, select the filter you want to remove in the Report Selection window, then click the Remove button. The filter disappears from the Filters field.

Viewing Reports

With the Windows Reporter, once you click the Generate button, your report appears on the screen as a data table. You can also view the report as a summary table or a graph. net.Analysis allows you to label pie graphs with any column in the data table, generate subreports directly from the report you are working with, and see a snapshot of statistics on your Web site. net.Analysis also allows you to manipulate the appearance of your report in a wide variety of ways using the Report Palette. Once you are satisfied with the appearance of your report, you can print it or export it file to a variety of applications.

Viewing the Report as a Graph or Summary Table

With the Windows Reporter, you can view a report as a graph or as a summary table, and you can modify it in a variety of ways with the functions of the

Report Palette. To view the report as a graph or summary table, select either Graph or Summary Table from the View menu. You can see the graph and summary table simultaneously by selecting both options in the View menu.

You may want to label your graphs with the information in the data table to create a graph that is easier to understand. To do so, double-click a column header of the data table and label the graph with the contents of that column. net.Analysis allows you to choose any one of the columns in the data table to label the graph.

Generating Subreports

In some cases, net.Analysis allows you to create more detailed reports directly from the report you are working with. For example, you just generated a report for the top domains visiting your site, and your report tells you that your heaviest users are from the commercial domain. You now want to find out the top 10 subdomains (which are often the company names) of users from the commercial domain, so you click the "commercial" row in the data table to generate a subreport.

To generate a subreport:

1. Click a row in the data table to generate a subreport for that domain. Clickable rows appear in red.

2. Click Yes. The subreport window appears, containing the details of the row you clicked. You can also click a row in the subreport's data table to get a sub-subreport.

Note: *When you are generating a sub-subreport to find out the top hostnames, they may not appear on the graph as labels because the names are long. If you enlarge the sub-subreport window to the right, they will appear.*

Taking a Database Snapshot

A database snapshot can tell you the bandwidth utilization for the last hour, the database net.Analysis is connected to, the first and last hit in your database, and the name and path of the logs net.Analysis is getting its information from. To take a snapshot of your database, choose Snapshot from the View menu. A Database Snapshot window similar to the one shown in Figure 14.5 will appear. You can refresh the information in the snapshot at any time by clicking the Now! button or by setting the refresh interval.

Printing Reports

To print a report, select Print from the File menu. net.Analysis will print the report in the active report window using a preformatted report style.

Exporting Reports

The net.Analysis Reporter allows you to export to a number of different file formats for applications including Microsoft Word, Excel, and Lotus 1-2-3.

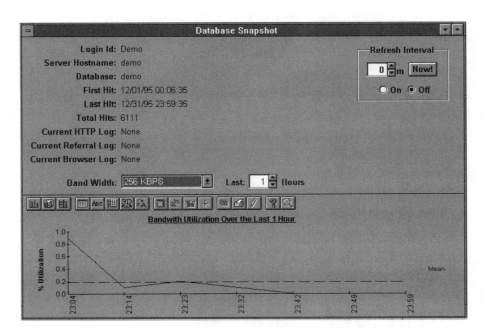

FIGURE 14.5 A sample Database Snapshot window.

You can also export reports directly to HTML for display on your Web site. Linking net.Analysis's exporting ability with the capabilities of a forms editor, such as net.Form (a forms-processing engine from net.Genesis), allows you to display up-to-the-minute dynamic reports on the usage of your Web site in response to user queries. (See Chapter 15 for more information on net.Form.)

To export a report to a file, follow these steps:

1. Select Export from the File menu. The File Options dialog box appears (Figure 14.6).

2. From the Type drop-down menu, choose the file type for your report.

3. In the To field, enter the path and name for the file.

4. Click the Elipse button. (If you click OK instead, the file will be saved in the current directory or the directory you specified, with the name you assigned.) The Save As window appears.

5. Choose the directory in which to save the file.

6. Click Save. The Save As window closes.

7. Click OK on the File Options window.

8. Click the Generate button on the Report Selection window. The report will be exported to a file.

FIGURE 14.6 The File Options dialog box.

Creating Custom Filters

Creating custom filters allows you to conduct a powerful, targeted analysis of the traffic on your Web site. You can include or exclude information from the access log by creating a new filter or editing an existing filter. When creating or editing a filter, you have the ability to define the resource classes and domain classes and include specific browser types and referrals in the filter. For example, you own an automobile company and want to know which of your competitors are accessing your homepage. To find out, you create a domain class that includes *.ford.com, *.mercur.com, and *.toyota.com. This tells net.Analysis to look at hits to your site only by any users from those domains. You create a resource class that contains only the name of your homepage, "Welcome.htm." You then include all browsers and all referrals in your filter and call your filter "Competitors' Hits to My Homepage." Finally, you generate a report and look at the data table to see which of your competitors are visiting your homepage.

Follow these steps to create a custom filter:

1. From the Edit menu, choose Filter. The Filter Editor dialog box appears (Figure 14.7).

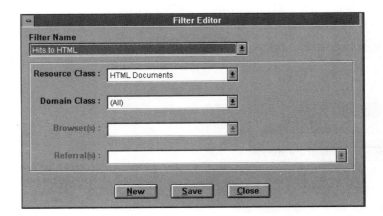

FIGURE 14.7 The Filter Editor dialog box.

2. Click the New button. The New Filter dialog box appears (Figure 14.8).

3. Enter the filter's name and a description of the filter.

4. Click OK. The Filter Editor reappears with your new filter in the Filter Name field.

5. Choose which resources on your site to analyze. Select a Resource Class from the Resource Class drop-down menu.

6. Choose which type of users to analyze. Select a Domain Class from the Domain Class drop-down menu.

7. Choose the browser you want to include in your analysis. Select a browser from the Browser drop-down menu.

8. Choose from the locations that people use to get to your site. Select one or more referrals from the Referrals drop-down menu.

9. Click the Save button to save your filter.

10. Click the Close button. Your filter appears in the Filter menu on the Report Selection window.

To delete a custom filter:

1. In the Filter Editor, select the filter you want to delete from the Filter Name drop-down menu.

2. From the Filter menu, select Delete.

3. Click OK.

FIGURE 14.8 The New Filter dialog box.

Analyzing Hits to the Site

A resource is a particular file on your Web site, such as your homepage or an image map. By modifying the resources or groups of resources (resource classes) included in a filter, you can analyze the user traffic on particular files on your site. Resource classes are useful because one document or document type may be identified by multiple resource names. For example, the resource class "HTML documents" contains all resources that end with .htm *and* .html. You can select a resource class from those already defined, edit an existing resource class, or create a new resource class.

For example, you have two catalogs on your Web site, and you want to see which is more popular with the online audience. Using net.Analysis, you create two resource classes, one for Catalog A and the other for Catalog B. You name them "Catalog A" and "Catalog B." The Catalog A resource class contains all resources from Catalog A, which you define as MySite/CatA/*. The Catalog B resource class contains all resources from Catalog B, which you define as MySite/CatB/*. You then create two filters, called "Hits to Catalog A" and "Hits to Catalog B," including all domains and all browsers. The Catalog A filter contains the resource class Catalog A, and the Catalog B filter contains the resource class Catalog B. You generate two reports using the report type Sessions per *Time*, with the time range All Time—one with the Catalog A filter and the other with the Catalog B filter. Finally, you compare the number of sessions to see which of the two catalogs is attracting more online attention.

To select a resource class, do the following:

1. From the Edit menu, choose Filter. The Filter Editor dialog box appears.

2. Select one of the resource classes from the Resource Class drop-down menu. The resource class is now part of the filter. (A * appears in the title bar to indicate changes have been made to the filter.)

3. Click the Save button to save the changes.

─── **Note:** *To select multiple resource classes, create a new resource class comprising other resource classes.*

To create a new resource class, follow these steps:

1. From the Edit menu, select Resource Class. The Resource Class Editor window appears (Figure 14.9).

2. Click the New button. The New Resource Class window appears.

3. Enter the name for the resource class you are creating in the Class Name field.

4. Click OK. The Resource Class Editor reappears with the name of your resource class in the Resource Class Name field.

5. Search for the resources to include in your resource class:

a. Enter the resource in the Wildcard Expression field and add to the Selected field by clicking the Filters button. Or search for

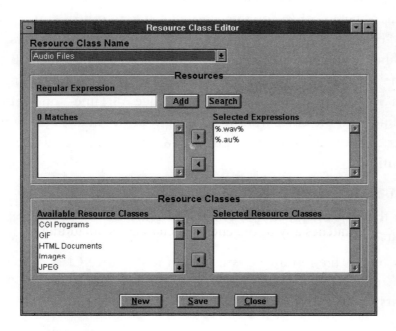

FIGURE 14.9 The Resource Class Editor window.

the particular resource you want to include by entering a search term into the Wildcard Expression field and clicking the Search button. You can use the characters in Table 14.2 to make your search more powerful.

b. If your search was successful, select a resource from the Matches field.

c. Click the right arrow to move it to the Selected field. Click the left arrow to remove a resource class from the Selected field.

6. Select any resource classes to include. Select a resource class from the Available Classes field. Click the right arrow to move it to the Selected field. Click the left arrow to remove a resource class from the Selected field.

7. Click the Save button to save your resource class.

8. Click the Close button. Your new resource class will now appear at the end of the Resource Class drop-down menu in the Filter Editor.

TABLE 14.2 Wildcard Characters for Refining Your Search

Character	Search Function
*	"Wildcard." Matches any number of characters. For example, enter *htm to match all files with the .HTM extension.
?	Matches any single character. For example, enter gr?y to match either "grey" or "gray."
\	Removes the special significance of the next character. For example, enter * to match an asterisk (*).
[...]	Matches any of the enclosed characters, including character ranges. For example, [a-z] matches any letter, from a to z. A caret as the first character matches any character not listed. For example, [^abc] matches any character not a, b, or c.

Analyzing the User Population

A domain is the name used on the Internet for a user's machine. For example, jdavis@amber.toyota.com is the user jdavis from the domain amber.toyota.com. By modifying which domain classes are included in a filter, you can analyze the traffic on your Web site from a particular type of user. For example, you advertised your Web site in a newspaper in Spain last week, and you want to see if more Spanish users are now accessing your site. You create a new domain class called "Spanish Users" that contains the domain *.es (*.es includes all Spanish users). You then create a filter with the report type Sessions per *Time*, time interval of All Time, and the filter Spanish Users. If the number of Sessions per *Time* increased since your ad ran, more Spanish users are accessing your site.

Follow these steps to select a domain class:

1. From the Edit menu, choose Filter. The Filter Editor appears.

2. Select one of the domain classes from the Domain Class dropdown menu. The domain class is now part of the filter. (A * appears in the title bar to indicate changes have been made to the filter.)

3. Click the Save button to save the changes.

To create a new domain class, do the following:

1. From the Edit menu, select Domain Class. The Domain Class Editor window appears (Figure 14.10).

2. Click the New button. The New Domain Class window appears.

3. Enter the name for the domain class you are creating in the Class Name field.

4. Click OK. The Domain Class Editor reappears with your new filter name in the Domain Class Name field.

5. Search for the domains you want to include in your domain class.

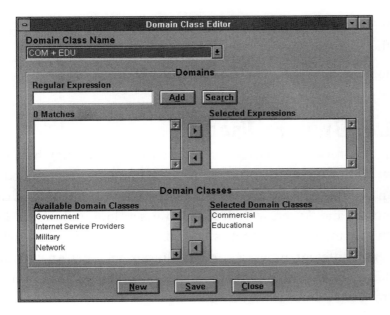

FIGURE 14.10 The Domain Class Editor.

    a. Enter the resource in the Wildcard Expression field and add it to the Selected field by clicking the Filters button. Or search for the particular resource you want to include by entering a search term into the Wildcard Expression field and clicking the Search button. You can use the characters listed in Table 14.2 to make your search more powerful.

    b If your search was successful, select a domain from the Matches field.

    c. Click the right arrow to move it to the Selected field. Click the left arrow to remove a domain from the Selected field.

6. Select any domain classes you want to include.

    a. Select a domain class from the Available Classes field.

    b. Click the right arrow to move it to the Selected field. Click the left arrow to remove a domain class from the Selected field.

7. Click the Save button to save your domain class.

8. Click the Close button.

Your new domain class will now appear in the Domain Class drop-down menu.

Analyzing Browser Usage

A browser is the software (such as Netscape Navigator or Mosaic) that people use to look at your Web site. By modifying which browsers are included in a filter, you can determine if you are attracting users based on the HTML capabilities of your site and if users with different browsers look at different documents or you can analyze the activities of AOL or Prodigy users as a whole. There are over 90 different browsers currently in existence. net.Analysis automatically adds each new browser that requests information from your Web site to the Browser(s) drop-down menu.

To select a browser follow these steps:

1. From the Edit menu, choose Filter. The Filter Editor appears.

2. Select a browser from the Browser(s) drop-down menu. (Click Any to see all the browsers that have requested information from your Web server.) If the Browser(s) field is inactive, you do not have browser information in your access log.

——**Note:** *The format of the access log depends on the Web server software you are using. To fully utilize the capabilities of net.Analysis, your Web server should be configured to create an access log, a referrer log, and a user agent (or browser) log. See your system administrator if you have questions about what types of logs are being generated by your Web server.*

Analyzing User Entry to the Site

A referral is a page on another server that has a link to your Web site. By modifying referrals included in a filter, you can determine how many people are getting to your Web site from a particular location. Referrals are added automatically to the Referral drop-down list as users come to your site. For example, you paid to advertise your Web site on Yahoo and NetSearch two weeks ago, and now you want to find out which of the two ads is routing more traffic to your site. To do this, you create two filters, one called "Yahoo" and another called "NetSearch." Both have All as the Domain Class, Resource Class, and Browser, but the Yahoo filter has the location of your ad on the Yahoo site, and the NetSearch filter has the location of your ad on the NetSearch site. You then generate two reports using your two different filters and compare the number of hits to determine which is generating more.

To select a referral page(s), do the following:

1. From the Edit menu, choose Filter. The Filter Editor appears.

2. Select a choice from the Referral(s) drop-down menu. If the Referral(s) field is inactive, you do not have an access log that contains referral information.

Chapter 15

Creating Forms and Integrating Databases

Forms are the basis of a dynamic HTML site and a static document-based site, providing a foundation for interactivity at the basic text input level. A document is dynamic because the HTML document is generated at the time it's delivered by a program called a script, which is stored on the server side. The Web server executes the script.

A form is a way of allowing Web users to send information to your Web server from their client programs. The server can either store that information for later analysis or act on it immediately to generate a new document on the fly, customized for the user based on user input from the form. Using HTML forms lets users become more involved in transactions and other activities.

Beyond One-Way Documents with Forms

Through the use of forms, you can add two-way communication to your HTML pages. Forms allow a user to enter information, provide a method to supply that information to a database program of your choosing, and return results to a user via regular HTML page construction. All the Web browsers support forms, which are used to elicit responses from users through a graphical user interface consisting of fill-in blanks, buttons, checkboxes, and other features. After the user fills in form values, the entries can be used by a script or executable (gateway) program. This gateway program can then access databases, other software, or any other program or data that the implementor designates. Based on the results, an HTML document can be displayed in the user's browser, showing the results of the gateway program execution. These scripts or programs are written with C or perl. Beyond the HTML form itself, the sending of the input information to another program for processing is where CGI (Common Gateway Interface) and APIs come into play, as explained later.

Having a Form Do Something

Once the form's front end or graphical user interface has been created, the next step is to create an executable script to be referred to in the Action attribute of the Form element. For some Web servers, having a script execute through a form requires permission to a directory designated for gateway programs (usually the cgi-bin directory or other directory designated in the Web server setup). Users without permission to this designated directory will *not* be able to execute a program through a form.

Common Gateway Interface

The Common Gateway Interface, or CGI, is the means for the HTTP server to interact with other programs on your, or someone else's, machine. The idea is that each server and client program, regardless of the operating system platform, adheres to the same standard mechanisms for the flow of data between client, server, and gateway program, enabling a high level of portability.

Although a CGI program can stand alone, it can also act as a mediator between the HTTP server and any other program that can accept at runtime some form of command line. This means that, for example, an SQL database program that has no built-in means for talking to an HTTP server can be accessed by a gateway program. The gateway program can usually be developed in any number of languages, irrespective of the external program.

CGI programs go beyond the static model of a client issuing one HTML request after another. Instead of passively reading server data content one prewritten screen at a time, the CGI specification allows the information provider to serve up different documents depending on the client's request. CGI also allows the gateway program to create new documents on the fly—that is, at the time that the client makes the request.

How CGI Works

When a Web user fills out a form and submits the information from client to server, the server receives it and then hands the request to the CGI program for execution. Output (if any) is passed back to the server then sent back to the client.

For HTML forms to be functional (for data submitted by the user to go anywhere useful) the developer must provide a custom program designed to properly handle user responses. To interact properly with Web servers, these programs must conform to the CGI standard set of rules. A CGI-compliant application can do almost anything with the data from the form, including the following:

- E-mail the response to a specific e-mail address
- Request information from a database
- Incorporate submitted data into a database
- Check the form's contents for valid information

Each form generally requires a custom CGI script tailor-made to the form's specific function. Providing forms support is expensive because it consumes valuable technical resources to write, test, and implement CGI scripts. Sites with few or poorly implemented forms lack interactivity and are often disregarded by users. Commercial-quality CGI scripting requires trained, experienced staff familiar with both the HTML 2.0 and CGI specifications.

Working with net.Form

net.Form adds the CGI programming component so that you don't have to do your own CGI programming. The CGI scripting is handled at the HTML authoring level. net.Form acts as a universal CGI script, which eliminates the need for writing, testing, and implementing the majority of existing custom scripts. Common tasks, such as checking contents of particular fields and mailing results to a specific user or group, are automated through net.Form. Webmasters can design forms and embed instructions describing how the contents of each form should be processed without having to write CGI scripts. net.Form takes information that is passed to it and acts as a generalized CGI-script to handle the form appropriately. All information concerning form processing is in the form itself, making maintenance easier. net.Form can also be used to perform standard error checking on contents of a form. As an enabler and a time saver, it enables nonprogrammers to create completely functional HTML forms without any programming. net.Form features include the following capabilities:

- Communicates with ODBC-compliant databases
- Automatically sends e-mail containing the form data submitted by users
- Enforces type checking on specified fields
- Validates credit card numbers
- Writes form contents to database-readable files

- Returns plain English error reports to users when they fail to fill out a form properly

- Sends form contents to auxiliary scripts after performing field checking

- Works with all CGI-compliant servers, HTML Level 2.0-compliant browsers

Note: *You may want to know the basics of the database application that you are working with, although this information is not necessary to use net.Form. To create queries to the database, you should have some knowledge of SQL.*

Getting Started with net.Form

After installing net.Form, you can quickly get started using forms. net.Form comes with several pre-made form templates that you can use as a basis for creating your own forms. You can display these forms by moving the HTML document files into any directory your Web server uses for accessing HTML document.

For example, if you're using the WebSite Professional, copy the HTML document files from the netgen\net.Form\examples directory to the Website\htdocs directory. Open a Web browser and enter *http://yourserver/ HTML_document_name.* Entering http://yourserver/order.html displays the order form, as shown in Figure 15.1. The following lists the form templates that are bundled with net.Form:

application.html	order.html	type_checking_negative.html
database.html	sequence.html	type_checking_positive.html
exec.html	survey.html	
feedback.html	template.html	

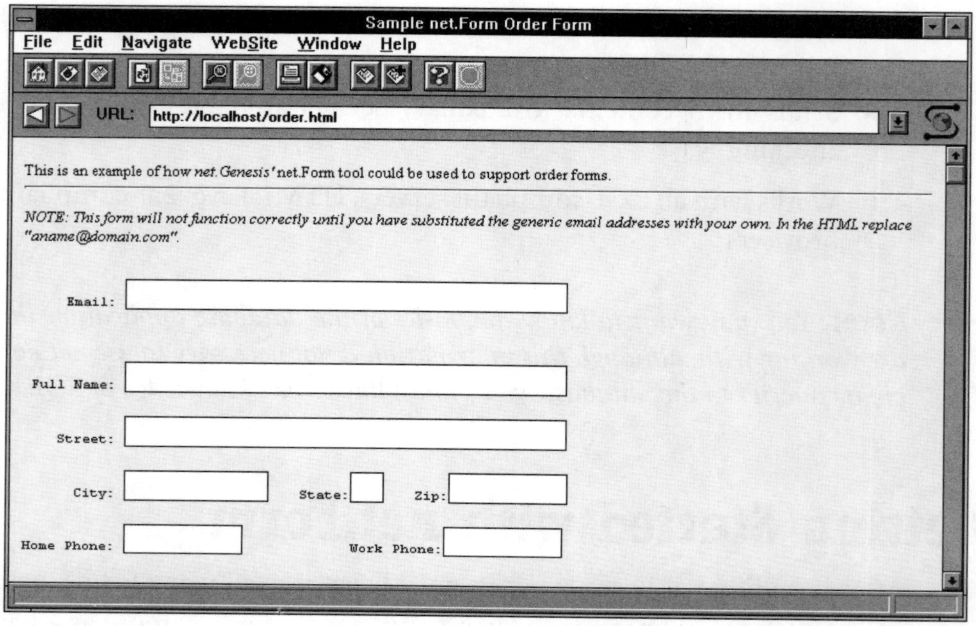

FIGURE 15.1 The net.Form order form template.

To see the HTML tags behind any of these forms, you can choose to view the source file from your Web browser. For example, Figure 15.2 shows the HTML document for the order form as it appears in a Web browser.

You can modify any of these templates using any HTML editor. For example, if you use the HotDog HTML Editor that comes with WebSite Professional, the survey form template appears as shown in Figure 15.3.

To activate any of these forms so that they work with net.Form, you must change the following line at the top of each form:

```
form method=POST action=/cgi-bin/net.Form.pl
```

to the directory containing the net.Form program. For example, using WebSite professional, change the line to the following:

```
form method=POST action=/yourserver/cgi-shl/net.Form.pl
```

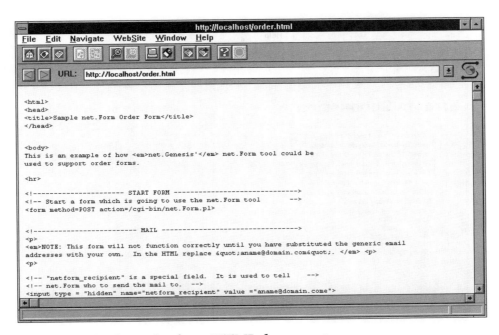

FIGURE 15.2 The order form HTML document.

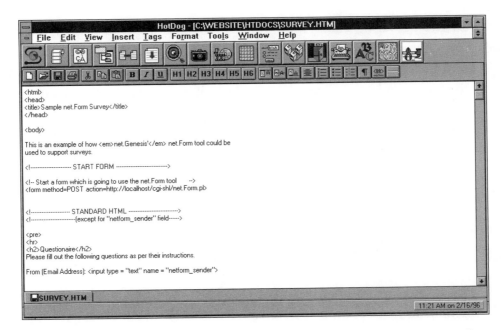

FIGURE 15.3 The Survey form as it appears in the HotDog HTML editor.

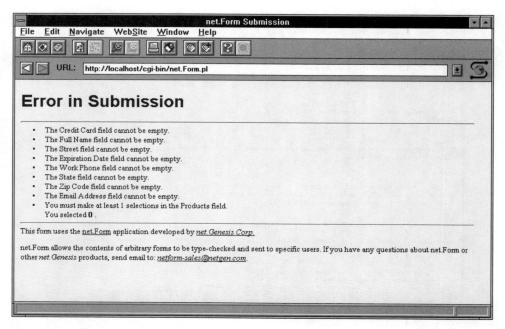

FIGURE 15.4 Error in Submission document generated by net.Form.

To test net.Form, enter http://yourserver/survey.html to display the survey form. Fill out the entries in the survey form, then click on the Send Request button at the bottom of the form. If you incorrectly entered information in the form, net.Form's error checking kicks it back to you with a document like the one shown in Figure 15.4. Use the back button to return to the previous screen in your Web browser and make the corrections. If you filled out the form correctly, net.Form generates a form similar to the one shown in Figure 15.5.

Creating Your Own net.Form-Enabled Form

You can create your own net.Form enabled forms using any HTML editor. net.Form includes an extensive collection of HTML tags for creating forms

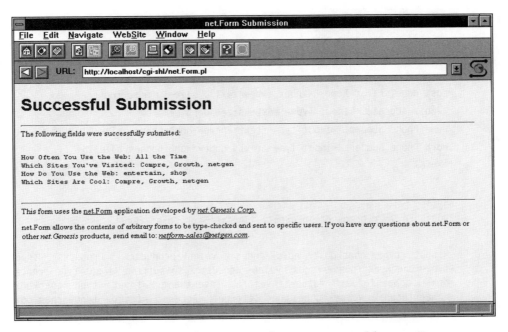

FIGURE 15.5 A successful Submission form generated by net.Form.

and connecting them to net.Form's universal CGI script. The following sections highlight key HTML tags used with net.Form.

The contents of netform.feedback.html have been reproduced below. Notice that the text contains only standard HTML attributes.

```
<html>
<head>
<title>Sample net.Form Feedback Form</title>
</head>

<body>
<h1>Sample net.Form Feedback Form</h1>
```

This tutorial demonstrates how net.Genesisl net.Form tool can be used to support feedback forms.

```
<hr>
<form method=POST action="myUrl">
```

```
<input type="hidden" name="send_to"
value='jane@nowhere.com>

<pre>
Last Name, First Name: <input type="text", size=30 name="name">
E-mail Address: <input type="text" size=30 name="from">
Home Phone Number: <input type="text" name="home_phone" size=13>
Work Phone Number: <input type="text" name="work_phone" size=13>
</pre>

<hr>
What are your areas of interest? (Choose 3 or less):<br>

<input type="checkbox" name="focus" value="products"> Products <input
type="checkbox" name="focus" value="consult"> Consulting <input type="check-
box" name="focus" value="invest"> Investment <input type="checkbox"
name="focus" value="access"> Internet Access <input type="checkbox"
name="focus" value="support"> Support <P>

What products are you interested in? (Choose 1 or more):<br>

<input type="checkbox" name="product" value="form"> net.Form <input
type="checkbox" name="product" value="thread"> net.Thread <input
type="checkbox" name="product" value="report"> net.Report
<hr>

Do you have any specific questions? <textarea rows=4 cols=60 name="comments">
</textarea>

<input type="submit" value="OK">
</form>

<hr>
This form uses <a href="http://www.netgen.com/"><em>net.Genesis</em></a>
net.Form product.

</body>
</html>
```

Adding the E-mail Support Using net.Form Tags

This section shows you how to take the tutorial file and add commands that instruct net.Form to send mail out when users fill out the form. In particular, net.Form allows you to control to whom the mail is sent, from whom it appears to come, and what the subject line is for the message. All net.Form commands must appear within the <form> portion of the HTML. If net.Form commands appear before the <form> tag or after the </form> tag, they will not be passed to the net.Form processing engine.

Specify net.Form as the Form's Processor

The first step to taking advantage of net.Form's capabilities is to tell the browser where to send the data submitted by the user. As with any form, the HTML must specify which CGI script will process the form. To accomplish this, change the line

```
<form method=POST action="myURL">
```

to

```
<form method=POST action="directory path for the net.Form.pl file">
```

The entry "*directory path for the net.Form.pl file*" assumes that net.Form has been installed in your server's cgi-bin directory. For example, if you're using WebSite, the path will be /cgi-shl/net.Form.pl.

Specifying an E-mail Address

One of the simplest and yet most useful functionalities performed by net.Form is mailing the contents of a form to specific individuals. net.Form uses a special field, netform_recipient, to specify to whom it should send e-mail. To configure the sample form so that net.Form will mail you the results, change

```
<input type="hidden" name=send_to"value="jane@nowhere.com">
```

to

```
<input type="hidden" name="netform_recipient" value="you@yourserver.com">
```

The net.form_recipient e-mail addresses must match at least one of permissible addresses specified during installation. This setting allows system administrators to control who may receive e-mail passed through net.Form. Also, the values of netform_recipient must be valid e-mail addresses.

Specifying the Subject Line for an E-mail Message

net.Form allows you to easily control the appearance of the header file of the e-mail generated by the form. The e-mail's header information includes fields such as From, To, and Subject. You can set the Subject field using the netform_subject field name. To specify a subject line in our sample feedback form, add the following line of HTML to the file:

```
<input type="hidden" name="netform_subject" value="net.Form Feedback Tutorial">
```

The net.form_subject field is not required to be a hidden input element. You could use another input element type to provide the user with a list of values to choose from or a text field to input any value.

Specifying the From Field of an E-mail Message

In addition to specifying the To and Subject fields for an e-mail message, net.Form allows you to set the From field that shows from whom the mail appears to come through the netform_sender field. To use the user's e-mail address in the From field of the message in our sample form, change the following line of HTML to the file:

```
E-mail Address: <input type="text" size=30 name="from">
```

to

```
E-mail Address: <input type="text" size=30 name="netform_sender">
```

This change will create an input box labeled E-mail Address, which represents the netform_sender field. Any text entered in this field by the user will be used as the value for netform_sender. The e-mail generated by the form will contain the netform_sender value in the From field.

Configuring the Appearance of the E-mail's Body Text

One of the more common uses of net.Form is to allow users to provide Webmasters with feedback about their site, their products, and their services. In such a case, the only piece of information that actually needs to be sent in the body of the e-mail message would be the user's comments. Other information the user enters—e-mail address and the nature of the feedback—can easily be integrated into other parts of the message such as the From field and the Subject line.

Accordingly, the net form_body field is ideal for allowing users to send comments to you. When it is output, the netform_body is specially formatted for this purpose. To take advantage of this special formatting, change the following line in the template file:

```
<textarea rows=4 cols=60 name="comments">
```

to

```
<textarea rows=4 cols=60 name="netform_body">
```

Configuring net.Form's Error Messages

In order to provide plain English error reporting, net.Form allows you to specify labels to use when referring to each of the fields in a form. These labels refer to fields whenever net.Form produces a field-specific error message and when net.Form outputs the contents of a field. To specify a label for a particular field, append the suffix_label to the original field name. Adding a label to the netform_sender field is as easy as adding the line

```
<input type="hidden" name="netform_sender_label" value="E-mail Address">
```

Now, anytime net.Form needs to reference the value of the netform_sender field, the string "E-mail Address" will be displayed as the field's title.

To label the other field names, add the following lines:

```
<input type="hidden" name="name_label" value="Your Name">
<input type="hidden" name="home_phone_label" value="Home Phone">
<input type="hidden" name="work_phone_label" value="Work Phone">
<input type="hidden" name="netform_body_label" value="Body Text">
<input type="hidden" name="product_label" value="Products">
<input type="hidden" name="focus_label" value="Interesting Areas">
```

Now every field name in the form has a useful label for error reporting.

Configuring net.Form's Field Validation Functionality

Now that the form is properly configured to send out e-mail, you can explore another of net.Form's time-saving features: field type checking. net.Form's type-checking capabilities allow you to require that information entered in certain fields be of a specific format. Type-checking options are controlled with the netform_config field.

For example, you may configure net.Form so that it requires that the user enter text in both the netform_sender and home_phone fields before the form is accepted. Also, you can further require that the contents of the netform_sender be in a valid e-mail address format and that the home_phone field obeys the syntax for valid phone numbers. To accomplish this, simply add the following line to your HTML document:

```
<input type="hidden" name="netform_config" value="netform_sender required,
e-mail home_phone required, phone">
```

By adding this single line to your HTML, you have configured net.Form to process the fields of this form appropriately. Without net.Form, you would have had to write a program that validated the fields itself and returned appropriate error messages.

Using still more field configurations, you can require that the name field be filled in and contain only text. The work_phone field can be configured to be optional, but still enforce the requirement that any non-blank value is in the format of a valid phone number. The focus and product checkbox fields can also be given quantitative configurations. Specifying a configuration of "3 –" for the focus field instructs net.Form to require that three or fewer values must be provided. Likewise, specifying the configuration of a product as "1 +" indicates that at least one product checkbox must be checked. You specify all these additions by adding the following line to the HTML:

```
<input  type="hidden"  name="netform_config"  value="name  required,  alpha
work_phone phone focus 3- product 1+">
```

For convenience, all these configurations can be combined into a single command:

```
<input type="hidden" name="netform_config" value="netform_sender required,
e-mail name required, alpha home_phone required, phone work_phone phone focus
3- product 1+">
```

Returning a Prepared HTML Document Upon Successful Submission

Finally, you can specify the URL of a page to be returned upon successful completion of the form. This URL is defined by the netform _success_message field. To configure net.Form to return a success message, add the following line to your file:

```
<input   type="hidden"   name="netform_success_message"   value="http://
www.netgen.com/products/net.Form/ sample_success.html">
```

If you want, you can specify a different document to be returned by simply modifying the value of netform_success_message.

Save the netform. feedback.html File

Once you save the net form. feedback.html file to disk, you will have success-fully transformed a simple, script-dependent HTML form into a robust, fully

net.Form-enabled feedback form. The contents of net.form.feedback.html
should now read as follows:

```
<html>
<head>
<title>Sample net.Form Feedback Form</title>
</head>

<body>
<h1>Sample net.Form Feedback Form</h1>
This tutorial demonstrates how <em>net.Genesis</em> net.Form tool can be used
to support feedback forms.
<hr>
<form method=POST action ="http://www.your-server.com/cgi-bin/net.Form.pl">

<input type="hidden" name="netform_recipient, value=you@your_server.com">
<input type="hidden" name="netform_subject" value="net.Form Feedback Tutor-
ial">

<pre>
Last Name, First Name: <input type="text" size=30 name="name">
E-mail Address: <input type="text" size=30 name="netfom_sender">
Home Phone Number: <input type="text" name="home_phone" size=13>
Work Phone Number: <input type="text" name="work_phone" size=13>
</pre>

<hr>
What are your areas of interest? (Choose 3 or less):<br>
<input type="checkbox" name="focus" value="products"> Products <input
type="checkbox" name="focus" value="consult"> Consulting <input type="check-
box" name="focus" value="invest"> Investment <input type="checkbox"
name="focus" value="access"> Internet Access <input type="checkbox"
name="focus value="supportf"> Support
<P>

What products are you interested in? (Choose 1 or more):<br>
<input type="checkbox" name="product" value="form"> net.Form <input
type="checkbox" name="product" value="thread"> net.Thread <input
type="checkbox" name="Product" value="report"> net.Report
```

```
<hr>

Do you have any specific questions?

<textarea rows=4 cols=60 name="netform_body"> </textarea>

<input type="submit" value="OK">
<input type="hidden" name="name_label" value="Your Name">
<input type="hidden" name="home_phone_label" value="Home Phone">
<input type="hidden" name="work_phone_label" value="Work Phone">
<input type="hidden" name="netform_sender_label" value="E-mail Address">
<input type="hidden" name="netform_body_label" value="Body Text">
<input type="hidden" name="product_label" value="Products">
<input type="hidden" name="focus_label" value="Interesting Areas">
<input type="hidden" name="netform_config" value="netform_sender required,
e-mail name required, alpha home_phone required, phone work_phone phone focus
3- product
1+">
<input            type="hidden"            name="netform_success_message"
value="http://www.netgen.com/products/netform/
sample_success.html">
</form>
<hr>
This form uses <a href="http://www.netgen.com"> <em>net.Genesis</em></a>
net.Form product.
</body>
</html>
```

Accessing the net.Form-Compatible Form

Once you have completed all the modifications and saved the file down, you can test net.Form by using a Web browser to load the form—either by opening the file locally or by accessing it through your Web server and submitting the form. The easiest way to test the behavior of a net.Form-compatible form is to submit it without any information. The resultant error messages will demonstrate the form's field configurations as well as its field labels.

net.Form Fields

net.Form acts as a generalized CGI library. All net.Form functions are controlled via special fields and values encoded in standard HTML. net.Form recognizes certain reserved field names. For clarity, all of net.Form's reserved fieldnames begin with the string netform. Because net.Form treats these fields specially, you should not use any fieldnames beginning with the string netform unless you are invoking a net.Form command. Examples of reserved fieldnames include netform_sender and netform_recipient. net.Form supports reserved field names that are used to support the following functions:

- Data Pre-Processing/Validation
- Data Post-Processing
- Sending E-mail
- Formatting the output
- Connecting to databases

Data Pre-Processing/Validation

net.Form allows form authors to specify restrictions on what data should be considered valid inputs from a form. This allows the contents of a form to be validated before any further processing is performed. Using net.Form's data validation mechanism can ensure that all necessary data is provided by the form user and is in a usable format. All the data pre-processing and validation are controlled through the netform_config field. net.Form includes a large collection of type-checking options that you use in conjunction with the netform_config field.

Data Post-Processing

After net.Form successfully performs data validation, the contents of the form can be further processed. net.Form's post-processing features allow form authors to control the server's response upon form submission. The post-processing reserved fields include the following:

- netform_exec
- netform_database_file
- netform_database_layout
- netform_process_script
- netform_success_message
- netform_recipient

Sending E-mail

One of net.Form's primary response mechanisms is e-mail. Using reserved fields, net.Form offers you the ability to e-mail a form's contents and to specify the recipients, sender, and subject. As a result, you can control the appearance of e-mail using HTML. The reserved e-mail configuration fields are as follows:

- netform_recipient
- netform_sender
- netform_subject
- netform_body
- netform_date

Formatting the Output

net.Form allows a user to specify formatting information that will control how net.Form outputs the contents of form fields. All the formatting mechanisms are controlled through the following fields:

- netform_sequence
- Field Labels
- netform_database_file

- netform_database_layout
- netform_database_format
- netform_database_delim

Connecting to Databases

net.Form allows users to connect to ODBC-compliant databases to perform a number of actions. The mechanisms for this interaction are controlled through the following field and files:

- netform_template_file
- Template files
- Query files

Overview of Connecting to Databases

net.Form provides the ability to communicate with ODBC-compliant databases. To use this functionality, you must meet the following conditions:

- You must already have ODBC drivers properly installed on the machine you are using to run net.Form for each database server with which you want to communicate.

- You must already have an ODBC administrator properly installed on the machine you are using to run net.Form.

- You must already have defined the data sources to which you want to connect.

If this is the first time you are setting up your ODBC drivers, consult your ODBC driver installation documentation for instructions on establishing connectivity. After you have established an ODBC connection between the database server and your computer, you can use net.Form to connect your databases to the Web.

Including Database Interaction in Forms

The netform_template_field is used to specify the name of a template file that net.Form should read after the form is submitted successfully. A template file contains the queries, the form, and the variables requested from the database and displays them in a table of drop-down menus and text fields.

The syntax for this entry is as follows:

```
<input type="hidden" name="netform_template_file" value="template_filename">
```

For example, assuming that file named sales.htx exists in the default template directory specified in the net.Form configuration file, you might enter the following:

```
<input type="hidden" name="netform_template_file" value="sales.htx">
```

where sale.htx is the template file to which net.Form writes the values from the input form.

Chapter 16

Customer Support Using Discussion Groups

Discussion groups within a Web site operate in a manner similar to that for the Internet's network newsgroups. Users post messages to forums centered on specific topics or functions. Using a discussion program, you can enhance your Web site by creating moderated discussion groups for your customers, vendors, or visitors. The big advantage of discussion groups is they give your business the opportunity to communicate directly with people connecting to your Web site. You can glean valuable feedback from users and add content to your site at the same time.

Opening Up Your Web Site to Discussions

Most companies today have established Web sites and use them as sources of customer interaction and feedback. To attract large numbers of repeat users, sites must be dynamic and interactive. Enabling site users to easily interact with companies and each other requires improved site quality and communications. Along with this discussion group functionality, site providers need an easy, efficient means of managing discussion areas.

Using a third-party Web server application, such as WebBoard or net.Thread, allows you to host discussion forums accessible through a Web browser interface. In addition to providing a threaded, outline-view organization of messages in a forum, these products allow you to structure any number of forums within a hierarchy, as well as to perform numerous administrative functions. You can use these products for specialized discussion forums, online customer support, internal project planning, and tracking.

From the user perspective, working with discussion groups in a Web site creates a friendly and easy-to-use communications medium. Navigating and working these discussion groups is made easy with the use of forms and buttons for point-and-click correspondence, letting users can communicate with your business or with other users. These tools provide a collection of administrative tools to allow you control over the content of messages to keep out the "crazies." The friendly user interface of Web-based discussion groups enables users to easily follow and navigate through online discussions.

net.Thread Overview

net.Thread links discussion groups into a Web site's existing HTML structure. Users select messages to view, based on message titles, posters, and time stamps. The message text appears in its entirety, along with any responses or replies, and users can investigate a different thread, navigate the current thread, or post their own message. A site administrator can create and manage net.Thread discussion areas using any Web browser. After a simple login procedure, net.Thread displays a hierarchical message tree that illustrates conversation flows.

Basic Definitions

Before you begin working with net.Thread, it's a good idea to become familiar with the basic terminology used for discussion groups. The following are the key terms to understand for working with net.Thread.

Hierarchy

net.Thread information is organized in a tree-structured hierarchy similar to an organization chart or outline structure. Each message has a parent message above it in the hierarchy and may have any number of child messages that represent replies to the message (in the example below, NBA is the parent of Message 1). For consistency, discussion forums and groups are also part of this hierarchy and make up the top-most levels of it. By starting at the top-level group in the hierarchy, you can access any message maintained by net.Thread by successively choosing child messages (or groups) until you reach the desired message. For example:

net.Genesis Sports Information Service

    NBA

        (Message 1)

        (Message 2)

    NFL

        (Message 1)

           (Reply to Message 1)

        (Message 2)

MLB

NHL

World Wide Web Discussions

   (Message 1)

   (Message 2)

General Discussion

   HTML 3.0 Standard

Group

A group is a set of messages or groups used for organizing the discussion topics in your net.Thread installation. The top level of the hierarchy is a group, as are all the items immediately below it in the hierarchy. In the example above, all the items not in parentheses are groups. Groups that have actual messages as their immediate children are referred to as discussion forum groups. In the example above, NBA and NFL are discussion forum groups, both containing messages.

Message

A message is the basic unit of information in net.Thread. It contains a title, message contents, author, and a date. Located within the net.Thread message hierarchy, a message has a parent message above it and may have children (replies) below it.

Parent

The parent is the message or group above a given message in the hierarchy. Every message and group, except at the top level, has a parent. In the example above, the parent of MLB is Sports Information Service.

Child

A message or group below a given message or group in the hierarchy is called a child. Any message or group can have any number of children. Messages and discussion forum groups may have only messages as children, while nondiscussion forum groups may have only other groups as children. In the example above, MLB is a child of Sports Information Service.

Discussion Forum Group

A discussion forum group has messages as children. Real discussion activity takes place in these groups; other groups are used to organize specific topics. In the example above, NFL is a discussion forum group.

Post

Posting creates a new message at the top of a discussion forum group, or for the Webmaster, it creates a new group within a group. There is no functional difference between post and reply, but at the top of a discussion forum a post generally represents a new discussion thread initiated by the user. In the NFL discussion forum group, Message 1 is a post.

Reply

Replying creates a new message in response to an existing message. This continues and adds to a discussion thread. There is no functional difference between reply and post, but reply is generally used to represent the continuation of a discussion thread rather than the initiation of one. In the NFL Discussion Forum Group, Reply to Message 1 is a reply.

Buttons in net.Thread

net.Thread uses HTML forms as its interface for both Webmasters and users. These forms include buttons that perform a variety of functions. Table 16.1 describes the functions of all the buttons in net.Thread forms.

TABLE 16.1 Button Reference for net.Thread

Button	Function (s)
Post	Creates a new message or group as a child of the currently viewed group.

TABLE 16.1 Continued

Button	Function (s)
	Users: Available only when viewing the top level of a discussion group.
	Webmaster: When viewing a group that is the parent of other groups, allows the creation of a new group or forum. When viewing the top level of a discussion forum, functions normally.
Reply	Creates a new message as the next "child" of the currently viewed message.
	Users: Available only when viewing a message.
	Webmaster: Functions normally.
Next	Views the next message (goes down one message in the outline display) from the message currently viewed.
	Users: Available only when there is a next message.
	Webmaster: Functions normally.
Previous	Views the previous message (goes up one message in the outline display) from the message currently viewed.
	User: Available only when there is a previous message.
	Webmaster: Functions normally.
Up	Allows users to go to the most immediate parent group of the current message.
	Users: Not available at the top level of the group to jump to the next highest group.
	Webmaster: Takes webmaster to the next highest group when at the top of one group.
Thread	Views the very top level of the site's thread hierarchy.
	Users: Not available at top level of hierarchy.
	Webmaster: Functions normally.
Help	Views a static help display.
	Users: None.
	Webmaster: Functions normally.

TABLE 16.1 Continued

Button	Function (s)
Depth +	Increases the display depth (the number of levels of hierarchy shown in the outline below the current message) by one unit. **Users:** Available only when viewing a message or a discussion forum. **Webmaster:** Functions normally.
Depth -	Reduces the display depth (the number of levels of hierarchy shown in the outline below the current message) by one unit. **Users:** Available only when viewing a message or a discussion forum. **Webmaster:** Functions normally.
Settings	Accesses the login screen so that the login name, display depth, and last login date can be modified. Returns to currently viewed message after settings are changed. **Users:** None. **Webmaster:** Should not be used to leave administrator mode (see "Logout").
Edit	Modifies a message or a group. **Users:** Not available. **Webmaster:** If viewing a message, accesses the message update form; if viewing a group, accesses the group update form.
Delete	Deletes a message or a group. **Users:** Not available. **Webmaster:** Marks a message as deleted, such that the message (and any responses to hierarchy below it) is no longer displayed anywhere in the outline. A confirmation is required. Deleted messages are not completely lost until they are purged.
Delete Old	Deletes messages older than a specified number of days. **Users:** Not available.

TABLE 16.1 Continued

Button	Function (s)
	Webmaster: Checks all messages at or below the one currently viewed to determine whether they are older than specified age. Displays a list of titles and requires confirmation. Messages are only deleted due to age if all messages below them in the hierarchy are also old.
Purge	Permanently removes deleted messages.
	Users: Not available.
	Webmaster: Operates on messages at or below the one currently viewed. Displays a list of titles and requires confirmation. Once messages are purged, they are irretrievably lost.
Logout	Cancels administrator access.
	Users: Not available.
	Webmaster: Cancels the administrator access and returns to the Login form at the top level of the site's hierarchy. For security reasons, it is important to log out rather than change the login name or exit the Web browser.

The Login Form

The login form is presented to both users and the webmaster for entering discussion areas. Figure 16.1 shows the net.Thread Login form as it appears for users, and Figure 16.2 shows the expanded net.Thread Login form.

The following describe the fields in the login form:

- **Login Name:** For administration, this field must be "webmaster."

- **Maximum Display Depth:** This field shows number of outline levels to display under the currently viewed message. It may be useful to set this to a high number, perhaps 10, while operating as the administrator.

- **Last Login:** Messages posted on or after the Last Login date will be marked as New when displayed.

- **Password:** The administrator password, initially webmaster, should be changed at time of installation.

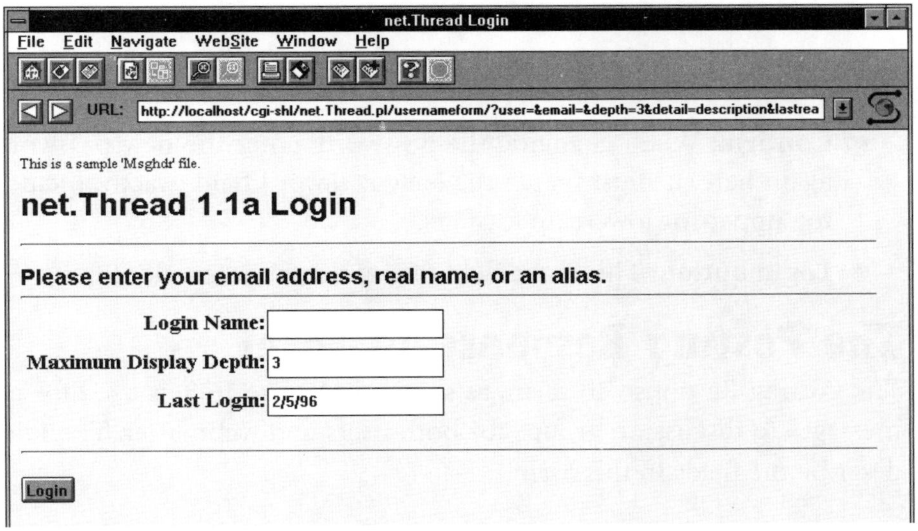

FIGURE 16.1 The standard user net.Thread Login form.

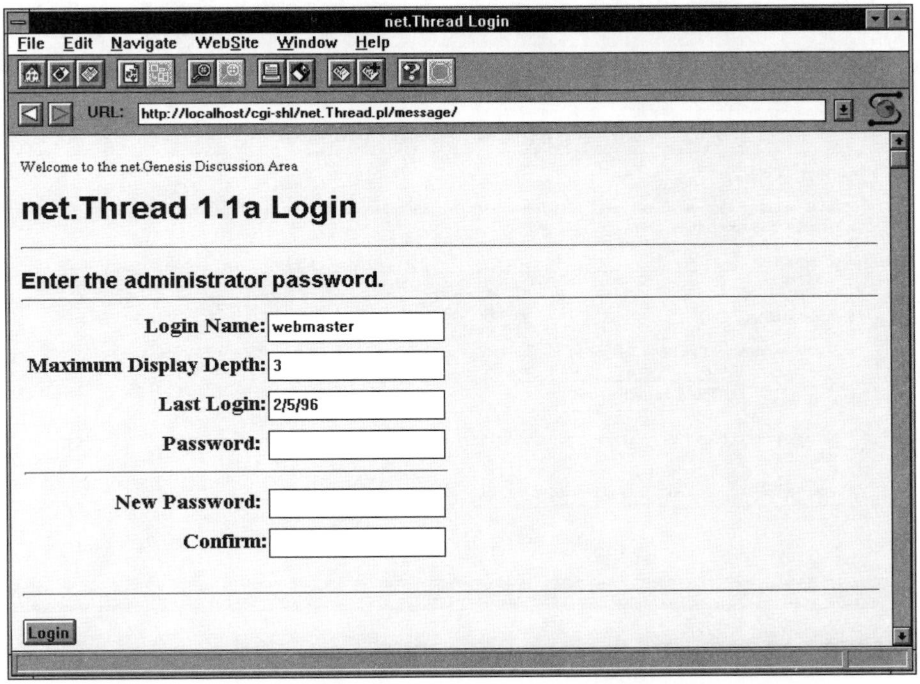

FIGURE 16.2 The expanded webmaster net.Thread Login form.

- **New Password:** When changing the password, enter the new password here. The current password and confirmation must be correctly entered.

- **Confirm:** When changing the password, enter the new password again here. It must match the New Password field exactly, including upper- or lowercase formats.

- **Login button:** This is the field that executes webmaster login.

The Posting Response To Form

The Posting Response To form, as shown in Figure 16.3, is used for posting messages to discussion groups for both users and webmaster. The following describe the fields in this form:

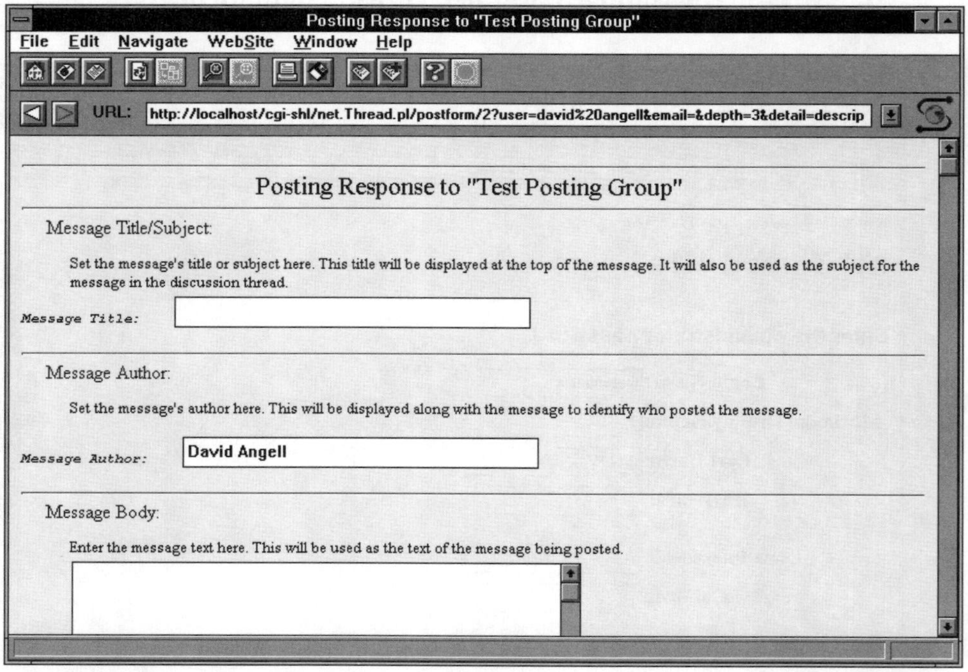

FIGURE 16.3 The Posting Response To form.

- **Message Title/Subject:** This field defaults to the existing message title and allows any changes. Unlike in the post message, any changes are interpreted as HTML.

- **Message Author:** This field defaults to the existing author of a message. Unlike in the post message form, any changes are interpreted as HTML.

- **Message Body:** This field defaults to the existing contents of a message. This will include any HTML codes that were added by net.Thread in initially formatting the message. The contents will be interpreted directly as HTML.

- **Formatting Options:** This field specifies the desired formatting for the message.

- **Post this message:** This button posts the form. Note that there is no preview for the Update form because if you want to, you can simply back up and edit again.

- **Clear Form:** This field restores all fields to their original values from when the form was first displayed. This may or may not function as you expect if you have already pressed Update.

The Group Configuration Update Form

The Group Configuration Update form, as shown in Figure 16.4, is available to the webmaster for defining discussion groups and forums, and it's accessed via the Edit button. The following describes the fields in this form:

- **Group Title:** This field will be displayed in the group and message hierarchy but not when the group is viewed. It is also used as the document title for the returned HTML.

- **Group Header:** This field is shown at the top of the display when the group itself is viewed. It can include text, HTML codes, references to images, links, etc. The group display can be thought of as a "homepage" for the group, and the group header is where you would enter the contents of this homepage.

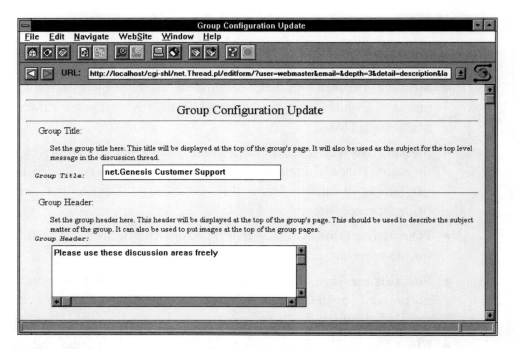

FIGURE 16.4 The Group Configuration Update form.

- **Group Footer:** The group footer is similar to the header, except that it is displayed immediately after (below) the message outline.

- **Message Header:** This field contains text, HTML codes, references to images, links, etc., to be displayed at the top of every message in the group and on the Login form when you are logging in to any message in the group. For a parent group, the only time the message header is displayed is when you are logging in directly to that parent group.

- **Group Password (Optional):** This field specifies the password for restricting access to a group.

- **Users will post messages to this group:** Select this radio button if this group represents a discussion forum of messages posted by users and will not have any other groups below it in the hierarchy. It is available only when the group is initially created.

- **This group will be the parent of subgroups:** Select this radio button if the group will have more specific groups beneath it in the hierarchy and will not have any messages posted directly to it by users. It is available only when the group is initially created.

- **Update this Group:** Store your changes or entries in this field.

- **Clear Values:** Select this radio button to restores all fields to their original values when the form was first displayed.

Setting Up net.Thread

A net.Thread site is administered through your Web browser. It provides for a password-protected administrative mode, which is similar to the normal user mode but provides additional button selections. To access the administrator mode, do the following:

1. Using your Web browser go to one of the following URLs depending on your Web server software:

   ```
   http://yourserver/cgi-shl/net.Thread.pl for O'Reilly's WebSite
   Professional
   ```

   ```
   http://yourserver/cgi-bin/net.Thread.exe for Netscape's Commerce Server
   ```

A sample "Title" file form appears, as shown in Figure 16.5.

2. Click on the Settings button. The net.Thread Login Form appears (see Figure 16.1).

3. In the Login Name field, type webmaster. This field is case sensitive, so make sure you type entirely in lowercase.

4. Click on the Login button. The form will be refreshed, this time displaying the expanded net.Thread Login form with Password, New Password, and Confirm fields.

5. In the Password field, enter your administrator password. Remember that the password is case sensitive.

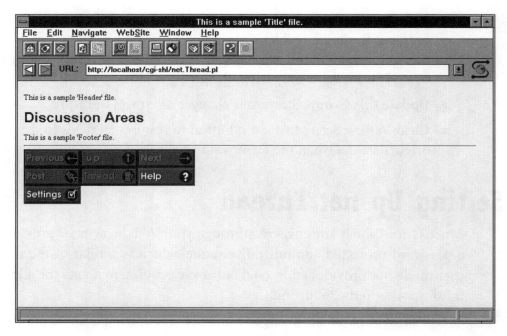

FIGURE 16.5 This is a sample "Title" file form.

6. Press Login again. You are now logged in for secure administrator access. The form in Figure 16.6 appears.

Note: *As a security precaution, your administrator login is valid for 15 minutes. If this time period expires and you attempt to execute an operation, net.Thread will request that you log in again. You need only type the password and press Login, and the operation you selected previously will proceed. Upon your successful login, the net.Thread root appears. You can change this default setting by editing the net.Thread configuration file.*

7. Click the Edit button to display the Group Configuration Update form to create an active net.Thread area.

8. Replace the text in the Group Title field with the text you would like to appear as the root document's HTML title (for example, "net.Genesis Customer Support"). This title will appear in the browser, on hotlists, and in other places.

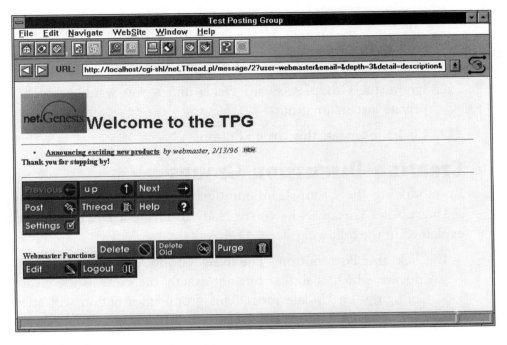

FIGURE 16.6 The webmaster form.

9. Move to the Group Header text field. The information you enter here appears at the top of the group's page. Note that this header information is interpreted as HTML, so any HTML tags in the header field will be rendered appropriately. For example, you can enter:

```
<strong>Please use these discussion areas freely</strong><br>
```

10. Move to the Group Footer field. Footer information appears at the bottom of the Group (but before the button bar). The footer information is also interpreted as HTML. Replace the text in the Footer field with your own. For example, enter:

```
<em>Thank you for visiting!</em><p>
```

11. Move to the Message Header field. The information you enter here appears at the top of the login screen. The message header is

interpreted as HTML. Replace the text in the Message Header field with your own. For example, enter:

Welcome to the net.Genesis Discussion Area

12. Ignore the Group Password Fields unless you want to create a private discussion group.

13. Click the Update this Group button.

Creating Discussion Groups

By modifying the Group Configuration Update form, you have finished setting up net.Thread. Now you're ready to create a Discussion Group as explained in the following steps;

1. Click the Post button. The New Group Configuration form appears, which is similar but not exactly the same as the Group Configuration Update form. This group information will affect the Discussion Groups you create beneath the root Group.

2. Replace the text in the Group Title field with your own text. For example, enter Test

Posting Group

3. Change the text in the Group Header field. For example, enter:

```
<h1><img src="/thread-images/logo.gif">
```

Welcome to the TPG</hl><hr>

The /thread/images entry reflects the default storage of net.Thread images that was established when you installed net.Thread.

4. Add text to the Footer field. For example, enter:

```
<strong>Thank you for stopping by!</strong><p>
```

5. Leave the Message Header field blank. When you are creating new groups, the Message Header is displayed when a user attempts to access the group directly from outside net.Thread, as well as at the top of each posting.

6. Leave the Users will post messages to this group radio button selected. This specifies that there will be a discussion forum group, as opposed to a group containing further groups.

7. Click the Create this Group button.

8. Click on the Thread button. You will go back to the root Group and see the that Test Posting Group has been added to the root hierarchy. You have created a discussion group that allows users to post new messages to your net.Thread discussion area.

To create a group of groups, follow the above procedure until step 6. Instead of leaving Users will post messages to this group selected, select This group will be the parent of subgroups. The resulting group can contain only other groups, as opposed to messages. This setup is useful for creating hierarchical discussion areas, such as the following:

General Discussion

Sports

    Soccer

    US

    Europe

    South America

Basketball

    NCAA (messages)

    NBA

        Teams

            Boston (messages)

            Chicago (messages)

            Sacramento (messages)

        Leagues

Football

   NCAA

   NFL

   CFL

———**Note:** *Creating a group will be your only opportunity to specify the group type. Once the group is created, this status cannot be changed. Note also that the top level is always setup as the parent of subgroups.*

Posting Messages

You've created a discussion group, but there isn't any content to it. To get things rolling, you should enter a few messages. The following explains how to post messages to a discussion group.

1. From the root Discussion Areas page, enter the Test Posting Group by clicking on it.

2. Click on the Post button. The Posting Response to form appears.

3. In the Message Title/Subject field, enter your message subject line.

4. Leave the Message Author field as webmaster unless you want to use another name.

5. In the Message Body field, enter your text message.

6. Leave the Format the text nicely for me radio button selected. This will autoformat the text for you so that net.Thread renders your message.

7. Leave the Post without previewing box unchecked.

8. Click the Post this message button. You will see a preview of the message, as shown in Figure 16.7.

9. If you want to change your message, use your browser's Back button. Otherwise, click the Post button.

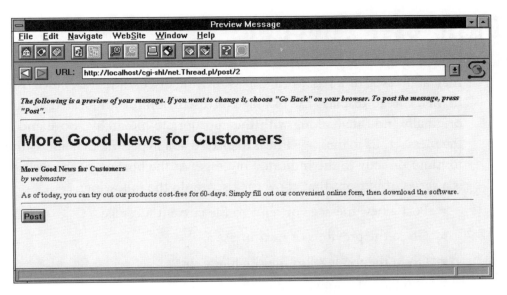

FIGURE 16.7 The Preview Message form.

10. Click the Test Posting Group link at the top of the document. This will return you to the top of the Test Posting Group hierarchy. Notice that your post now appears in the group's message hierarchy.

Deleting Old Messages

Occasionally, you'll need to delete messages from the hierarchy. Remember that deleting a message also deletes all of its replies as well. To delete a message, do the following:

1. View the post by clicking on the link.

2. When the message is displayed, check the Delete button. net.Thread will confirm that you want to delete the displayed message and all its replies.

3. To delete the message and remove it from the hierarchy, click the Delete button at the top of the confirmation page. You will then be returned to the top level of the Test Posting Group.

Basic User Functions

Users log into the net.Thread discussion areas by using their real names, e-mail addresses, or a password, if it's a private discussion area. Once users log in, net.Thread displays the message or discussion forum located at the URL originally indicated, along with the appropriate hierarchy above and below the message. Each message title is displayed as a hyperlink that allows the user to jump directly to the indicated message. At the bottom of the web display is a series of buttons that allow the user to do the following:

- Post a new message or reply to the current message
- Go to the previous or next message
- Go to the top level of the site hierarchy
- Display help information
- Change login settings

Posting a Message

Users post new messages by pressing either the Post button (from the top level of the Forum) or the Reply button (from a specific message). A form is displayed that allows the user to enter a title (which will appear on the message outline as well as when the message is displayed), the sender (defaulting to the name used for login, but allowing changes), and the text of the message. The user can specify whether the message is one of the following types:

- Normal text in which double-blank lines will be treated as HTML paragraphs, words surrounded by asterisks will be displayed <strong> (*strong* = **strong**), and words surrounded by under-scores will be displayed emphasized (_emphasize_= *emphasized*)
- HTML, in which net.Thread assumes that HTML codes are already included in the message
- Preformat, in which net.Thread displays the message in a fixed-pitch font exactly as entered by the user

Unless the user indicates otherwise with the provided checkbox, the message will be previewed before it is actually posted. This is particularly useful in the case of HTML messages, which might not display as expected.

Changing Settings

The user can change certain settings related to the display of messages. Specifically:

- Login name: This is used as the default value for the From field when a message is posted.

- Level: By pressing the appropriate button. (See Table 16.1 for a complete listing of net.Thread buttons and their functions.)

- Maximum display depth: This is the number of levels of message hierarchy to display below the currently viewed message. The default is three. Note that the maximum display depth can also be directly increased or reduced by one.

- Last Login: Messages posted on or after the date specified here will be indicated as New!

Administering net.Thread

Your net.Thread site is administered through your Web browser. You use the same password-protected administrative mode you used to configure net.Thread. Using your Web browser, go to the URL for your net.Thread, then click on the Settings button. In the Login Name field, type webmaster and click the Login button. Enter your password and click on Login again. You are now logged in for administrator access.

Your administrator login is valid for 15 minutes. If this time period expires and you attempt to execute an operation, net.Thread will request that you log in again. You need only type the password and press Login, and the operation you selected previously will proceed. This feature is designed to enhance the security protection afforded by the system.

You can change your webmaster password at any time after logging in as webmaster by entering a password in the New Password field, then entering the new password again in the Confirm field.

Setting Up Groups and Forums

You can create any number of forums and organize them in a hierarchical, tree-structured fashion. This hierarchy is best determined in advance. For example:

Sports Discussions

    NBA

        Celtics

        76ers

        Bulls

    NFL

        Patriots

        Eagles

    NHL

        Bruins

    MLB

        Red Sox

        White Sox

To begin, log in as webmaster. To create a new branch of the discussion-forum tree, press the Post button. The form that appears is the same as that used to edit group information, with one exception: at the very bottom of the form is a pair of radio buttons where you indicate whether the new group will be a discussion forum in which users will post messages or a parent group that has other groups branching from it. This is your only opportunity to specify the type of group. Once the group is created, this status cannot be changed. In the example above, when creating the groups NBA, NFL, NHL, and MLB, you would select "This group will be the parent of subgroups." For the other groups, such as Celtics, Bruins, and Red Sox, you would select "Users will post messages to this group." Note that the top level is always set up as the parent of subgroups. Enter the group information and press the Update the Group button. The group will be created and displayed. You can modify the group information at any time by pressing the Edit button.

Editing and Deleting Messages

While logged in as webmaster, you can modify and delete any message or group in the hierarchy (except that you may not delete the top level). You may wish to do this because a group or message thread is no longer in use or because you want to exercise editorial control over the message content.

To edit a message, view that message by selecting it from the hierarchy. Press the Edit button, and a form will be displayed with the current contents of the message. Modify the contents of the message as desired and press Update. If you wish to erase the contents of the message, but want to retain its responses in the message outline, click the checkbox "Check here to erase message" prior to pressing Update.

To delete a message, view the message and press the Delete button. net.Thread will redisplay the message and will ask you to confirm the deletion by pressing the Delete button a second time.

Note: *Because of the hierarchical nature of discussion forums, deleting a message also deletes the entire hierarchy below it (all children associated with the deleted message). Be sure to use this feature carefully.*

Purging Messages

Deleted messages are not completely removed from the system until they are purged. Use net.Thread's purge feature only when you're confident that all the messages you've deleted won't be needed in the future. Purge operates only on the message hierarchy below the message currently viewed, so if you wish to purge an entire forum you must be viewing the top level of that forum. To purge the entire message database, go to the top level of the hierarchy by clicking on the Thread button, then use the Purge button from there.

net.Thread also provides a Delete Old capability so that you can more easily manage the size of the message database. Like Purge and Delete, Delete Old operates on the entire hierarchy below the message you are currently viewing. View the desired message and click on the Delete old button. net.Thread will ask you how many days old a message must be to be included in the deletion, and when you press Proceed, it will display the titles of the messages it intends to delete. You must press Delete old again to confirm the deletion of these messages.

Updating the Group Hierarchy

The hierarchy of your discussion forums can be modified to a large extent after it has been created. In certain cases, however, it will be necessary to delete and re-create groups to achieve the desired new hierarchy. When logged in as webmaster, you can do the following:

- Delete a group. View the group and press the Delete button. All groups and messages below the indicated group in the hierarchy will be deleted.

- Modify group information. View the group and press the Edit button.

- Create new groups. View the group that will be the parent of the new group, and press the Post button. Note that the parent must have been specified as the parent of groups rather than as a place where users post messages (if not, when you press the Post button, you will simply be posting a message to the group).

It is not possible to create a group below a point where users post messages. If you must modify the hierarchy in this way, it will be necessary to delete the affected messages and groups and create them from scratch.

Providing Users with Access URLs

To advertise your discussion forums, you must provide a URL in which each forum can be accessed. To determine the appropriate URL, simply view the desired discussion forum or message. Provide the entire URL up to but not including the question mark Typically, this URL will be something like this:

```
http://www.netgen.com/cgi-bin/net.Thread/message/3/1
```

net.Thread will automatically request that users log in and will then direct them to the indicated message location. Keep in mind that once you have advertised this URL, you will want to avoid deleting it or else users will experience an error condition when they try to access it.

Changing net.Thread Default Settings

net.Thread's configuration file lives in the directory with the net.Thread program files, which you specified during its installation. For example, if you installed net.Thread for use with WebSite Professional, the configuration file is in the directory WebSite/cgi-shl/. The configuration file named net.Thread,config.pl is a text file that you can bring up in Notepad. Figure 16.8 shows the net.Thread configuration file in Notepad. Each of the settings is described in this file.

The following describe some of the net.Thread features that can be activated in its configuration file:

- **Message Sort Direction.** The administrator can now specify how threads are sorted, choosing least recent to most recent or vice versa.

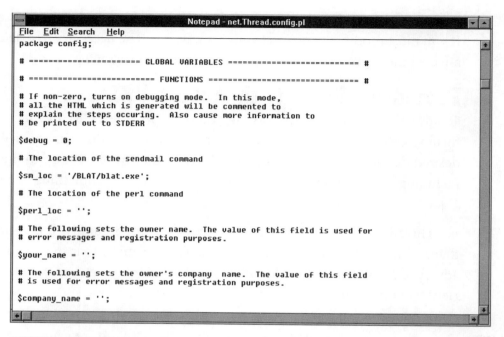

FIGURE 16.8 The net.Thread.config.pl configuration file in Notepad.

- **Strict HTML Checking.** net.Thread can explicitly restrict which HTML tags users can use when posting messages to net.Thread. If this option is turned on, net.Thread scans all incoming messages and automatically strips them of any prohibited HTML tags.

- **Moderation.** net.Thread has full moderation abilities. If you turn on moderation, all messages that are posted will be queued for approval from the Webmaster. When the Webmaster logs into net.Thread, he or she will be able to see all the messages awaiting approval and can approve or reject them.

- **Undelete.** net.Thread can undelete messages that were previously deleted (but not purged). The Webmaster logging into net.Thread will be able to see all those messages and can undelete any of them.

- **Button Bar Location.** net.Thread allows you to place the button bar at the top or bottom of the screen.

- **Administrative E-mail Notification.** net.Thread lets the webmaster or other listed users automatically receive e-mail each time a new message is posted. This is intended to make it easier to administer the threads.

- **Button suppression.** net.Thread's appearance can be simplified if many of the nonessential buttons in net.Thread are suppressed. These include the detail buttons (Depth+ and Depth-), the Next and Previous buttons, and the Settings button.

- **Configurable User Login.** This feature lets Webmasters control whether users have to log into net.Thread and allows them to turn off the standard user login screen.

- **Configurable List Element.** This feature lets you specify whether net.Thread should present the threads using numbered lists or bulleted lists.

Chapter 17

Bells, Whistles, and Future Directions

Beyond the core tools for creating forms, offering discussion groups, and tracking Web site usage, there is a growing number of enhancement tools to improve the delivery of information to Web users. Additionally, new technologies are just over the horizon, promising to have a big impact on Web sites. This chapter surveys the key enhancement tools and future technological directions of the Web.

Bells and Whistles

HTML documents are fine for basic information delivery, but they're just a starting point. Three new tools stand out as promising add-ons for delivering multimedia information via Web sites: RealAudio, Shockwave, and Acrobat. The following sections provide an overview of these tools.

The Web Is Alive with the Sound of RealAudio

RealAudio, an audio product from Progressive Networks (http://www.realaudio.com/), is a sound player for Windows. When you select a link to a normal sound file, like the Web's ubiquitous ".au" format, you normally have a long wait before you can hear it because a sound file is generally large and you must completely download the sound before a player will begin playing it. But a RealAudio file (the extension is ".ram" or ".ra") begins playing within just a few seconds of your initiating the transfer. It doesn't matter whether it's 10 seconds or 10 hours of sound—playing begins almost immediately, and the sound is played directly as it comes over the network.

What's amazing about RealAudio is the small amount of bandwidth you need to play a RealAudio sound live over the Internet. The bandwidth requirement is only about 10Kbps, just within range of a tiny 14.4K modem. Even better, you can go off and do other things while the sound is playing. RealAudio achieves its efficiency by massively compressing the audio. For example, a 14.0MB au file in RealAudio format takes only about 1.8MB of space. That is a little over 30 minutes of audio. The new version 2.0 has greatly enhanced sound quality over 28.8Kbps connections. You can now hear FM (mono) quality sound and music.

You can add RealAudio capability to your Web server using the RealAudio Server package. Pricing for the server software varies according to the volume it supports. To support 10 simultaneous RealAudio connections, the list price is $1,495. The RealAudio player is distributed free of charge to end users.

MacroMedia's Shockwave

Director and Shockwave for Director together provide powerful tools for creating multimedia on the Internet. Shockwave enables the playback of high-impact multimedia on the Web, transforming Web pages into dynamic, interactive multimedia productions that load as quickly as static image. Shockwave for Director leverages existing multimedia content and converts it for delivery via the Internet at lower bandwidths. Advanced compression speeds delivery over the Net with compression rates of 40 to 60 percent. Macromedia (http://www.macromedia.com/) provides free Shockwave plug-ins for Netscape Navigator and most other browsers.

Electronic Publishing with Adobe Acrobat

HTML is fine for creating documents for Web browsers, but to deliver sophisticated documents that mimic slick publications from the real world, you need to go beyond HTML. The other major criterion for distributing these documents is that they need to be platform independent. In other words, they should be accessible for users operating from Microsoft Windows, Macintosh, and Unix platforms.

Adobe's Acrobat software family of universal electronic publishing tools fits these criteria. Acrobat provides companies the flexibility for adding documents to a Web site without having to learn a new publishing tools. This family of tools lets Webmasters provide documents with the look and feel of those created using desktop publishing programs such as Adobe Photoshop, Adobe PageMaker, FrameMaker, and others. Figure 17.1 shows an example of a Portable Document Format (PDF) document.

These tools allow people to use virtually any authoring application to create information that can be viewed, searched, and printed across all the major platforms. The Adobe PDF, an open, cross-platform file format created by Acrobat software, preserves the fidelity of electronic documents, enabling information to be distributed in a single format across a broad range of media including the World Wide Web, e-mail, intranets, CD-ROM, and print-on-demand systems. The Acrobat software family includes the following tools:

- Acrobat Reader lets users view, navigate through, and print PDF files and includes support for embedded Web links, movies, and sound clips. The Acrobat Reader software is available free of charge from Adobe's Web server at http://www.adobe.com/.

- Acrobat Exchange lets you add value to documents and share them with other Acrobat software users. Beyond the viewing and printing of documents, Exchange lets you annotate, build navigational links into, and add security controls to PDF files.

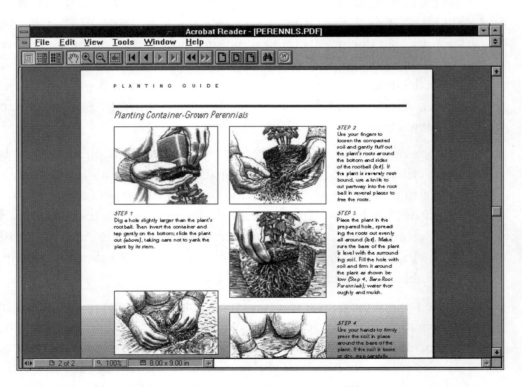

FIGURE 17.1 A sample PDF document as viewed online.

- Acrobat PDF Writer is a driver that enables you to create PDF files from common business applications, such as word processing, spreadsheets, and presentation programs. Creating PDF files is as easy as printing from your application.

- Acrobat Search program provides full-text search capabilities for PDF files that have been indexed with Acrobat Catalog software. Search using Keywords or Boolean logic, or choose special search options, including Thesaurus, Word Stemming, Proximity, Match Case, and Sounds Like.

- Acrobat Distiller converts any PostScript language into PDF. Use it with layout or image editing programs, documents containing high-resolution or Encapsulated PostScript (EPS) artwork or images, or documents containing complex blends or gradient fills.

- Acrobat Catalog creates full-text indexes for collections of PDF files stored on CD-ROM or network servers. Indexes let you find information instantly using Acrobat Search, and they can be automatically updated at regular time intervals of your choice.

- Acrobat Capture is a powerful tool for turning printed documents into PDF files. It converts a scanned image of the printed page into a complete electronic document with word-for-word accuracy and full graphic fidelity. It includes a copy of Acrobat Exchange.

Adobe Acrobat also includes Weblink, a plug-in application for Web publishing, and Movie Tool, which allows multimedia elements to be added to PDF files. Weblink lets authors embed URLs within PDF files, allowing users to access Web links via PDF documents. With Movie tool, authors can easily incorporate multimedia elements into PDF files including QuickTime, AVI video, and audio files. Acrobat includes built-in support for Adobe Type fonts.

Future Technologies

The World Wide Web is the medium for internetworking and intranets, and it will continue to have a bright and exciting future. The leading technologies that promise to have a big impact on the Web and Web servers are Java, virtual reality, and multimedia capabilities. The new HTML 3.0 draft specifications should prove much more robust than the current HTML 2.0. For virtual reality, the Virtual Reality Modeling Language (VRML) promises to transform the Web into a fully interactive 3-D environment. Web servers will be navigated, moving through simulated worlds. Advances in real-time audio and video are making them options for the next generation of bandwidth beyond the 14.4Kbps modems, which still dominate Web connections.

Sun Microsystems' Java

Java is a full-fledged programming language developed by Sun Microsystems. In a typical scenario, a Java program (called an applet) is stored on the Web server. When a Web browser finds a document with a Java applet embedded in it, the applet is transferred over the Internet to the user's computer. The connection to the server is then severed, and the applet begins to run, communicating directly to the Web browser. Think of a Java applet as an inline program, much like the inline images in Web documents. Java applets eliminate the need for helper applications. Figures 17.2 and 17.3 show examples of simple Java applets.

However, the delivery of Java into the hands of the nonprogrammer is not here yet. Java is an interpreted programming environment, and the language is object oriented and comparable to C++. Java programming is simpler than C++ coding for a number of reasons. Most importantly, programmers do not deal with pointers, which are among the most difficult aspects of a C++ program to debug; and the Java interpreter manages memory, not the program. A Java program can be a simple collection of classes and methods to control them. The language was designed specifically to move objects across a heterogeneous network and was adopted for the Internet. Disk access information does not exist; instead, Java comes with a library of routines designed to handle standard Internet protocols like FTP and HTTP. Java transfers include byte-code verification, guarding against the addition of

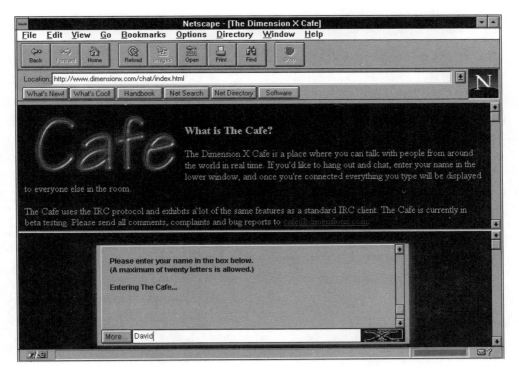

FIGURE 17.2 The Cafe applet lets users chat at a Web site.

viruses or Trojan horses (that means if the packet's size is changed along the way, it will be aborted).

Web browsers that are Java ready must contain an interpreter, a program licensed from Sun that translates Java instructions into an executable program that runs on your system. Netscape's Navigator 2.0 is Java ready. Most Java applets you'll come across on the Web are self-contained programs that Web browsers will identify as MIME (multipurpose Internet mail extensions) types requiring the Java interpreter (sometimes referred to as a virtual machine). Well-designed Java applets will query the browser to determine whether the Java interpreter is present. If it is, the program will execute on your system. If not, a still image or text message should be displayed or a hole appears in the page where the applet should run. This architecture allows Java

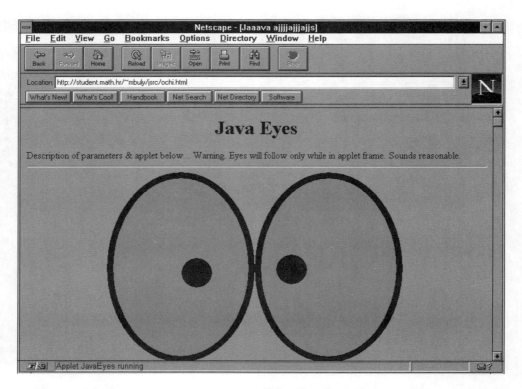

FIGURE 17.3 The Java Eyes applet follows your mouse pointer on the screen.

to be platform independent. The programmer, Web server, and browser can be running different operating systems, but the application will run without modification as long as a Java interpreter was written for that architecture. Sun distributes versions of the compiler and interpreter for the Macintosh, Solaris, Windows NT, and Windows 95 platforms.

Early demos of Java applets have focused on flashy motion video and animation effects. In the long run, Java provides a powerful way to distribute interactive applications. A Java program can allow users to enter selections, process the data locally, and generate a response that can be passed back to the host. The biggest immediate impact on Web sites is that Java is almost certain to surpass awkward CGI interactive processing techniques because, by design, it's more efficient and more powerful. CGI scripts are host based, requiring server processing for every Perl script launched. Java puts the local processor to work; the server simply sends data to the client system. In graphics-intensive applications, that's a significant benefit because millions of bytes won't have to move across the network; instead, they'll be generated locally.

As a nonprogrammer Webmaster, you need to follow the Java developments toward enhancement products you can add to your Web server or incorporate into the Web server software. In release 1.1, Java will support RSA's public-key encryption standards, making it possible to safeguard transactions against snooping. Java will also be compatible with Netscape's Secure Sockets Layer (SSL) and the Visa/MasterCard SET standard. Netscape plans to include the Java interpreter in its Commerce Server, making it possible to develop advanced applications, such as automated fulfillment of orders sent by e-mail or Web forms.

Most users will need to know only two things about Java: Is my browser capable of running Java programs and where can I find Java applets? Java applets are opened with a simple link from an HTML page, so providing a Java-animated effect can be as simple as copying a Java byte-code (the format that is interpreted by Java-ready Web browsers) file to the server and editing an existing HTML code to add the link. For more information on Java, visit Sun's Java's home page (http://java.sun.com/).

Microsoft's Visual Basic

Visual Basic 5.0, scheduled for release in the fourth quarter of 1996, is Microsoft's challenge to Sun's Java. Visual Basic will support an OLE Document Objects specification that will let Visual Basic applications be launched from Web browsers as part of the Sweeper API extensions for Windows NT. The Sweeper APIs will be used in concert with OLE extensions to let users read Web server documents, including Visual Basic applications in their native format. The crux of Visual Basic's Web push is the ability to create OCXes (OLE Custom Controls), which are the equivalent of Java applets.

Microsoft is leveraging the large installed base of Visual Basic developers to challenge Java.

HTML 3.0

The next generation of HTML, the HTML 3.0 draft, attempts to make up for all the shortcomings of the current HTML 2.0 draft. You've already seen one of HTML 3.0's new features, tables (as implemented by Netscape), but there are quite a few others: inline figures, support for proper display of mathematical formulas and equations, customized lists, better control over text and graphic positioning, static banners that stay at the top or bottom of the document regardless of scrolling, and style sheets.

With all the uncertainty surrounding the stability of the HTML 3.0 draft at any particular time, the Web community is growing more and more impatient. Browsers like Netscape Navigator are attempting to make up for the void that HTML 3.0 has been promising to fill for so long. HTML 3.0 is a long way from being completed, but it will be a big step forward for the Web if the draft is ever finished. It's much more robust than HTML 2.0, but also more involved. The learning curve will be a lot higher for 3.0. At this stage, it's probably wise to sit back and wait for things to calm down on HTML 3.0.

Virtual Reality on the Web

3-D virtual reality promises to transform the Web into computer-generated worlds that immerse network users so that they can visualize, manipulate, and interact with a network's contents. Already, a growing number of prototypes are operating on the Internet using the World Wide Web as the conduit. In these worlds, users represented by avatars (animated 3-D digital personas) operate within a network's contents and communicate in real time with other users or agents. Imagine a cyberspace alive with grand piazzas, public squares, cafes, beer halls, or bazaars, where people gather to socialize and transact in real time. Figures 17.4, 17.5, 17.6, 17.7, and 17.8 take you through a virtual world designed by Worlds Inc. This world allows avatars to communicate with each other in real time.

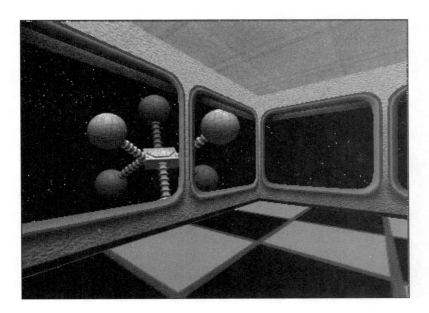

FIGURE 17.4 An observation deck.

FIGURE 17.5 Into a gallery of avatars.

FIGURE 17.6 Up a moving escalator.

FIGURE 17.7 Down a hallway.

FIGURE 17.8 Into a room full of other avatars.

VRML

Virtual reality (VR) is being implemented on the Web via VRML (Virtual Reality Modeling Language) and other competing VR languages. With VRML, programmers can encode data into 3-D scenes that let users navigate through it. VRML 1.0 is the language that specifies the construction of 3-D scenes that are built from individual objects. It also provides the methods to link the component objects to other objects, such as other scenes or conventional Web hyperlinks. Currently, VRML supports only navigation within 3-D worlds, not the interaction of avatars.

The VRML specification is currently based on SGI's Open Inventor format for rendering 3-D environments. However, several other specifications are also being considered. One of the biggest benefits of Open Inventor is that you are not forced to transfer large quantities of bitmapped graphics, but instead transfer instructions that your VRML browser uses to reconstruct the world on the client machine. A typical VRML document is very small, often as little as 5K for a small object or 400K for a more complex environment.

This is certainly within the reach of current networking technology, with a 400K document taking less than two minutes to transfer with a 28.8K modern connection. Inline objects can be embedded in a world, much as inline images can be embedded in a regular HTML document, so worlds can be split among many servers.

A number of special VRML-based browsers that work as helper applications with your Web browser have been released. The first generation of VR browsers is still in its infancy, and the products are a little clunky, but still they represent a look at the future of Web servers. One of the leading resources for VR and VRML information is at http://www.yahoo.com/Entertainment /Virtual_Reality_Modeling_Language_VRML_/ or http://www.lightside.com /3dsite/cgi/vrml/index.html.

Appendix

Webmaster Resources

This appendix provides a listing of Webmaster resources.

Windows NT Web Commerce Servers

Microsoft Internet Information Server

Microsoft Corporation

URL: http://www.microsoft-com

Netscape Commerce Server

Netscape Communications Corporation

URL: http://home.netscape.com

Commerce Builder

The Internet Factory

URL: http://www.aristosoft.com/

Purveyor Encrypt

Process Software Inc.

URL: http://wwwprocess.com/

WebSite Professional

O'Reilly & Associates Inc.

URL: http://www.ora.com/

Web Commander

Luckman Interactive Inc.

URL: http://www.luckman.com/

InterWare

Consensys

URL: http://www.consensys.com/

Internet Office Web Server

CompuServe, Inc.

URL: http://www.compuserve.com/

Automatic CGI Scripting Programs

net.Form

net.Genesis

URL: http://www.netgen.com/

Cold Fusion

Allaire, Inc.

URL: http://www.allaire.com/

Web Usage Tracking Programs and Services

net.Analysis

net.Genesis

URL: http://www.netgen.com/

Web Trends

e.g. Software Inc.

URL: http://www.egsoftware.com/

Market Focus

Interse Corporation

URL: http://www.interse.com/

NetCount

NetCount

URL: http://www.netcount.com

Web-Based Conferencing Systems

net.Thread

net.Genesis

URL: http://www.netgen.com/

WebBoard

O'Reilly and Associates Inc.

URL: http://www.ora.com/

About

AEX Software

URL: http://www.aex.com/

Web-Based Chat Systems

ichat

ichat

URL: http://www.ichat.com

Netscape Community Chat Server

Netscape Communications Corporation

URL: http://home.netscape.com

Online Publishing and Multimedia Tools

Adobe Acrobat

URL: http://www.adobe.com

Shockwave for Director

Macromedia

URL: http://www.macromedia.com/

QuickTime for Windows &
QuickTime Development Kit (APDA, #RO453LL/B)

URL: http://www.apple.com

RealAudio

Progressive Networks

URL: http://realaudio.com/

Web Site Development and Database Connectivity Tools

Netscape LiveWire

Netscape

URL: http://home.netcape.com/

Microsoft Internet Studio

Microsoft

URL: http://www.microsoft.com/

Excite for Web Servers

Architext Software Inc.

URL: http://www.excite.com/

BestWeb Pro

Best-Seller Inc.

URL: http://www.bestseller.com

WebWATCHER

Caravelle Inc.

URL: http://home.caravelle.com/

Electronic Commerce and Security Resources

DigiCash

URL: http://www.digicash.com/

CyberCash

URL: http://cybercash.com/

NetChex

URL: http://www.netchex.com/

First Virtual Holdings Inc.

URL: http://www.fv.com/

VeriSign

URL: http://www.verisign.com/

Terisa Systems

URL: http://www.terisa.com/

NetCash

URL: http://www.netbank.com/

CommerceNet

URL: http://www.commerce.net/

Eagle Firewall

Raptor Systems, Inc.

URL: http://www.raptor.com/

Firewall/Plus

Network-1 Software

URL: http://www.network-1.com/

Leading World Wide Web Browsers

Enhanced NCSA Mosaic for Windows

Spyglass Inc.

URL: http://www.spyglass.com/

Netscape Navigator

Netscape Communications Corporation

URL: http://home.netscape.com

Microsoft Internet Explorer

Microsoft Corporation

URL: http://www.microsoft.com/

HTML Editors

HoTMetaL PRO

SoftQuad Inc.

URL: http://www.sq.com

NaviPress

NaviSoft

URL: http://www.naviservice.com/

Microsoft Internet Assistant

Microsoft Corporation

URL: http://www.microsoft.com/

WebAuthor

Quarterdeck Office Systems Inc.

URL: http: / /www.qdeck.com

Spider

InContext

URL: http://www.incontext.ca

ISDN Equipment Vendors

NT1 Ace

AdTran

URL: http://www.adtran.com/

NT1U-100TC

NT1U-220TC

Tone Commander Systems Inc.

URL: http://www.halcyon.com/tcs/

BitSURFR Pro

Vanguard 310

Motorola

URL: http://www.mot.com/

ADAK 221

ADAK 421

ADAK Communications Corporation

URL: http://www.adak.com/

SuperNT1

Alpha Telecom Inc.

URL: http://www.iquest.com/~ati_usa/

Impact

3Com Corporation

URL: http://www.3com.com/

Pipeline 25

Pipeline 50 ISDN

Pipeline 50HX

Ascend Communications Inc.

URL: http://www.ascend.com/

Sportster ISDN 128K

U.S. Robotics

URL: http://www.usr.com/

Elite 2864D

Elite 2864DI

ZyXEL

URL: http://www.zyxel.com

LANLine 5242i

LANLine 5250i

Gandalf Technologies Inc.

URL: http://www.gandalf.ca

Cyberspace Internet Card

ISDN*tek

URL: http://isdntek.com

Cisco 201/202/203/204

Cisco Systems

URL: http://www.cisco.com/

NetCommander ISDN

Diamond Multimedia

URL: http://www.diamondmm.com/

DataFire

Digi International

URL: http://www.digibd.com

IBM WaveRunner

7845 ISDN Network Terminator Extended

International Business Machines

URL: http://www.ibmlink.ibm.com/

PowerLink 128 ISDN Modem

Livingston Enterprises

URL://www.livingston.com/

Microcom SoLIS-L

Microcom SoLIS-F

Microcom

URL:http://www.microcom.com/

ISDN Basic Rate Adapter

Xircom

URL: http://www.xircom.com/

Netopia

Farallon Computing Inc.

URL: http://www.farallon.com/

Internet Service Providers

Dan Kegel's List of ISDN Internet Service Providers

URL: http://alumni.caltech.edu/~dank/isdn/isdn_ip.html

U.S. Internet Service Providers List

URL: http://www.primus.com/staff/peggy/provider.html

BBN Planet

150 Cambridge Park Drive

Cambridge, MA 02140

URL: http://www.bbnplanet.com/

Best Internet Communications Inc.

421 Castro Street

Mountain View, CA 94041

URL: http://www.best.com/

CCnet Communications

190 N. Wiget Lane, Suite # 291

Walnut Creek, CA 94598

URL: http://www.ccnet.com/

CERFnet

P.O. Box 85608

San Diego, CA 92186-9784

URL: http://www.cerf.net/

CICNet

2901 Hubbard Drive

Ann Arbor, MI 48105

URL: http://www.cic.net/

Colorado SuperNet

One Denver Place

999 18th Street

Denver, CO 80202

URL: http://www.csn.org/

Commuter Communications Systems

13706 Research Blvd., Suite 203

Austin, TX 78750

URL: http://www.ccsi.com/

CRL

Box 326

Larkspur, CA 94977

URL: http://www.crl.com/

CTS Network Services (CTSNet)

4444 Convoy Street, Suite 300

San Diego, CA 92111

URL: http://www.cts.net/

CyberGate

662 South Military Trail

Deerfield Beach, FL 33442

URL: http://www.gate.net/

DATABANK Inc.

1473 Hwy 40

Lawrence, KS 66044

URL: http://www.databank.com/

Digital Express: Group Inc.

6006 Greenbelt Road, Suite 228

Greenbelt, MD 20770

URL: http://www.digex.net/

Dimensional Communications

821 17th Street, Suite 804

Denver, CO 80202

URL: http://www.dimensional.com/

Echo

97 Perry Street, Suite 13

New York, NY 10014

URL: http://www.echonyc.com/

Global Enterprise Services

3 Independence Way

Princeton, NJ 08540

URL: http://www.jvnc.net/

Hawaii Online

737 Bishop Street, Suite 2350

Honolulu, HI 96813

URL: http://aloha.net/

HoloNet

Information Access Technologies Inc.

46 Shattuck Square, Suite 11

Berkeley, CA 94704

URL: http://www.holonet.net/

ICOnetworks

5617 Scotts Valley Drive

Scotts Valley, CA 95066

URL: http://www.ico.net/

IDS World Network

Area code(s): 401, 305, 407

3 Franklin Road

East Greenwich, RI 02818

URL: http://www.ids.net/

Institute for Global Communications/IGC Networks

18 De Boom Street

San Francisco, CA 94107

URL: http://www.igc.apc.org/

Interaccess Co.

9400 W. Foster Avenue, Suite 111

Chicago, IL 60656

URL: http://www.interaccess.com/

Internet Direct Inc.

1366 East Thomas, #210

Phoenix, AZ 85014

URL: http: / /wwwindirect.com/

Internet Express

1155 Kelly Johnson Boulevard, Suite 400

Colorado Springs, CO 80920

URL: http://usa.net/

InterNex Information Services Inc.

2302 Walsh Avenue

Santa Clara, CA 95051

URL: http://www.internex.net/

Kaildospace (Server Service)

P.O. Box 341556

Los Angeles, CA 90034

URL: http://kspace.com/

Macro Computer Solutions

1300 West Belmont, Suite 402

Chicago, IL 60657

URL: http://www.mcs.com/

Merit Network/MichNet

2901 Hubbard Pod G

Ann Arbor, MI 48105

URL: http://www.merit.edu/

MetroNet

300 B Street, Suite 203

Santa Rosa, CA 95404

URL: http://metro.net/

MiDnet

201 North 8th Street, Suite 421

Lincoln, NE 68588

URL: http://www.mid.net/

MRNet

511 llth Avenue Box 212 South

Minneapolis, MN 55415

URL: http://www.mrnet/

MSEN Inc.

628 Brooks Street

Ann Arbor, MI 48103

URL: http://www.msen.com/

MV Communications Inc.

P.0 Box 4963

Manchester, NH 03108

URL: http://www.mv.com/

NEARNET

BBN Technology Services Inc.

1 0 Moulton Street

Cambridge, MA 02138

URL: http://www.nearnet/

Neosoft

3408 Mangum Street

Houston, TX 77092

URL: http://www.neosoft.com/

Netcom On-Line Communications Services

4000 Moorpark Avenue, Suite 209

San Jose, CA 95117

URL: http://www.netcom.com/

Netillinois

1840 Oak Avenue

Evanston, IL 60201

URL: http://www.illinois.net/

North Bay Network

20 Minor Court

San Rafael, CA 94903

URL: http://www.nb.com/

North Shore Access

Voice: (617) 593-3110

URL: http://www.shore.net/

NorthWestNet

15400 S.E. 30th Place, Suite 202

Bellevue, WA 98007

URL: http://www.nwnet.net

Nuance Network Services

904 Bob Wallace Avenue, Suite 119

Huntsville, AL 35801

URL: http://www.nuance.com/

OARNet

1224 Kinnear Road

Columbus, OH 43212

URL: http://www.oarnet/

Panix Public Access UNIX & Internet

URL: http://www.panix.com/

Performance Systems International Inc. (PSI)

510 Huntmar Park Drive

Herndon, VA 12180

URL: http://www.psi.net/

Phantom Access

1562 First Avenue, Suite 351

New York, NY 10028

URL: http://www.phantom.com/

Pipeline

150 Broadway

New York, NY 10038

URL: http://www.pipeline.com/

Portal Communications Company

20863 Stevens Creek Boulevard, Suite 200

Cupertino, CA 95014

URL: http://www.portal.com/

PREPnet

305 S Craig Street, 2nd Floor

Pittsburgh, PA 15213

URL: http://www.cmu.edu/

QuakeNet Internet Services

830 Wilmington Road

San Mateo, CA 94402

URL: http://www.quake.net/

RustNet Inc.

6905 Telegraph, Suite 315

Bloomfield Hills, MI 48301

URL: http://www.rustnet.net/

Shouting Ground Technologies

P.O. Box 5039 Station A

Champaign, IL 61820

URL: http://www.shout.net/

Skylink Networks Inc.

4850 West Flamingo Road, Suite 23

Las Vegas, NV 89103

URL: http://www.skylink.net/

South Coast Computing Services Inc.

1811 Bering, Suite 100

Houston, TX 77057

URL: http://www.sccsi.com/

SURAnet

8400 Baltimore Blvd.

College Park, MD 20740

URL: http://www.sura.net/

Teleport

319 SouthWest Washington #803

Portland, OR 97204

URL: http://www.teleport.com/

Telerama Public Access Internet

P.O. Box 60024

Pittsburgh, PA 15211

URL: http://www.telerama.com/

Texas Metronet

860 Kinwest Parkway, Suite 179

Irving, TX 75063-3440

URL: http://www.metronet.com/

TerraNet Inc.

729 Boylston Street

Boston, MA 02116

URL: http://www.terra.net/

The Internet Access Company

175 The Great Road

Bedford, MA 01730

URL: http://www.tiac.com/

UUNET Technologies Inc.

3060 Williams Drive

Fairfax, VA 22031

URL: http://www.uu.net/

VNet Internet Access Inc.

1206 Kenilwratch Avenue

PO. Box 31474

Charlotte, SC 28231

URL: http://www.vnet.net/

XNet Information Systems

3080 East Ogden Avenue, #202

Lisle, IL 60532

URL: http://www.xnet.com/

Other Resources

The Webmasters Guild

URL: http://www.webmaster.org/

InterNIC Registration Services

URL: http://rs.internic.net/

Index